DATELINE
SUNDAY, U.S.A.

The Story of Three and a
Half Centuries of Sunday-law
Battles in America

by Warren L. Johns

Pacific Press Publishing Association

Mountain View, California
Omaha, Nebraska

DEDICATION

"Hi! I'm Ed O'Brien."

The hand was outstretched. A broad grin sparkled across an open Irish face. Keen intellect laced with a magnificent sense of humor glistened in the steel-blue eyes.

It was September, 1955, and the first day of school for the freshman law class at the University of Southern California. That informal meeting with Ed marked the beginning of a rich friendship between us.

Friends were important to Ed. He had a genuine feeling for people, an attitude that never recognized a barrier of color, language, religion, or economics. His type of friendship epitomized the American tradition. He was a Catholic and a Democrat, I a Protestant and a Republican. Political disagreements became a source of good-humored kidding, while religious differences seemed only to produce sincere understanding.

Under the stress of scholastic competition, law students are exposed to unusual tensions. A standard gimmick for relieving those tensions was Ed's rather shopworn anecdote about the old grad who had never needed to study in law school because of his self-admitted "inherent ability." The absurdity of it all evoked peals of laughter when Ed, with feigned seriousness, would assure his fellow students of their good fortune in being able to rely on "inherent ability."

When Ed opened his law practice in Los Angeles, it was an immediate success. When he invited me to join this practice, I considered this the ultimate compliment. Only other serious commitments prevented my acceptance.

But there was always time for a midweek luncheon and an exchange of views on the challenges of our profession. We both revered our American heritage of law and justice which expresses a deep concern for the individual.

Ed relished the adventure of living. As a merchant seaman he had sailed oceans. He had tried parachute jumping and had driven an Army tank in the California desert. There was the family trip to Hawaii; an Alaskan adventure on the Alcan highway (movies showed him catching fish in the shallow streams with his bare hands); the motorcycle excursion into Mexico; an occasional evening patrol ride with friends on the police force. He flew his own light plane around metropolitan Los Angeles, and his friends had a standing invitation to join him as he soared above the city.

On Friday, September 18, 1964, a jetliner brought me back to Southern California from New York. At home in Santa Ana, my wife pointed to a headline in the Los Angeles *Times,* with an accompanying picture. Ed O'Brien had made his last airplane flight, and the wreckage had been spotted in the Santa Monica mountains.

The world was the loser! Though his achievements were many, thirty-three years is not long enough for a soul endowed with the talents and human warmth that lived in Ed O'Brien.

This book provides my own memorial to his memory. Although some of my interpretations of history may not parallel his, it is certain that the underlying fabric which emphasizes individual dignity and human rights in a free society would eptomize his thinking.

To the reader whose theology embraces a concept of a better world in the hereafter, I suggesst that it will be only a matter of time before you may be confronted with an outstretched hand, a pair of keen blue eyes, and an Irish grin as their owner says,

"Hi! I'm Ed O'Brien."

PREFACE

The Sunday-law problem has been with mankind for quite a few centuries now—since Constantine's first civil Sunday code of A.D. 321. The theological dimensions of the Sabbath-Sunday controversy have even more venerable beginnings, dating to pagan sun worshipers who worshiped on the "venerable day of the Sun" half a millennium or more before Christ. For nearly sixteen centuries church councils and civil courts have dispensed decrees and exemptions, and citizens ranging from a Roman peasant to the first President of the United States have run afoul of Sunday laws.

Among the books on Sunday laws and the related theological issues occupying two central shelves of my bookcase are venerable tomes written in Old English, and contemporary treatments more flippant than formidable. Peter Heylyn's *History of the Sabbath,* in a 1636 edition, leans its tired covers against Dr. Fr. White's *A Treatise of the Sabbath-day, containing a defence of the Orthodoxall Doctrine of the Church of England, against Sabbatarian-Novelty,* printed in 1635. Hiley H. Ward's 1960 edition of *Space-Age Sunday,* a literary astronaut's-eye view of the problem condensed into 160 pages, is supported by Dr. Leo Pfeffer's definitive *Church, State, and Freedom,* 675 pages of lucid scholarship. Warren Johns's *Dateline Sunday* will sit somewhere to the right of center—a popularly written history of Sunday blue laws, with major emphasis upon the rationale behind the United States Supreme Court decisions of 1961 and their subsequent legislative fallout. I found his explanation of how Sunday laws came to be regarded as civil legislation with welfare benefits to the public, and thus capable of being rationalized as within the legitimate police power of the state, particularly lucid.

As a practicing attorney-at-law, and legal director of the Church-State Council, a nonpartisan educational organization dedicated to religious freedom and separation of church and state,

Mr. Johns is qualified to treat the legal issues. As a frequent contributor to secular and religious magazines, he adds a popular writing style that makes *Dateline Sunday* a treat instead of a treatment. What fourth-century Roman emperor authorized the first exemption from a Sunday law? Do automatic coin-operated laundries, with no one employed on the premises, infringe on Canada's Lord's Day Act? Why did Michigan's unique two-day (Saturday-Sunday) law not only tickle the funnybone of that state's reporters but also incur the judicial frown of all eight justices of Michigan's highest tribunal? Johns has the instructive and often entertaining answers.

The defender of Sunday laws will not like this book, for Johns does not masquerade as an objective appraiser. He dislikes laws that make otherwise law-abiding citizens criminals for a day and punctures illusions with the sharp lance of reason and the quick strike of wit. It will take a reader of the Lord's Day Alliance breed to come through the reading with convictions unshaken.

The author does not ignore the laudable social objectives of those who support Sunday laws. He pays his respects to a day of rest from labor, and family and community togetherness. He shows clearly, however, that Sunday laws are designed more to protect and honor the observance of a day than to protect and benefit the individual.

As editor of *Liberty,* a magazine specializing in church-state affairs, I found Johns's book valuable enough to request permission to reprint a number of its chapters in successive issues of *Liberty.* Johns does not solve the Sunday-law problem, and he largely evades the theological issues; but he does clarify, interestingly, many of the historical and judicial issues.

ROLAND R. HEGSTAD.

Washington, D.C.
January 3, 1967.

CONTENTS

As George Washington, newly elected President, journeyed by horseback in Connecticut one Sunday morning, a tithingman challenged him, demanding that he travel no farther than the town where he planned to attend church.

1. "SOMETHING BORROWED, SOMETHING BLUE"

The sharp order of the tithingman, "Halt!" split the Sunday-morning Connecticut air.

The distinguished-appearing stranger reined in his horse and turned to face the austere official.

The sun had already risen high above the treetops, and the tall traveler was anxious to complete his journey to a town in New York in time to attend church, as was his custom. He had forgotten about the "blue laws" governing Sunday travel in the state of Connecticut.

"What license have you to travel upon the Lord's Day?" the tithingman demanded.

"I am on my way to New York to attend church," the stranger responded courteously. "I planned to reach the city yesterday, but my journey took longer than I anticipated."

It was not until the stranger "promised to go no further than the town intended that the tithingman would permit him to proceed on his journey."[1]

This event was not particularly newsworthy in itself, since the tithingman of that day could arrest anyone who "walked or rode unnecessarily" on the first day of the week. But in this case the blue-law violator was George Washington, newly elected President of the United States.

1

DATELINE SUNDAY, U.S.A.

By Washington's time—this incident took place in 1789—sturdy patriots had gone far in breaking the shackles of the Old World and creating a government of the people. But the free air of the new continent was still tainted by something old, borrowed, and very blue.

Upon their arrival in America, the persecuted Congregationalist minority from the Old World adjusted quickly to their new role of dominance. John Cotton, of Massachusetts Bay Colony, declared that "toleration made the world anti-Christian" and that if a man is shown the path to truth but "shall still persist in the error of his way and be punished, he is not persecuted for cause of conscience, but for *sinning against his own conscience*."[2] He insisted that "persecution is not wrong in itself; it is wicked for falsehood to persecute truth, but it is the sacred duty of truth to persecute falsehood."[3]

Nowhere in the colonies was the battle for freedom more intense or its defeat more complete than in Massachusetts. By 1629 the Congregationalist majority had gained complete control. The law of Plymouth stated that because "Wee would be loath that any Person should be permitted to pass that Wee suspected to affect the Superstition of the Chh of Rome, Wee do hereby declare that it is our Will and Pleasure that none be permitted to pass."[4] A Jesuit was assured of banishment, and if "taken the second time within this Jurisdiction, upon lawful trial and conviction, he shall be put to Death."[5] Jews and Catholics were denied the right to vote or to hold public office.

In 1682 Cotton Mather learned of a ship christened *Welcome,* curiously enough. It was headed in his direction carrying "100 or more of the heretics and malignants called Quakers, with W. Penn, who is the chief scamp at the head of them."[6] In a letter to John Higginson, Mather confided a cunning plot conceived by the General Court. The brig *Porpoise* was to waylay the *Welcome* near Cape Cod and sell the "whole lot to Barbados, where slaves fetch good prices in rum and sugar, and we

2

shall not only do the Lord great good by punishing the wicked, but we shall make great good for His minister and people."[7]

Apparently William Penn managed to elude the *Porpoise,* but other Quakers, such as Mary Dyer, met death in Boston by hanging. More than an idle threat, the penalty was codified by a statute which explained that the "cursed sect of the Quakers" were to be "sentenced to banishment upon pain of death."[8]

The 1644 act of the General Court, ordering banishment for those opposed to infant baptism, rebuked Baptists who believed in immersion at the age of accountability. A Mr. Painter was whipped for refusing the sprinkling rite for his child.[9] Obadiah Holmes, another Baptist, had ministered to a fellow believer and was beaten so unmercifully that he aroused the sympathy of the people, and "in spite of the danger, numbers flocked about him when he was set free, in sympathy and admiration."[10]

Despite the demands of the Crown in 1665 that freedom of worship be given to Episcopalians, the General Court of the Massachusetts church-state government replied that Episcopal worship "will disturb our peace in our present enjoyments." It added piously, "We have commended to the ministry & people here the word of the Lord for their rule therein."[11] No wonder some of their own brethren sympathized with persecuted settlers.

There was the unfortunate George Burroughs, himself a former clergyman, who was accused of witchcraft during the 1692 hysteria. Someone recalled seeing Burroughs lift a musket at arm's length with his finger in the barrel. This feat of strength, considered something beyond human capability, was introduced at his trial as evidence that he practiced witchcraft.

Although he was found guilty, many of the people had reservations about hanging this man, particularly when they heard his final dramatic plea for mercy from the scaffold. But Cotton Mather was there to assure the public that "justice" was being done. The noose took the life of George Burroughs on August 19, 1692.

DATELINE SUNDAY, U.S.A.

Then there was Anne Hutchinson, a resident of Boston. Religious meetings in her home, in which she showed how the Scriptures reveal that the road to the good life is by faith and not mechanical works, were a thorn in the side of the local clergy.

Though she was an expectant mother, in November, 1637, she was callously tried for heresy and evicted from the colony. Witty and intelligent, Anne Hutchinson was also direct and outspoken. The weekly teas at her home for the prominent ladies of Boston had provided a strategic platform from which to discuss views of the "inner light" versus the ritualistic forms of Puritanism. Her sympathizer, Governor Vane, was defeated for reelection; then her brother-in-law, John Wheelwright, was convicted of similar heresy. When her turn came in 1637, this mother of fourteen faced her accusers without flinching and declared: "Now if you do condemn me for speaking what in my conscience I know to be truth, I must commit myself unto the Lord."[12]

It comes as no surprise that Sunday blue laws blossomed in this fertile soil of intolerance, where clergy dominated church and state. In 1629 the Massachusetts Bay Colony decreed: "To the end the Saboth may bee celebrated in a religious manner, we appoint, that all that inhabite the plantacon, both for the generall and pticuler imployments, may surcease their labor every Satterday throughout the yeare at 3 of the clock in the afternoone, and that they spend the rest of that day in catechising and preparacion for the Saboth as the minister shall direct."[13]

In November of the following year, John Baker was whipped for "shooteing att fowle on the Sabboth day."[14]

The Virginia Sunday law of 1610 prohibited Sunday "gaming" and required attendance at "diuine seruice" in the morning and "in the afternoon to diuine seruice, and Catechising, vpon paine for the first fault to lose their prouision, and allowance for the whole weeke following, for the second to lose the said allowance, and also to be whipt, and for the third to suffer death."[15]

4

The iron fist of the clergy-dominated state was an everyday fact of colonial life. Strict Sunday laws were a weekly reminder of this union.

DATELINE SUNDAY, U.S.A.

Although not codified in statute, questions answered by certain of the Massachusetts Bay Colony elders on November 13, 1644, included a declaration that "any sinn committed with an high hand, as ye gathering of sticks on ye Saboth day, may be punished with death, wn a lesser punishment might serve for gathering sticks privily, & in some neede."[16]

Fortunately for the "worldly-minded" among the colonists, most colonial Sunday blue laws did not carry the death penalty. The General Court, meeting in Boston October 19, 1658, took note that "the sunn being set, both euery Saturday & on the Lords day, young people & others take liberty to walke & sporte themselves in the streets or fields . . . and too frequently repajre to publicque houses of entertajnment, & there sitt drincking."[17] Resident violators were liable to a five shilling fine for this type of conduct. The mere threat of fine proved an inadequate deterrent, so in 1665 the General Court recommended corporal punishment for those "refusing or neglecting to submitt to the Courts sentence."[18]

Sunday traveling on horseback, on foot, or by boat to an out-of-town meeting or assembly not specifically provided for by law was illegal. Tradesmen, artificers, and laborers could not conduct business or perform work on land or water. Games, sports, play, and recreation were taboo, "works of necessity and charity only excepted."

In Plymouth Colony church attendance was required, and "such as sleep or play about the meetinghouse in times of the public worship of God on the Lord's day" could expect to have the constable report their names to the court. Violent riding was banned, as was smoking tobacco.[19]

The cage, the stocks, heavy fines, and whipping customarily recompensed violators. A man named Birdseye from Milford, Connecticut, was reportedly sentenced to the whipping post for scandalously kissing his wife on Sunday."[20]

"SOMETHING BORROWED, SOMETHING BLUE"

According to Mrs. Alice Morse Earle's history, *The Sabbath in Puritan New England,* one of the leading characters in the enforcement of the Puritan Sunday "was the 'tithingman,' . . . who entered private houses to assure himself that no one stayed at home on the 'Sabbath' [Sunday] and hustled up any loiterers. . . . He was empowered to stop all Sunday work." In fact, the tithingman was always busy on Sunday doing sleuth work, spying out other people's liberties, and haling them before the civil magistrate for neglect of religious duties.

In 1670 "two lovers, John Lewis and Sarah Chapman, were accused and tried for 'sitting together on the Lord's day under an apple tree in Goodman Chapman's orchard.'" "A Dunstable soldier, for 'wetting a piece of old hat to put in his shoe' to protect his foot—for doing this heavy work on the Lord's day, was fined, and paid forty shillings." "Captain Kemble, of Boston, was in 1656 set for two hours in the public stocks, for his 'lewd and unseemly behavior,' which consisted in kissing his wife 'publicquely' on the Sabbath day, upon the doorsteps of house," on his return from a three years' voyage. An English sea captain was "soundly whipped" for a like offense. A man who had fallen into the water and absented himself from church to dry his only suit of clothes, was found guilty and "publicly whipped." Smoking on Sunday was forbidden. To stay away from church meant "cumulative mulct." Other equally foolish and drastic laws prohibited the people from walking, driving, or riding horseback on Sunday, unless they went to church or to the cemetery.[21]

The iron fist of the clergy-dominated state was an everyday fact of colonial life. Stringent Sunday laws were a weekly reminder of this union. Freedom of individual conscience had a long way to go.

But apart from the excesses of theocracy, to the everlasting credit of the Puritan settlers, as honest, hardworking, self-disciplined men they conquered an untamed wilderness and contributed largely to the creation of a new and free society in a new world. Their many sterling qualities provided the spark that ulti-

7

mately pushed the new civilization across prairies, deserts, and mountains to the Pacific.

Not to be overlooked is the spiritual evolution in the heart of the individual citizen early in the seventeenth century. The authoritarian clergy could not forever rest in the comfort of a captive audience. Sympathy for the Anne Hutchinsons of America became a mighty undercurrent that churned to the surface with ever-increasing frequency and intensity.

The early settlers were seeking more than civil and religious subjugation. Men like Williams, Jefferson, Madison, and Mason helped to give positive direction to that quest for freedom. The colonists had undertaken a monumental struggle with tyranny that would rendezvous with a massive victory for freedom late in the eighteenth century.

REFERENCES

1. "The President and the Tithingman," *Columbian Centinal,* December, 1789. In *American State Papers,* Third Revised Edition (Washington, D.C.: Review and Herald Publishing Association, 1943), page 51.
2. Sanford H. Cobb, *Rise of Religious Liberty in America* (New York: The Macmillan Company, 1902), pages 68, 69.
3. John Fiske, *Beginnings of New England,* page 178. In *American State Papers,* page 231.
4. Francis Newton Thorpe, "The Charter of New England," 1620. In *The Federal and State Constitutions, Colonial Charters, and Other Organic Laws* (Washington, D.C.: Government Printing Office, 1909), Vol. 3, p. 1839.
5. "The General Laws and Liberties of the Massachusetts Colony" (1672 revision), page 67. In *American State Papers,* page 31.
6. Frank H. Yost, *Let Freedom Ring* (Mountain View, California: Pacific Press Publishing Association, 1945), page 56.
7. *Ibid.*
8. "The General Laws and Liberties of the Massachusetts Colony," page 48. In *American State Papers,* page 30.
9. Thomas Hutchinson, *The History of Massachusetts* (Boston: Thomas C. Cushing for Thomas and Andrews, 1795-1828), Vol. 1, p. 208.
10. Adams, *The Emancipation of Massachusetts* (1887), pages 114, 115.
11. *Records of the Governor and Company of the Massachusetts Bay in New England* (Boston, 1854), Vol. 4, Part 2, pp. 200, 201.
12. William L. Roper, "The Saintly Heretic," *Liberty,* Vol. 57 (1962), No. 4, p. 22
13. *Records of the Governor, etc.,* Vol. 1, p. 395.
14. *Ibid.,* p. 82.
15. Peter Force, *Tracts Relating to the Colonies in North America* (Washington, D.C., 1844. Published Gloucester, Massachusetts: Peter Smith, 1963), Vol. 3. No. 2, pp. 10, 11.

16. *Records of the Governor, etc.,* Vol. 2, p. 93.
17. *Ibid.,* Vol. 4, Part 1, p. 347.
18. *Ibid.,* Vol. 4, Part 2, p. 276.
19. *The Compact With the Charter and Laws of the Colony of New Plymouth* (Boston, 1836), pages 93, 157, 158.
20. See Ralph Nader, "Blue Law Causes Examined," *Harvard Law Review,* November 25, 1959.
21. "The Blue Laws of New England," *Liberty,* Vol. 58 (1963), No. 1, pp. 18, 19.

Brought to trial in Boston, Roger Williams declared his opinion that the magistrate might not punish a breach of the Sabbath.

JOHN STEEL, ARTIST; © P. P. P. A.

2. NEW WORLD, OLD LAWS

The influential pen of Augustine, fifth-century church father, proclaimed, "It is, indeed, better that men should be brought to serve God by instruction than by fear of punishment, or by pain. But because the former means are better, the latter must not therefore be neglected." He reasoned that many require "the rod of temporal suffering, before they attain to the highest grade of religious development."[1]

John Calvin added the arm of the state to his arsenal of weapons to be used in spiritual coercion, maintaining that "godly princes may lawfully issue edicts for compelling obstinate and rebellious persons to worship the true God and to maintain the unity of the faith."[2]

America's Puritans inherited this paradox, vigorously enforcing a doctrine of "love" by civil laws, with their accompanying threats and punishments.

What George Washington was to the political future of his country, Roger Williams was to religious liberty in America—its father. One of the first dissenters to be heard, Williams came perilously close to being silenced.

As a young man in England he had observed the atrocities of the Star Chamber. "He had been particularly shocked by the treatment given Alexander Leighton, a celebrated Scottish physician and clergyman, who had been tried for religious noncon-formity. Leighton had been sentenced to life imprisonment, fined 10,000 pounds, and facially disfigured, his ears being cut off, his nose slit, and his face branded with a hot iron."[3]

Ordained in the Episcopal Church, Williams had espoused Separatist doctrines by the time of his arrival in Boston in 1631. He accepted an offer to serve as minister for the Salem congrega-tion. Once in Salem, he boldly mounted the pulpit to condemn the "practice of punishing those who failed to attend Sunday church services. Civil magistrates, he declared, had no right to enforce church discipline."[4] This reckless talk was too much for the insecure Salemites to accept, so Williams took his heresies to Plymouth, where his ministry included the Indians.

Back in Salem in 1633, he launched a verbal assault against the theocratic government of Boston. He advocated absolute separation of church and state, attacked the civil use of the reli-gious oath, and challenged the right of the British Crown to appropriate Indian lands without adequate compensation.

The General Court read "subversion" in the latter declaration and called him to account. In the fall of 1635, the court formally charged Williams with denying that individual conscience lies within the sphere of government. Governor Winthrop, in the first volume of his 1631 journal, had observed:

"At a court holden at Boston . . . Mr. Williams . . . had declared his opinion that the magistrate might not punish a breach of the Sabbath, nor any other offense [that was religious], as it was a breach of the first table [of the law of God]."[5]

Williams refused to abandon his views and was found guilty of disseminating "newe & dangerous opinions." His sentence was banishment from the Bay Colony, effective the following spring. Now that the theocrats had made a martyr of the man, loyal hearts in Salem were bound closer to his cause, and Bay Colony leaders determined to arrest him and deport him to Eng-land. But when officers arrived from Boston, Williams had vanished. In midwinter he had escaped to the sheltering woods and the protection of friendly Indians. Here his dream of a colony where freedom of conscience would be protected by law blossomed into reality. Away from the Plymouth and Massachusetts colonies, he bought land from the Indians and founded "Providence," the beginning of Rhode Island.

"In his colony, dissenters were welcome. No oaths regarding a person's religious beliefs were required. Citizens were not compelled by law to attend church, and there were no taxes for support of a state church."[6] Even the Jew, the Catholic, and the Quaker were openly accepted in Providence.

Rhode Island law beckoned to the colonists, "All men may walk as conscience persuade them, every one in the name of his God."[7] Historian George Bancroft has written:

> At a time when Germany was the battle-field for all Europe in the implacable wars of religion; when even Holland was bleeding with the anger of vengeful factions; when France was still to go through the fearful struggle with bigotry; when England was gasping under the despotism of intolerance; almost half a century before William Penn became an American proprietary; and two full years before Descartes founded modern philosophy on the method of free reflection —Roger Williams asserted the great doctrine of intellectual liberty. It became his glory to found a state upon that principle. . . . He was the first person in modern Christendom to assert in its plenitude the doctrine of liberty of conscience, the equality of opinions before law. . . . Williams would permit persecution of no opinion, of no religion, leaving heresy unharmed by law, and orthodoxy unprotected by terrors of penal statutes.[8]

Shortly before Williams's trek through the wilderness, Cecil Calvert founded the Maryland settlement. Although it was established primarily as a refuge for persecuted Catholics, Christians of all faiths were welcomed. This philosophy of toleration was codified by the Maryland Assembly in 1649. It proclaimed that "noe person . . . within this Province, . . . professing to believe in Jesus Christ, shall from henceforth bee any waies troubled . . . for . . . his or her religion . . . soe as they be not unfaithfull to the Lord Proprietary or molest or conspire against the civill Government established."[9]

While this *Toleration Act* of 1649 protected minority Christian persuasions, it offered little comfort to the non-Christian and fell miserably short of the Williams philosophy. In the same breath, the legislature curtailed Sunday activity by decreeing that anyone who would profane "the Sabbath or Lords day called Sunday by frequent swearing, drunkenness or by any uncivill or disorderly recreacion, or by working on that day when absolute necessity doth not require it"[10] would be subject to fine, imprisonment, and public whipping.

These early pioneers were followed by William Penn and the Pennsylvania Quaker colony. Advised to "tremble at the Word of the Lord," the dissenting religionists in England who relied on the "inner light" rather than exterior sacrament, were first nicknamed "Quakers" in 1650. William Penn, son of an English admiral, joined the group, and in 1670, at the age of twenty-six, he made religious and legal history.

In 1664 Parliament outlawed all religious meetings but those sanctioned by the Church of England. Roman Catholics and other dissenters suffered from the vengeance of this and similar rigid regulations established by a hostile government. Quakers went to jail by the thousands, and scores died in prison.

Young Penn himself was no stranger to the prison cell. Thus the threat of imprisonment held no real terror for him when he found soldiers barring the entrance to the Quaker meeting hall on Gracechurch Street, London, on August 14, 1670. Penn simply preached to the believers in the street and was haled into court for "disturbance of the peace."

The indictment which came on September 1 was filled with double-talk and such gibberish as "contempt of the said Lord the

14

Though not granting absolute religious freedom, William Penn's colony offered liberty to all professing belief in God.

King, and of his Law" as well as terror and disturbance to his people and subjects and "against the Peace of the said Lord the King, his Crown and Dignity."[11]

To protect the "dignity" of the Crown, the inept Lord Mayor, Sir Samuel Starling, was summoned. Sitting with him was "the Recorder, John Howel, the chief criminal judge of the City of London, equally unlearned in the law which he was supposed to administer, a stupid man with little to sustain him except a few worn-thin Latin proverbs which he took delight in misapplying. He was a dull, heavy man, who was soon angry when the trial came alive, and kept his hot temper simmering; he suspected that Penn was making fun of him—which indeed Penn was."[12] These giants of jurisprudence were joined by aldermen and sheriffs. The twelve-man jury was expected to do its duty and find a guilty verdict.

With his codefendant, William Meade, Penn erected a stout and vigorous defense, punctuated with spicy exchanges with the court. At one point Penn demanded to know upon what law his indictment was based.

"Upon the Common-Law," the Recorder snapped.

"Where is that Common-Law?" persisted Penn.

The Recorder retorted, "You must not think that I am able to run up so many Years, and over so many adjudged Cases, which we call Common-Law, to answer your Curiosity."

"This Answer I am sure is very short of my Question, for if it be Common, it should not be so hard to produce," Penn taunted.[13]

The Recorder called Penn "impertinent" and invoked *les non scripta*. In turn, Penn accused the court of "sinister and arbitrary designs."

Meade, the codefendant, spoke of the Quaker tenet of peace to which he subscribed, in contrast to an "unlawful assembly" as defined by Lord Coke. The Lord Mayor bristled. "You deserve to have your tongue cut out."[14]

16

Penn and Meade held their ground through the acid exchanges, and the jury of twelve ordinary men was impressed. To the dismay of the court, it returned a verdict of "not guilty" to the unlawful-assembly charge.

"Members of the court threatened the jury with fines and hinted at torture if they did not bring in a verdict to the judge's taste—but they would not yield: 'NOR WILL WE EVER DO IT!' their foreman shouted in answer to Penn's impassioned appeal, 'Give not away your right!' "[15]

Repeatedly the jury was sent out for a revised verdict. Repeatedly it returned with an unaltered opinion despite the court's threat to keep the jury "lock'd up, without Meat, Drink, Fire, and Tobacco."

When a defiant jury returned for the fifth time with the same verdict, Penn challenged the court.

"What hope is there of ever having Justice done, when Juries are threatened, and their Verdicts rejected?" he exclaimed.

"Stop his Mouth; Jaylor, bring Fetters and stake him to the Ground," Lord Mayor shouted.

Penn clung to his aplomb, "Do your Pleasure, I matter not your Fetters."

"And the recorder in his exasperation disclosed the real basis of the prosecution and fitted the proceeding expressly into the history of religious intolerance in Europe: 'Till now,' he said, 'I never understood the Reason of the Policy and Prudence of the *Spaniards,* in suffering the Inquisition among them: And certainly it will never be well with us, till something like unto the *Spanish* Inquisition be in *England'!*"[16]

For their obstinacy, each juryman was fined forty marks and imprisoned, along with the defendants, until the fine had been paid. Thus ended the trial of William Penn and William Meade. And thus was born the soul of a leader whose principles of toleration would find expression in the new world. Although short of absolute religious freedom, the Pennsylvania colony took a giant step forward and offered liberty to all who believed in God.

Even here, however, all who deserved liberty of conscience had to profess faith in Jesus Christ.[17] And, inspired by the Sunday law of the twenty-ninth year of Charles II, honest labor and business on Sunday were declared to be criminal acts. To protect against "looseness, irreligion, and atheism," people were ordered by law to "devote themselves to religious and pious exercises" which included the reading and hearing of the Holy Scriptures and the attendance at worship services.

Baptists and Quakers found rough going in New England. "Connecticut Baptists converted from Congregationalism moved into northern North Carolina. . . . They spread with astonishing rapidity both toward the south and the north into Virginia. . . . The Episcopal Church was the established church in that colony. Other churches were denied official permission to conduct the rites of their faith. The Baptists, Quakers, and Presbyterians became active in their opposition."[18]

By the time of the Revolution, the Anglican Church's position in the South was also "weakened by the fact that theirs was the official church of England in a period when independence from the mother country was about to become the paramount fact of current history. For, whatever their doctrinal differences in religion, all of the Founding Fathers were political revolutionaries, determined to enact a new formulation of the idea of government by consent of the governed."[19]

By the mid-eighteenth century, the ground had been broken for a noble experiment in self-government built on a foundation of complete separation of church and state. The most influential skirmish in the political battle for disestablishment would be fought on the soil of Virginia.

NEW WORLD, OLD LAWS

REFERENCES

1. Philip Schaff, *History of the Christian Church* (Grand Rapids, Michigan: Wm. B. Eerdmans Publishing Company, 1950), Vol. 3, Section 27, pp. 144, 145.
2. Charles M. Snow, *Religious Liberty in America* (Washington, D.C.: Review and Herald Publishing Association, 1914), page 37.
3. William L. Roper, "Roger Williams, The Man and His Dream," *Liberty,* Vol. 58 (1963), No. 1, p. 27.
4. *Ibid.*
5. *Winthrop's Journal,* Vol. 1, pp. 52, 53. In *American State Papers,* Third Revised Edition (Washington, D.C.: Review and Herald Publishing Association, 1943), page 57.
6. Roper, *Op. cit.,* p. 29.
7. *Proceedings of the First General Assembly and the Code of Laws* [Rhode Island], 1647, page 50.
8. George Bancroft, *History of the United States of America* (Boston: Charles C. Little and James Brown, 1846), Vol. 1, pp. 254, 255.
9. "Proceedings and Acts of the General Assembly of Maryland (1637/38-1664)," *Archives of Maryland* (Baltimore: Maryland Historical Society, 1883), Vol. 1, p. 246.
10. *Ibid.*
11. Eberhad P. Deutsch, "Hugh Latimer's Candle and the Trial of William Penn," *American Bar Association Journal,* Vol. 51 (1965), No. 7, pp. 627, 628.
12. Francis Biddle, "The Ordeal of William Penn," *American Heritage,* Vol. 15 (1964), No. 3, p. 31. Used by permission.
13. See Deutsch, *Op. cit.,* pp. 628, 629.
14. Biddle, *Op. cit.,* p. 30.
15. Deutsch, *Op. cit.,* p. 629.
16. See *Ibid.,* pp. 629, 630.
17. See *American State Papers,* pages 39, 40.
18. Alvin W. Johnson and Frank H. Yost, *Separation of Church and State in the United States* (Minneapolis: University of Minnesota Press, 1948), page 3.
19. E. M. Halliday, "Nature's God and the Founding Fathers," *American Heritage,* Vol. 14 (1963), No. 6, p. 5. Used by permission.

Jefferson declared that he contemplated "with reverence" the act that built a wall of separation of church and state.

3. "BUILDING A WALL OF SEPARATION"

Dateline: PHILADELPHIA, November 3, 1791. Today the first ten amendments to the United States Constitution became a part of the supreme law of the land. The first sentence of the first amendment rejected centuries of precedent, guaranteeing that religion was to be neither the slave nor the master of the state.

Thomas Jefferson observed, "I contemplate with sovereign reverence that act of the whole American people which declares that their legislature should 'make no law respecting an establishment of religion or prohibiting the free exercise therof,' thus building a wall of separation between church and state."[1]

This was no paper philosophy. Though Christianity flourished in the minds of the citizens and leaders of the new nation, neutrality in matters of religion had become official government doctrine. This philosophy appeared in the "Treaty of Peace and Friendship" with Tripoli, executed November 4, 1796 during the administration of George Washington. This document declared that "the government of the United States of America is not, in any sense, founded on the Christian religion."[2]

A revolution in both thought and action had taken place. A noble experiment in civil and religious liberty had been conceived.

21

DATELINE SUNDAY, U.S.A.

Centuries marked with martyrdoms and bloody persecutions foisted on ancestors across the Atlantic, offered a shabby chronicle. New World settlers recalled the lions of the Roman coliseum; the Spanish Inquisition; the massacres of the Waldenses in their mountain hideaways; the Tower of London; the "holy" wars; the rack, the screw, and the stake; fines, imprisonments, and executions.

Overzealous early colonists had not been reluctant to use the dock, the pillory, and the lash. Yet, paradoxically, the stringent character of the colonial Puritan was one factor which assured the eventual demise of government by clergy. As early settlers struggled to survive in a new and hostile land, stalwart individualism was essential, and a self-reliant citizenry chafed under the heel of oppressive clericalism. Citizens nearly succeeded in preventing the clergy-inspired hanging of George Burroughs, and even the teachings of Roger Williams found sympathetic Puritan ears. The scope of the land itself encouraged freedom. Where political or religious ostracism had occurred, there was always the refuge of the new frontier.

The fifty-five men who met in Philadelphia in 1787 to construct a new system of government had been exposed to the philosophical thought of theorists like Locke, Montesquieu, and Voltaire, who wrote from philosophical bent and from bitter experience as well. Ideas such as "That government which governs least, governs best," and "I may disagree with what you say, but I will defend to the death your right to say it," appealed to the founding fathers.

Finally, inherent in the origins of the American Revolution was the diversity of the national heritage. Patterns of religious thought were equally diverse:

> The growth of religious freedom might have had a different story but for America's novel situation of having no majority religion. Puritan New England, which clung longest to the old intolerance, and Anglican Virginia, which was

22

hardly less intolerant in the early days, were the only areas dominated by single religious groups. The Quaker colonies —Pennsylvania, New Jersey, and Delaware—none of which had religious establishments, came nearest, after Rhode Island, to realizing complete religious liberty, but the Proprietary colonies in general developed liberal tendencies. Business considerations would naturally operate to induce Proprietors to grant a measure of tolerance, for they needed to attract industrious settlers and promote peace and prosperity. This was at least partly responsible for writing liberty-of-conscience clauses into the charters of New York, New Jersey, the Carolinas, and Georgia.

Aside from the increase of dissenters, the growing number of the unchurched was a factor. Even in Puritan New England the majority of the masses were not church members, and the wave of popular resentment against the magistrates prevented the continuance of severe persecution of Quakers. Indeed, the increasing strictness of the Puritan legislation attests the inability to enforce such laws on the population at large.[3]

Stephen Mumford, a member of the Bell Lane Seventh Day Baptist Church in London, settled in Roger Williams's Newport, Rhode Island, colony in 1664. When five members of the Newport First Baptist Church joined the Mumfords in worshiping on the seventh day of the week rather than Sunday, they were called before the church officials to answer for their deviation.

Samuel Hubbard, one of the five, later wrote the details of his appearance: "I answered, 'I believe there is but one God, Creator of all things by His word at first and then made the 7th day and sanctified it; commanded it to be kept holy, etc., that Christ our Lord established it, Math 5 [Matthew 5]; the holy apostles established it, did not say it *was* holy, but *is* holy, just and good.' "[4]

Seven years after this brush with established religion, the Baptist group founded its own meeting place in Newport and counted among its members some of the most prominent, influential citizens of Rhode Island. Samuel Ward, Rhode Island

23

governor and first colonial governor who refused to enforce the 1765 Stamp Act, was a Seventh Day Baptist and a delegate to the Continental Congress that met in Philadelphia on September 5, 1774. Had he not died on March 26, 1776, he likely would have been one of the signers of the Declaration of Independence.

The case of Governor Ward and the Seventh Day Baptists is a clear illustration of the position of minority groups in some colonies:

> While full freedom of belief was not legally protected in any of the colonies at the start of the Revolution, and most of them had an established church supported by the government, minority groups and nonconforming individuals were in fact granted considerable leeway. Catholics were strong in Maryland; Quakers, in Pennsylvania. In New England, the evolution of a Congregational doctrine had moved toward freedom of conscience for more than a century, so that there was a kind of paradox in the legal establishment of a church so nearly democratic in its organization. The supremacy of the Anglicans in the South, moreover, was weakened by the fact that theirs was the official church of England in a period when independence from the mother country was about to become the paramount fact of current history. For, whatever their doctrinal differences in religion, all of the Founding Fathers were political revolutionaries, determined to enact a new formulation of the idea of government by consent of the governed.[5]

With the Baptists, Quakers, and Presbyterians moving into the South, the time had come to consider more carefully the establishment of religion in a political context. These minorities were present in Virginia, a colony dominated in its religious affairs by the Church of England and the home of some of the most astute political leadership of the Revolution, George Mason, James Madison, and Albermarle County's Thomas Jefferson.

Jefferson believed that complete personal freedom of conscience was inseparable from "the principle of majority rule." This principle "depended on the premise of a well-informed public, each member of which could choose among moral or political alternatives with absolute freedom from mental coercion. This is the key to Jefferson's lifelong insistence on complete separation of church and state."[6]

The Virginia House of Burgesses, meeting in Williamsburg, was a forum for issues affecting civil and religious liberty. Here constant demands were heard for the recognition of basic human rights. A steady stream of petitions and requests to protect these rights flowed to the legislature from Virginia citizens. By 1776, the year that James Madison of Port Conway arrived as a delegate, the House of Burgesses was reviewing the entire structure of Virginia government.

Madison served on a committee to draw up a bill of rights which would provide the philosophical base for the new government. "The great George Mason of Gunston Hall was chief author of the articles in this bill, which was to become the prototype for similar manifestos in other states as well as, eventually, for the Bill of Rights of the United States Constitution."[7]

The last of a sixteen-section "Declaration of Rights," adopted by the House of Burgesses on June 12, 1776, reflected the thoughts of Jefferson, and its final draft carried the influence of Madison's thinking as well. It declared: "That religion, or the duty which we owe to our Creator, and the manner of discharging it, can be directed only by reason and conviction, not by force or violence; and therefore all men are equally entitled to the free exercise of religion, according to the dictates of conscience."[8]

Patrick Henry penned the original draft of this article, which included a reference to "the fullest *toleration* in the exercise of religion." Madison was committed to nothing short of *"free exercise"* and succeeded in having "toleration" dropped from the final draft. He reasoned that a state which could "tolerate" could also prohibit.

The Anglican Church still remained the established religion

of the Virginia colony. "Government salaries for Anglican ministers had been suspended. . . . [But] it was impossible to be legally married . . . unless the ceremony was performed by an Anglican clergyman, and heresy against the Christian faith was still a crime."[9]

Presbyterians pushed for abolition of the establishment. In October, 1776, just after the Declaration of Independence had been signed, the Presbytery of Hanover presented a memorial to Virginia's General Assembly asking for the removal of "every species of religious as well as civil bondage," and noting that "every argument for civil liberty gains additional strength when applied in the concerns of religion." Then they added this statement:

> We ask no ecclesiastical establishment for ourselves, neither can we approve of them and grant it to others. . . . We are induced earnestly to entreat that all laws now in force in this commonwealth which countenance religious domination may be speedily repealed,—that all of every religious sect may be protected in the full exercise of their several modes of worship, and exempted from all taxes for the support of any church whatsoever, further than what may be agreeable to their own private choice or voluntary obligation.[10]

When Patrick Henry championed a general tax labeled "A Bill Establishing a Provision for Teachers of the Christian Faith" in 1784, Madison denounced it as "chiefly obnoxious on account of its dishonorable principle and dangerous tendency."[11] Madison opposed any concept which gave Christianity a legal preference over other religious persuasions and which was in any way short of absolute separation of church and state.

In response to a suggestion from George and Wilson Cary Nicholas, members of the General Assembly, Madison took his pen in hand to arouse a public which already had freedom on its mind. In "A Memorial and Remonstrance," which was printed and circulated for signatures in 1785, he warned, "It is proper to take alarm at the first experiment on our liberties." He cited the free men all over America who refused to wait until usurped power had strengthened itself through exercise. Then he applied this logic to the religious freedom issue at hand, asking:

> Who does not see that the same authority which can establish Christianity, in exclusion of all other Religions, may establish with the same ease any particular sect of Christians, in exclusion of all other sects? that the same authority which can force a citizen to contribute three pence only of his property for the support of any one establishment, may force him to conform to any other establishment in all cases whatsoever?[12]

The impact of Madison's precise logic created a public reaction so intense that proponents of the "Provision for Teachers of the Christian Religion" measure conceded defeat. The memorial had been signed by several different religious sects, even including a considerable number of the old hierarchy.

Madison seized this moment to push for the adoption of an "Act for Establishing Religious Freedom," written by Jefferson in 1779 but shelved at that time for lack of support. So prized was the content of this document that Jefferson chose it, coupled with his authorship of the Declaration of Independence and his founding of the University of Virginia, as the outstanding achievements of his life which were to be carved on his tombstone.

But the mood of 1785 contrasted with the mood of 1774. Seasoned by a hard-fought and costly conflict with Great Britain, political reformers were prepared to make religious liberty as absolute as the desired political freedom which the people sought. The act was passed by the Assembly in December of 1785:

> No man shall be compelled to frequent or support any religious worship, place, or ministry whatsoever, nor shall be enforced, restrained, molested, or burthened in his body

The Liberty Bell, hidden during the Revolutionary War, was returned to Philadelphia to proclaim the birth of a free nation.

or goods, nor shall otherwise suffer on account of his religious opinions or belief; but that all men shall be free to profess and by argument to maintain their opinions in matters of religion, and that the same shall in nowise diminish, enlarge, or affect their civil capacities.[13]

28

"BUILDING A WALL OF SEPARATION"

Church-state separation had achieved legal status in Virginia!

The Virginia act of disestablishment was published widely, even in foreign countries. But when Jefferson urged New England political leaders to move for disestablishment in their colonies, he received little encouragement. John Adams reported the mood of some: "I knew they might as well turn the heavenly bodies out of their annual and diurnal courses, as the people of Massachusetts at the present day from their meetinghouse and Sunday laws."[14]

The time was ripe for Federal intervention. Men of philosophical orientation like Jefferson sensed that this was the moment to establish "every essential right." The voice from Monticello cautioned:

> The spirit of the times may alter, will alter. Our rulers will become corrupt, our people careless. A single zealot may commence persecution, and better men be his victims. It can never be too often repeated, that the time for fixing every essential right on a legal basis is while our rulers are honest, and ourselves united. From the conclusion of this war we shall be going downhill. It will not then be necessary to resort every moment to the people for support. They will be forgotten, therefore, and their rights disregarded. They will forget themselves, but in the sole faculty of making money, and will never think of uniting to effect a due respect for their rights. The shackles, therefore, which shall not be knocked off at the conclusion of this war, will remain on us long, will be made heavier and heavier, till our rights shall revive or expire in a convulsion.[15]

When the Federal Constitutional Convention adjourned on September 17, 1787, it had produced an impressive document. It guaranteed that there would be no religious test for holding public office in the new government. But the Constitution had no bill of rights and no positive guarantees of church-state separation. George Mason was so distraught at this shortcoming that he refused to sign or approve the work of the convention. When

Jefferson saw the final draft, he, too, was disappointed at the lack of major religious freedom guarantees; but he found it otherwise acceptable and stated a willingness to trust to the "good sense and honest intentions of our citizens"[16] to obtain the desired amendments.

No sooner had local states initiated ratification procedures for the Constitution than the move for a bill of rights was launched. Virginia, New York, and New Hampshire asked for a declaration of religious liberty. As might be expected, James Madison was in the eye of the storm.

It was Madison who presented a long list of amendments to the First Congress, meeting in 1789. At the top of the list was a religious liberty amendment drawn by Madison himself. His colleagues subjected it to some reworking, but it was one of seventeen proposals sent to the Senate. Twelve amendments were finally sent to the states and ten ultimately ratified.

When the "Bill of Rights" was born in 1791, the wall of separation between church and state became the law of the United States of America. *"Congress shall make no law respecting an establishment of religion, or prohibiting the free exercise thereof."*

Meanwhile the battle for disestablishment in the new state governments got under way. Influential Virginia had pioneered the way. But "in the first [state] constitutions during the war period, only two of the thirteen new states, Rhode Island and Virginia, had complete religious freedom and separation. Six required Protestantism, two the Christian religion, and five a nominal establishment; and seven retained other provisions concerning such points as the Bible, the Trinity, and belief in heaven and hell. By the end of the Revolution nearly all the states had accepted the principle of separation of church and state."[17]

Not until 1833 did Massachusetts abolish some of the last significant remnants of religious establishment—and this state was the last of the original thirteen states to surrender the formal traditions of pseudotheocracy. Even then, disestablishment was not complete. One symbol of religious establishment, the Sunday blue law, remained on the books of most states.

In 1804 Thomas Paine voiced a bemused amazement at the patent incongruity of this traditional symbol:

> The word Sabbath means REST; that is, cessation from labor, but the stupid Blue Laws of Connecticut make a labor of rest, for they oblige a person to sit still from sunrise to sunset on a Sabbath-day, which is hard work. Fanaticism made those laws, and hypocrisy pretends to reverence them, for where such laws prevail hypocrisy will prevail also.
>
> One of those laws says, "No person shall run on a Sabbath-day, nor walk in his garden, nor elsewhere; but reverently to and from meeting." These fanatical hypocrites forget that God dwells not in temples made with hands, and that the earth is full of His glory.[18]

REFERENCES

1. *Reynolds* v. *United States*, 98 U.S. 145 (1878).
2. *United States Statutes at Large*, Vol. 8, p. 155.
3. *American State Papers and Related Documents* (Washington, D.C.: Review and Herald Publishing Association, 1949), pages 91, 92.
4. Charles J. Bochman, "Where Sabbathkeeping Began in North America," *Review and Herald*, Vol. 140 (1963), No. 22, p. 6.
5. E. M. Halliday, "Nature's God and the Founding Fathers," *American Heritage*, Vol. 14 (1963), No. 6, p. 5. Used by permission.
6. *Ibid.*, p. 7.
7. *Ibid.*, p. 100.
8. *American Archives*, Fourth Series, Vol. 6, pp. 1561, 1562. In *American State Papers*, Third Revised Edition (Washington, D.C.: Review and Herald Publishing Association, 1943), page 63.
9. Halliday, *Op. cit.*, p. 101.
10. "Dissenters Petition, 1776," from Bishop Meade, *Old Churches, Ministers, and Families of Virginia*, Vol. 2, Appendix, pp. 440-443. In *American State Papers*, pages 73, 74.
11. *Writings of James Madison*, Vol. 1, pp. 130, 131. In *American State Papers*, page 99.
12. *Ibid.*, pp. 84, 85.
13. *Writings of Thomas Jefferson*. In Norman Cousins, *In God We Trust* (New York: Harper & Brothers Publishers, 1958), pages 126, 127.
14. "Diary of John Adams." In *American State Papers*, page 101.
15. Thomas Jefferson, *Notes on Virginia*, Query XVII. In *American State Papers*, page 101.
16. *Reynolds* v. *United States* 98 U.S. 145 (1878).
17. *American State Papers and Related Documents* (1949 edition), page 92.
18. Thomas Paine, *Prospect Papers, 1804*. In *In God We Trust*, page 432.

"Religion flourishes in greater purity, without than with the aid of government," declared ex-president James Madison.

4. "WE ARE TEACHING THE WORLD"

Writing to Edward Livingston from his Montpelier home in the summer of 1822, ex-president James Madison declared: "We are teaching the world the great truth that Governments do better without kings and nobles than with them. The merit will be doubled by the other lesson that Religion flourishes in greater purity, without than with the aid of government."

Madison regretted that in some states disestablishment still had not been achieved. He felt that any alliance or coalition between government and religion imperiled the success of both. He argued that "religion and Government will both exist in greater purity, the less they are mixed together," and he supported his theory by citing the example of Virginia, "where it is impossible to deny that religion prevails with more zeal and a more exemplary priesthood than it ever did when established and patronized by public authority."

From its inception the Federal Government had no established religion or church tradition. Free of establishments, the new republic was consequently free of Sunday laws on a national level. James Madison liked it that way.

Madison approved of executive proclamations of fasts and festivals, providing they were merely "recommendatory," not

33

obligatory. Government has "a right to *appoint* particular days for religious worship throughout the state, without any penal sanction *enforcing* the worship."[1]

Madison's attitude was based upon commitment to individual property rights as well as independence of church and state. Among property rights, Madison included "time."

> If there be a government, then, which prides itself on maintaining the inviolability of property; which provides that none shall be taken *directly,* even for public use, without indemnification to the owner, and yet *directly* violates the property which individuals have in their opinions, their religion, their persons, and their faculties;—nay more, *which indirectly* violates their property, in their actual possessions, in the labor that acquires their daily subsistance, and in the hallowed remnant of time which ought to relieve their fatigues and soothe their cares, the inference will have been anticipated, that such a government is not a pattern for the United States.[2]

Madison, however, had powerful opponents who pushed for Sunday legislation on the Federal level. The matter boiled to the surface April 26, 1810, when Congress acted to require postmasters to provide service every day of the week, including the first day.

A deluge of petitions from clergymen and others demanded that Congress rescind the law and endorse "the strict observance of the first day of the week, as set apart by the command of God for His more immediate service."[3] No effort was made to conceal the religious motivation.

In 1815 the Thirteenth Congress reaffirmed its previous action, but the agitation continued. Chains anchored with padlocks were stretched across post roads in Philadelphia to halt the movement of mail coaches on Sunday. Roads that had brought representatives from thirteen colonies to forge a new government a few years before, now challenged the free spirit of that government. Defiance of the Federal authority carried the scent of something alien to the representative form of government that had been created.

As petitions continued to deluge Congress, that body again debated the issue, and again took a position opposed to national Sunday laws. Prominent in the opposition was Richard M. Johnson, a patriot's patriot. Born in Kentucky in 1780, after the colonies' formal break with England, Johnson's life began contemporaneously with that of his nation. His was the generation that bridged the era between the fledgling republic and the Civil War. His was a building, expanding generation; and as the country burst forth into new geographic areas, its formulas of freedom and justice gained new plateaus of expression.

Cast in the philosophical mold of Madison and Jefferson, Johnson reveled in the atmosphere of religious liberty enjoyed by the new country. He determined to preserve that liberty, and devoted his political career to the ideals of the free spirit of man. He earned distinction in the War of 1812, leading 1,900 volunteers against the British and Indian forces at the Battle of the Thames, October 5, 1813. Five years later his colleagues in Congress awarded him a sword of honor for his "daring and distinguished valor" in combat.

In the House of Representatives and the Senate, and later in the vice-presidency of the United States, Johnson gained a reputation as a man of unshakable convictions, who would not yield to pressure of any kind. He met the Sunday-law issue head on, declaring his conviction that 999 out of 1,000 citizens "were opposed to any legislative interference, inasmuch as it would have a tendency to unite religious institutions with the government." He saw in the proposals "the entering wedge of a scheme to make this government a religious, instead of a social and political, institution."

Senator Chambers of Maryland, a colleague of the Kentuckian, observed that the petitioners felt that "the observance

Patriot Richard Johnson urged that Congress not be called upon to try to settle which day should be kept as the Sabbath.

of the Sabbath was connected with the civil interests of the government."

Johnson replied that while he did not dispute the pure motives of the petitioners, "some denominations considered one day the most sacred, and some looked to another, and these petitions did, in fact, call upon Congress to settle what was the law of God. . . . Whether it was the first day or the seventh, the principle was wrong."[4]

In precedent-shattering actions taken in 1829 and 1830, both the Senate and the House adopted reports which followed the Johnson arguments and repudiated the Sunday legislation. The report Johnson submitted to the Senate was adopted in 1829. State legislatures in Indiana, Alabama, Illinois, and Kentucky joined with private citizens to celebrate its acceptance. A definitive declaration, this report emphasized that the United States Government is a "civil and not a religious institution," and as such "it is not the legitimate province of the legislature to determine what religion is true, or what false." Rather, the Government's proper function is to protect all persons "in the enjoyment of their religious as well as civil rights, and not to determine for any whether they shall esteem one day above another, or esteem all days alike holy."

Continuing the report, Johnson warned that in all past religious trials and persecutions victims suffered because they violated what some government had "denominated the law of God." He rejected the proposal that the Federal legislature could be an effective tribunal to interpret the laws of God, for once the principle is "established that religion, or religious observances, shall be interwoven with our legislative acts, we must pursue to its ultimatum." This, he contended, could lead to use of public monies for the construction of churches and salaries of the clergy.

Further, Johnson's report argued that, according to the principle of separation of church and state, all citizens of varying religious persuasions are equal under the law. "While the mail is transported on Saturday, the Jew and the Sabbatarian may abstain from any agency in carrying it, on conscientious scruples. While it is transported on the first day of the week, another class may abstain, from the same religious scruples. The obligation of government is the same to both these classes; and the committee can discover no principle on which the claims of one should be more respected than those of the other, unless it be admitted that the consciences of the minority are less sacred than those of the majority."

Johnson stressed national security in his plea to retain daily mail service. With heavy westward migration, any breakdown in communication would constitute a threat to operation of government on the fringes of the nation's new frontiers.

The report concluded by suggesting that persuasion offered the best means of enforcing religious observances. By means of a living religion, with meaningful deeds of benevolence, meekness, temperance, and holiness, the moral influence of the Sunday-law advocates would "then do infinitely more to advance the true interests of religion, than any measures which they may call on Congress to enact."[5]

In 1830 Richard Johnson again served in the House of Representatives. As before, his dynamic leadership was the inspiration behind a report on the same issue brought before the House on March 4 and 5 of that year.

Rarely has a political document been more profound in its impact and influence. As in the Senate report of the preceeding year, the need for uninterrupted communication with the West was cited. "To stop the mails one day in seven would be to thrust the whole western country, and other distant parts of this republic, one day's journey from the seat of government."

As if aware of the precedent-setting impact this Congressional confrontation would have on subsequent Federal Sunday-law proposals, Johnson expressed his relief that "the proposition should have been made at this early period, while the spirit of the Revolution yet exists in full vigor."

Recognizing the diversity of thought with respect to first-day versus seventh-day observance, the House Committee on the Post Office and Post Roads pointed to government's obligation to "protect all and determine for none," since "Congress acts under a constitution of delegated and limited powers. The committee looked in vain to that instrument for a delegation of power authorizing this body to inquire and determine what part of time, or whether any, has been set apart by the Almighty for religious exercises. On the contrary, among the few prohibitions which it contains is one . . . that Congress shall pass no law respecting an establishment of religion, or prohibiting the free exercise thereof."

Since the Sunday business hours observed by the post office had already been made flexible in order not to interfere with public worship, "the committee believe that there is no just ground of complaint, unless it be conceded that they have a controlling power over the consciences of others."

> If Congress shall declare the first day of the week holy, it will not convince the Jew nor the Sabbatarian. It will dissatisfy both, and, consequently, convert neither. Human power may extort vain sacrifices, but the Deity alone can command the affections of the heart."

The committee report recalled painful persecutions of the past and the reasons behind them. It noted that the Christian religion was opposed originally by human government.

> Banishment, tortures, and death were inflicted in vain to stop its progress. But many of its professors, as soon as clothed with political power, lost the meek spirit which their creed inculcated, and began to inflict on other religions, and on dissenting sects of their own religion, persecutions more aggravated than those which their own apostles had endured.
> The ten persecutions of pagan emperors were exceeded

39

in atrocity by the massacres and murders perpetrated by Christian hands; and in vain shall we examine the records of imperial tyranny for an engine of cruelty equal to the holy Inquisition. Every religious sect, however meek its origin, commenced the work of persecution as soon as it acquired political power. . . .

What did the Protestants of Germany, or the Huguenots of France, ask of their Catholic superiors? Toleration. What do the persecuted Catholics of Ireland ask of their oppressors? Toleration. Do not all men in this country enjoy every religious right which martyrs and saints ever asked? Whence, then, the voice of complaint? Who is it that, in the full enjoyment of every principle which human laws can secure, wishes to wrest a portion of these principles from his neighbor?

The report speculated as to the absurdities that might result once a Federal Sunday law were adopted. If it is sinful to carry letters, "it must be equally sinful for individuals to write, carry, receive, or read them." Therefore, "it would seem to require that these acts should be made penal to complete the system."

Ultimately, the committee warned, laws could be established to suppress travel on the Lord's Day, except for church attendance. Newspapers would be unobtainable, as printing, delivering, and receiving them would constitute transgression. Eventually even conversation would be limited, except on religious topics. Social relationships on the first day would cease. Eventually, even men's thoughts would cease to be their own.

The report concluded with an appeal to reason.

If the Almighty has set apart the first day of the week as a time which man is bound to keep holy, and devote exclusively to His worship, would it not be more congenial to the precepts of Christians to appeal exclusively to the Great Lawgiver of the universe to aid them in making men better —in correcting their practices, by purifying their hearts? Government will protect them in their efforts. When they shall have so instructed the public mind, and awakened the consciences of individuals as to make them believe that it is a violation of God's law to carry the mail, open post-offices, or receive letters on Sunday, the evil of which they complain will cease of itself, without any exertion of the strong arm of civil power.[6]

In the history of Sunday-law controversy there had never been a more devastating analysis than that developed by the eloquent Richard Johnson and adopted by the Congress of the United States in 1829 and 1830. So complete was the victory for religious freedom that not until 1888 was any serious move again made in Congress for a national Sunday observance. Despite this lull, most nineteenth-century state governments clung to Sunday blue laws in spirit and fact, and state courts still enforced first-day observance on a patently religious platform.

REFERENCES

1. *Letters and Other Writings of James Madison* (1865), Vol. 3, pp. 273 ff. In *American State Papers,* Third Revised Edition (Washington, D.C.: Review and Herald Publishing Association, 1943), pages 174, 175.
2. *American State Papers,* page 158.
3. *Ibid.,* p. 188.
4. *Register of Debates in Congress,* Vol. 5 p. 42. In *American State Papers,* pages 188, 189.
5. *Senate Report on Sunday Mails,* January 19, 1829. In *American State Papers,* pages 190-195.
6. *House Report on Sunday Mails,* March 4, 5, 1830. In *American State Papers,* pages 196-205.

William Lloyd Garrison declared, "Attempts to coerce an observance of the Sabbath . . . have been, must be, . . . nugatory."

5. "UPRIGHT PERSONS HAVE BEEN THRUST INTO PRISON"

The chill of the Pennsylvania winter would have slowed a less ambitious man. But not Charles C. Burleigh, flaming orator of the old school, intent on exposing the slavery that flourished in parts of midnineteenth-century America.

Arriving in West Chester in February, 1847, he was prepared to promote his cause through public lectures and printed pamphlets. The public listened willingly, but the crusader's efforts ground to an abrupt halt. Burleigh customarily distributed antislavery literature at the conclusion of his lectures. But when he sold this literature following a Sunday lecture in West Chester, he went to jail, not because of his progressive views on human freedom, but because selling *anything* on Sunday, even Christian literature, violated the local blue law. Twice during the month of February, 1847, he went to prison for this same cause, once for six days.[1]

While Congress had not succumbed to pressures to create Federal Sunday legislation, blue laws in the states had survived the general disestablishment of religion. In most cases the leaders of the antislavery movement were fighting both slavery and enforced Sunday worship as infringements on human rights. As early as 1836, William Lloyd Garrison, fiery editor of *The Liberator,* had editorialized: "Certain we are that all attempts to coerce an observance of the Sabbath by legislation have been, must be, and ought to be, nugatory."[2] He cried out against the utilizing of civil or ecclesiastical pains and penalties in order "to enforce its observances, as a peculiarly 'holy day.' "[3]

An attempt was made to arrest Garrison under a charge similar to that leveled against Burleigh. The abolitionists concluded the time had come to resist the Sunday-law flanking attack. In a statement drafted by Garrison and signed by Burleigh and other abolitionist spokesmen, an anti-Sunday-law convention was called in Boston, Massachusetts, for March 23 and 24, 1848. The convention call, addressed "An Appeal to the Friends of Civil and Religious Liberty," pointed to the widespread existence of "laws enforcing the religious observance of the first day of the week as the Sabbath, and punishing as criminals such as attempt to pursue their usual avocations on that day."

Citing recent so-called "crimes" of alleged Sabbath desecration in Massachusetts, Vermont, Pennsylvania, and Ohio, the call noted that "conscientious and upright persons have been thrust into prison for an act no more intrinsically heinous than that of gathering in a crop of hay, or selling moral or philanthropic publications." The Garrison-Burleigh document also referred to an organized religious combination that had been formed during the past five years under the name "The American and Foreign Sabbath Union," which hoped "to impose the Sabbatical yoke yet more heavily on the necks of the American people." "Religious bigotry and ecclesiastical tyranny" inspired these efforts, since there was a reliance upon brute force and penal law in the Union's effort "to crush by violence the rights of conscience, and religious liberty and equality." "Their real spirit," the document concluded, "is revealed as at war with the genius of republicanism and the spirit of Christianity."

Criticizing the blue law as "a shameful act of imposture and tyranny," these reformers denounced "all penal laws respecting the religious observance of any day as the Sabbath" as despotic and anti-Christian and demanded that they should be repealed promptly.[4]

Following such a massive uproar, it came as no surprise that the 1848 Boston convention produced a package of six resolutions calling for the abolition of all state Sunday blue laws. The resolutions charged that those "who are for subjecting to fine or imprisonment such as do not receive their interpretation of the Scriptures in regard to the observance of the first day of the week as the Sabbath, are actuated by a mistaken or malevolent spirit . . . which in various ages, has resorted to the dungeon, the rack, the gallows, and the stake, for the accomplishment of its purpose."[5]

Those in attendance at the convention reasoned that if there was a law indicating the proper day for religious worship and forcing abstinence from work on such a day, laws could eventually be established which would force the people to worship at certain places and times, all under government supervision. By the same token, laws might determine the doctrines to be preached and the ordinances to be observed. Since the young nation had proved a refuge from the scourge of church-state tyranny, and since the people were accustomed to making their own decisions regarding worship, liberation from Sunday legislation seemed a logical next step. Supporters of religious liberty were urged to petition their state legislators for blue-law repeal.

With characteristic articulation, Garrison spoke in vehement defense of the convention resolutions, likening the Sunday-law advocate to a thief that warns, "If you do not obey me, I will put my hands into your pocket, and take out as much as I please in the shape of a fine; or if I find nothing there, I will put you in prison; or if you resist enough to require it, I will shoot you dead."

"Passing a law, forbidding me or you to do on a particular day, what is in itself right . . . is nothing better than sheer usurpation," Garrison warned.

Garrison relegated blue laws to the class of "tyrannical legislation which formerly sent men to the stake, in the name of God and for His glory, because they did not agree in the theological views of those who burnt them to ashes."

"If it [Sabbatical observance] be of God, it does not need legislation to uphold it," Garrison reasoned. "There is no power which can prevail against it."

Since Christianity, as taught by its Founder, does not rely for its safety and prosperity "on the rack or the stake, the dungeon or the gibbet, unjust proscription or brutal supremacy," why not "let the first day of the week stand on its own basis, as the second or third day stands?"

If we do so, Garrison predicted, "it will be much more rationally observed than it is now."[6]

While the work of Garrison and others in the antislavery cause was successful, their efforts to defeat Sunday laws largely failed, perhaps because slavery and national union were the ultimate political concerns of the day.

Meanwhile, undeterred by the Federal Bill of Rights, local states continued to enforce Sunday observance. In a steady stream of decisions, the majority of state courts sanctioned blue laws for obviously religious objectives.

The Massachusetts Supreme Court in 1880 tied the statutes of that era to the Puritan pioneers when it observed:

> Our Puritan ancestors intended that the day should be not merely a day of rest from labor, but also a day devoted to public and private worship and to religious meditation and repose, undisturbed by secular cares or amusements. They saw fit to enforce the observance of the day by penal legislation, and the statute regulations which they devised for that purpose have continued in force, without any substantial modification, to the present time.[7]

An earlier Massachusetts court had accepted the religious establishment of Sunday because "the legislative power or the uniform usage of every Christian state has exacted the observance of it as such."[8]

Chief Justice English, of the 1856 Arkansas Supreme Court, defended Sunday laws in an opinion involving playing cards: "The object of the statute was to prohibit the *desecration* of the *Sabbath* by engaging in the vicious employment of playing *cards* on that day, which is set apart by Divine appointment, as well as by the law of the land, for other and better engagements; and whether the defendant played for a wager or amusement, he is alike guilty of a desecration of the Sabbath, and consequently of a violation of the law."[9]

Chief Justice Kent of New York described the Sunday law of his day (1811) as a statute which "consecrates the first day of the week, as holy time."[10] Decades later, in 1834, another New York jurist pointed to the obvious solemnity of the day.[11]

A short time prior to the abolitionists' anti-Sunday-law convention in Boston, the Alabama Supreme Court found the legislative intent clear to "advance the interest of religion, by prohibiting all persons from engaging in their common and ordinary avocations of business, or employment, on Sunday."[12] And it was in the year of the Boston convention that the Iowa case of *Davis* v. *Fish* was reported, attesting to the sacred character of Sunday as a Heaven-appointed institution which was "established by laws, both human and divine, for public worship and private devotion."[13]

A Minnesota Sunday law was enforced "to prevent a desecration of the day."[14] Just before the Civil War, a Georgia court described Sunday as "that holy day."[15]

Shortly after the war, the Georgia Supreme Court heard the case of *H. Karwisch* v. *The Mayor and Council of Atlanta*, relating to the rights of a citizen to keep the doors of his business open on the first day of the week. The court declared, "The law fixes the day recognized as the Sabbath day all over Christendom, and that day, by Devine injunction, is to be kept holy—'on it thou shalt do no work.' "[16]

In the case of *Judefind* v. *The State of Maryland*, in 1894, Judge Boyd argued that the spirit shown in the religious-liberty declaration of the Maryland constitution was satisfied as long as free exercise of religion was permitted, even though the Christian religion enjoyed preferred status. He admitted, "It is undoubtedly true that rest from secular employment on Sunday does have a tendency to foster and encourage the Christian religion."[17]

Mr. Judefind, a Seventh-day Adventist of Rock Hall, Maryland, had been arrested November 20, 1892, on a charge of husking corn on Sunday. Pastor Rowe, of the local Methodist Episcopal church, was the accuser. While passing by on an adjacent road, he testified, he spotted Judefind at work in his field. The warrant was issued and served later that same day, Sunday—an act in itself out of harmony with local legal practice. Although the justice of the peace who issued the warrant and tried the case later denied this procedure, the constable who served the warrant admitted to having done the work on Sunday.

The justice of the peace fined Judefind five dollars. Judefind appealed to the circuit court, and the case was heard in Chestertown, in April, 1893, with Attorney Ringgold of Baltimore acting for the defense. When judgment was withheld at time of trial, Ringgold gave notice of intent to appeal in the event of an adverse decision and returned to Baltimore expecting that he would be informed when the court was prepared to render its decision in the case.

"At the end of a week, Judge Wicks, in the absence of the counsel for the defense, delivered the opinion of the court, and committed the defendant to jail for thirty days. When Mr. Ringgold received notice of this fact, he journeyed to Chestertown and applied for a writ of release for the defendant, pending the appeal; but the judges refused to sign the release, and Mr.

Judefind had to serve his time out before the case was heard in the court of appeals, January 23, 1894."[18]

Judefind could find little comfort in the contention of Judge Boyd that, though the state law favored Sunday, free exercise of religion was permitted for all.

The Judefind case is not particularly refreshing either in its reflection on due process of law or respect for freedom of conscience. And it does not stand alone as a phenomenon of the times. In the nineteenth century, Sunday laws served as an active instrument of religious intolerance in more than one state.

Organized as a church in 1863, Seventh-day Adventists were committed to the doctrine of Sabbath observance from sundown Friday evening to sundown Saturday evening, as a memorial of creation. They were also committed to civil obedience, respect for government, and love of country. Their leaders counseled them honestly to endeavor to obey Sunday laws, however unjust.

Still there were some who, like Judefind, misjudged the zeal of their spies and critics. At Shady Side, Maryland, a "Watchman's Association" was formed for the avowed purpose of spying on the Sunday conduct of seventh-day observers in hopes of ferreting out "illegal" actions and sending them to jail "or driving them from the country. . . . The door and transom of their meetinghouse at this place were broken and their worship was disturbed." A Mr. Howard was arrested for taking two or three minutes to pick up some sticks in a churchyard Sunday morning before breakfast. A Mr. Bullen ran afoul of the law for inspecting his garden for five minutes one Sunday. This happened at a time when "axes were to be heard all around the neighborhood. Even their informants were caring for their boats, bailing out water, drying sails, etc., preparing to amuse themselves on the same 'Lord's day,' commonly called Sunday.' "

A Mr. Ford, of Queen Anne's County, Maryland, swore he would prosecute the first Seventh-day Adventist he could find at work on Sunday. Consequently he was instrumental in the arrest of his own brother on June 5, 1893. The crime was the act of "hauling some window sashes for the new Seventh-day Adventist church, from the steamer dock on Sunday, to prevent their being destroyed, threats to that effect having been made."[19]

Samuel Mitchel, a Seventh-day Adventist of Quitman, Brooks County, Georgia, was sentenced to thirty days in jail in 1878 for plowing his own field. Although in poor health, he served the sentence rather than pay the fine.

In 1889, Day Conklin of Bigcreek, Forsyth County, Georgia, was found guilty of chopping wood on Sunday. The Friday before, much of his family's possessions had been soaked in a cloudburst while moving. The weather turned bitter cold, and with his meager supply of firewood exhausted by Sunday, Conklin acted to preserve the health of his family.

Fine and court costs totaled $83! Eradicating all doubt as to the motive behind Conklin's conviction, one of the witnesses against him, and one of the jurors giving the verdict, "chopped wood at their own homes on the very next Sunday after the trial,"[20] apparently immune to any threat of prosecution. But Conklin was a Seventh-day Adventist.

Seventh-day observers were charged with a wide variety of Sunday-law violations. In Arkansas, J. W. Scoles, a clergyman, was seen painting the back of a church "out of sight of all public roads." James A. Armstrong dug potatoes in his field. William L. Gentry plowed on his farm. Fourteen-year-old John A. Meeks hunted squirrels. J. L. James did carpenter work as an act of charity. He worked in the rain to repair a house for a widow about to be evicted from her home. The widow was a Methodist. The informer was a minister of the Missionary Baptist Church who had a habit of chopping wood for his own use on Sunday. J. L. Shockly cleared land and hauled rails. Joe McCoy plowed his field. John Neusch picked some overripe peaches which threatened to spoil on the trees.

"UPRIGHT PERSONS . . . INTO PRISON"

In 1887, Arkansas State Senator R. W. Crockett, grandson of the legendary "Davy," made an impassioned plea to his cohorts to restore an exemption for seventh-day observers which would offer some relief from Sunday-law enforcement. The exception was restored after Crockett's dramatic plea which cited the hardship case of a Mr. Swearingen:

> He was a member of the Seventh-day Adventist Church, and after having sacredly observed the Sabbath of his people (Saturday) by abstaining from all secular work, he and his son, a lad of seventeen, on the first day of the week went quietly about their usual avocations. They disturbed no one—interfered with the rights of no one. But they were observed, and reported to the grand jury—indicted, arrested, tried, convicted, fined; and having no money to pay the fine, these moral Christian citizens of Arkansas were dragged to the county jail and imprisoned like felons for twenty-five days—and for what? For daring in this so-called land of liberty, in the year of our Lord 1887, to worship God!
>
> Was this the end of the story? Alas, no sir! They were turned out; and the old man's only horse—his sole reliance to make bread for his children, was levied on to pay the fine and costs, amounting to thirty-eight dollars. The horse sold at auction for twenty-seven dollars. A few days afterward the sheriff came again, and demanded thirty-six dollars,—eleven dollars balance due on fine and costs, and twenty-five dollars for board for himself and son while in jail. And when the poor old man—a Christian, mind you—told him with tears that he had no money, he promptly levied on his only cow, but was persuaded to accept bond, and the amount was paid by contributions from his friends of the same faith. Sir, my heart swells to bursting with indignation as I repeat to you the infamous story.[21]

Tennessee also had an unfortunate number of prosecutions which offered evidence suggesting that the law was being arbitrarily exercised against a religious minority. It was in Tennessee that convicted Sunday-law violators were reserved a place in line on the chain gang.

In Rhea County, Tennessee, Seventh-day Adventists were sentenced to the cha[i]n gang for Sunday-law violation. All in the picture except the three in fro[nt]

e Adventists. The man on the wagon at upper left is an ordained minister.
milar arrests for Sunday-law infraction occurred in several Southern states.

DATELINE SUNDAY, U.S.A.

Four Seventh-day Adventists were tried May 27, 1892, at Paris, Tennessee, on charges ranging from chopping and hauling firewood to plowing in a strawberry field. After being fined $25 apiece, three of the defendants were marched through the streets of Paris in the chain gang and forced to perform street labor. W. B. Capps served ninety-seven days in jail for performing ordinary farm labor in Dresden, Tennessee.

Then there was the case of R. M. King, a Tennessee farmer charged with cultivating his corn on a Sunday in June, 1889. Members of his community had urged King to forsake his beliefs and conform to the Sunday-keeping traditions of his neighbors. They suggested that he either change his ways, move away, or face prosecution.

It was no idle threat! Citizens signed a pledge late in 1888 to prosecute all observed Sunday violations. Hunting, fishing, ordinary farm labor, and urgent business were common Sunday practices in the neighborhood. But the vigilantes had eyes only for the seventh-day observers.

Obion County Justice J. A. Barker found King guilty on July 6, 1889. The fine and costs totaled $12.85, which King had to forfeit.

Next came a grand jury indictment for virtually the same offense for which he had been fined by Barker. He was charged with "plowing on Sunday, and doing various other kinds of work on that day [June 23] and on Sundays before that day without regard to said Sabbath days."

Judge Swiggart and a jury heard the matter in Troy, Tennessee, on March 6, 1890. The defense was not allowed to introduce evidence of the previous conviction for the June 23 offense. Within a half hour the jury was back with a guilty verdict. This time the fine was $75. The judge refused a new trial and warned that "Mr. King and all other men should and must obey" the laws of Tennessee "or leave the country."[22]

King appealed.

54

Colonel T. E. Richardson represented the appellant and submitted a brief to the state supreme court. But the trial verdict was sustained in 1891. Don M. Dickinson, Postmaster General in 1888-89, joined with Richardson in representing King's case on appeal before the United States Circuit Court for the western district of Tennessee.

In an August 1, 1891, decision, Federal Judge Hammond acknowledged that "by a sort of factitious advantage, the observers of Sunday have secured the aid of the civil law, and adhere to that advantage with great tenacity, and in spite of the clamor for religious freedom and the progress that has been made in the absolute separation of church and state, and in spite of the strong and merciless attack that has always been ready, in the field of controversial theology, to be made, as it has been made here, upon the claim for divine authority for the change from the seventh to the first day of the week,"[23] they cling to their advantage.

But the Federal Court refused to reverse the decision because, in the court's words, "The proper appeal is to the legislature. For the courts cannot change that which has been done, however done, by the civil law in favor of the Sunday observers."

Like the Judefind case of Maryland, the King case epitomized judicial recognition of enforced Sunday observance as a *religious institution*.

The decisions reflected an era pockmarked with widespread religious agitation on the issue. During the years 1895 and 1896 alone, "no less than seventy-six Seventh-day Adventists were prosecuted in the United States and Canada under existing Sunday laws. Of these, twenty-eight served terms of various lengths in jails, chain gangs, etc., aggregating 1,144 days."[24]

Not always did the Sunday-law violators lose their cases. The Sullivan Wareham family moved from Montana to Greenville, South Carolina, to farm. Worshipers on the seventh day, they were seen picking strawberries on Sunday, May 2, 1909, and

55

with others of like belief, charged with disrupting "the peace and dignity of the State of South Carolina."

This time, a friendly jury took only thirty minutes to return a "not guilty" verdict. The case drew wide attention and prompted the Washington *Post* of August 19, 1909, to editorialize:

> A few days ago a thoroughly orthodox Christian in one of the Southern States found five members of the Adventist faith working in the field on a Sunday. Deeply imbued with the gloomy faith of a John Balfour of Burley, this excellent and exemplary man, just from the sanctuary, where he worshiped in the name of Him who sat at meat with publicans and sinners and plucked green corn on a Sunday—this child of orthodoxy and cruelty swore out a warrant, and had the five arrested for breaking the Sabbath.
>
> The jury was composed of enlightened men, and the accused were acquitted on the plea that they kept one day of the week holy, a Saturday. And such is orthodoxy, that argues by the stake, the fagot, and the torch. This paper is not sectarian, though it is Christian, and as an observer of men, things, and events, it is ready to say that as few criminals, male and female, are recruited from the Adventists as from any other sect, numbers computed.
>
> They work Sundays, but they keep Saturdays, and that fulfills the law of God, as it should of man. These folk are earnest, sincere Christian men, women, and children. They may be wrong in faith, desperately wrong. That is a matter of conscience; but their consciences are about as likely to be right as yours or ours. "Leave thought unfettered every creed to scan," and take care of your own conscience. That will keep you busy without meddling with the consciences of other people.[25]

In 1848, William Lloyd Garrison had hopefully predicted the imminent demise of blue laws. "I am confident that, in the course of a few years, there will not be a Sabbatical enactment left unrepealed in the United States, if in any part of Christendom."[26]

"UPRIGHT PERSONS . . . INTO PRISON"

Logic gave substance to optimism, but the facts of history shattered the dream.

REFERENCES

1. See *Liberator*, Vol. 17, pp. 54, 59; *Pennsylvania Freeman*, March 25, 1847. Cited in *American State Papers*, Third Revised Edition (Washington, D.C.: Review and Herald Publishing Association, 1943), page 233.
2. *Liberator*, Vol. 6, p. 118; *Life of Garrison*, Vol. 2, p. 108. In *American State Papers*, pages 232, 233.
3. *Life of Garrison*, Vol. 2, pp. 111, 112. In *American State Papers*, page 233.
4. "The American Anti-Sunday-Law Convention of 1848." In *American State Papers*, pages 208-212.
5. "Resolutions Adopted by the Convention." In *American State Papers*, pages 212-214.
6. "Garrison's Speech Upon the Foregoing Resolutions." In *American State Papers*, pages 214-217.
7. *Davis* v. *Somerville*, 128 Massachusetts 594 (1880).
8. *Pearce* v. *Atwood*, 13 Massachusetts 324 (1816).
9. *Stockden* v. *State*, 18 Arkansas 186 (1856).
10. *People* v. *Ruggles*, 8 New York (Johnson's) 290 (1811).
11. *Boynton* v. *Page*, 13 New York (Wendell's) 425 (1835).
12. *O'Donnell* v. *Sweeney*, 5 Alabama 467 (1843).
13. *Davis* v. *Fish*, 1 Iowa (Green's) 406 (1848).
14. *Brackett* v. *Edgerton*, 14 Minnesota 134 (1869).
15. *Gholston* v. *Gholston*, 31 Georgia 625 (1860).
16. *Karwisch* v. *Atlanta*, 44 Georgia 205 (1871).
17. *Judefind* v. *State*, 78 Maryland 510 (1894).
18. *American State Papers*, page 556.
19. *Ibid.*, pp. 557, 558.
20. *Ibid.*, p. 554.
21. *Weekly Arkansas Gazette*, February 10, 1887, page 8. In *American State Papers*, pages 221, 222.
22. *American State Papers*, page 546.
23. *The Federal Reporter*, Vol. 46, pp. 905-916. In *American State Papers*, page 531.
24. *American State Papers*, page 562.
25. "A Matter of Conscience," Washington *Post*, August 19, 1909. In *American State Papers*, page 560.
26. *Liberator*, April 21, 1848, page 63.

Early players and fans little suspected that the baseball diamond would become a center of controversy over Sunday laws.

6.

PLAY BALL—
MAYBE!

Abner Doubleday, it is commonly believed, invented baseball.* He conceived what he thought to be a fun game, with players using a ball and a wooden club. The one with the ball threw it at the player with the club, who swung vigorously at the speeding missile. If he was lucky and hit the ball with the club, he could run around a 360-foot diamond back "home" to the point of his original departure. This success was termed a "run," and the team with the most runs won the game.

The scheme may have looked ridiculous to some, but participants discovered a unique thrill in blasting the ball over the heads of the fielders.

Baseball became a national pastime, played in the cow pasture, the corner lot, and the more sophisticated "diamond." Little did those early players suspect that electronic communications would one day create a multimillion audience for a single game, or that in Houston, Texas, one could lease a block of seats in the climate-controlled "Astrodome" for something like $18,000 a year. Nor did Doubleday dream of the antagonism or legal tests that would ensue as Sunday-law protagonists classified this form of recreation as "worldly amusement."

*The origin of the game is obscure. Some authorities trace it to the old English game of rounders, which was also played in colonial America. Others consider the resemblance to rounders coincidental.

DATELINE SUNDAY, U.S.A.

Years ago on a Sunday "in Plainfield, New Jersey, . . . a large crowd assembled to witness a baseball game. Certain of the clergy had determined that no more Sunday baseball should be played in that place, and those in favor of the game also determined that they would defy the decision of the clergymen."

"Play ball!" the umpire shouted.

The pitcher waited for the catcher's signal. The batter dusted his fingers and gripped his bat. Then the clergyman, accompanied by a deputy sheriff, entered.

"We have warrants for the arrest of anyone who participates in this game," announced the preacher. The deputy waved the legal papers. The clergyman and the ballplayers exchanged bits and pieces of rhubarb. But the crowd had come to see a ball game and began to hoot and holler. When this had no effect, they marched across the field and ousted the preacher and his deputy sheriff from the ball park. The deputy discreetly faded into the woodwork and allowed the crowd to chase the preacher, which they did, all the way to his house. The deputy persuaded the remaining spectators to depart the scene, and the game was called on account of Sunday laws![1]

Characteristically, blue laws banned labor, business, and "worldly amusements."

> In their laudable attempt to forsake worldliness and ritualism for the religion of the Bible, the Puritans committed the double error of applying the fourth commandment to the first day of the week and making the Mosaic legal code the basis for enforcement. In the Puritan colonies there arose the practice of applying to Sunday the sunset-to-sunset reckoning of the Biblical Sabbath, while the English law began Sunday at midnight.[2]

So severe was the Puritan attitude that religion appeared to offer more of a burden than a blessing. The devil received the credit for most of life's pleasures, while long faces were saved for the Lord. If something was enjoyable, it was suspect as also sinful and "worldly." Effort was made to eliminate even the possibility of such pleasures and amusements in order to fashion a spirit of worshipful sobriety for the first day of the week.

Sixteenth-century golfers in Scotland ran afoul of blue laws. In Edinburgh, on October 1, 1593, "John Henrie, Pat Bogie and others were accusit of playing the Gowff on the Links of Leith during the time of the sermonnes, were ordainit to be put in prison until a fine of fourty shillings wer payit and cautioned not to do lyke again no type heirefter under the paine of punishment at the discretion of the magestrates."[3]

Since statutory language in Scotland, the United States, or anywhere else, compels precision, Sunday-law proponents have compiled long lists of "worldly" pleasures to be prohibited on Sunday; and this theological programming has survived disestablishment. Organizations such as the "American Sabbath Union," a constituent of the "International Federation of Sunday Rest Associations of the United States and Canada," have helped perpetuate the pressure for the Puritan blue-law morality.

In Alabama, in the 1930's and 1940's, it was a misdemeanor to play baseball "in any public place," though there was an exemption for cities with more than 15,000 population. In Connecticut, professional baseball was allowed, providing local legislative enactment also approved and the game took place "after 2 p.m." on Sunday. The law did not specify whether the crowd could come early and watch the players practice. In Florida, the team manager could be held guilty of the same misdemeanor as the baseball player. Idaho did not name baseball, but conceivably the prohibition of "noise, rout, or amusement" might cover ball playing unless it could be played in a quiet and dignified manner. In Indiana, you could play Abner Doubleday's game fearlessly, providing you were under fourteen years of age. If fourteen or older, you had to wait until after 1 p.m. and play at least 1,000 feet from "any established house of worship." Presumably the Pony League could play in the front yard of a

Babe Ruth crosses home plate after hitting a grand slam at Shibe Park, Philadelphia, in a 1929 Yankees-versus-Athletics game.

church on Sunday morning without danger of prosecution.

The Kansas code said playing a "game of any kind" on Sunday was a misdemeanor, but here the court came to the rescue and suggested that baseball was outside the scope of this statutory prohibition. Kentucky exempted "amateur sports" and "athletic games." Maine banned "any sport, game, or recreation"—subject to local government option.

The sports-minded Maryland resident had to be particularly alert. A general prohibition prevented "gaming" or joining in any "unlawful pastime or recreation." If he lived in Hagerstown, baseball was allowed all day Sunday providing it was amateur. If commercial, baseball was permissible between the hours of 2 p.m. and 5 p.m. Montgomery County allowed "amateur" baseball and other "lawful" sport from 2 p.m. to 6 p.m.

Subject to local ordinance, "amateur" sports were lawful in some Massachusetts cities between 2 p.m. and 6 p.m., with "professional" sports allowed from 1:50 to 6:30 p.m. In Massachusetts and Michigan, attending a prohibited event was considered as much a violation as participating. Mississippi said No to "ball playing of any kind." Missouri forbade "games of any kind," specifying a fine of $50. Nebraska gave cities the local option to "prohibit all public amusements, shows, exhibitions."

New Hampshire gave the green light to baseball if approved by the "selectmen of any town" and not played before 1 p.m. "where admission is charged or donations accepted." New Jersey had a flat prohibition against "playing football" but ignored naming the national pastime except by inference under "any other kind of playing sports, pastimes, or diversions." New Mexico said No to any sports.

New York, with its "house that Ruth built," declared it "unlawful to play baseball" whether or not admission was charged, "but only after two o'clock in the afternoon." North Dakota specified that Sunday baseball might not be played closer than 500 feet to a church or at any other time than between

DATELINE SUNDAY, U.S.A.

1 and 6 p.m. Ohio forbade "sporting" to the fourteen-year-old and older, but since the next statutory words are "rioting" and "quarreling," it is questionable whether baseball was intended, if played with calm and decorum.

Pennsylvania required baseball to be played between 2 and 6 p.m., providing the voters of a municipality had given prior approval. South Carolina said No to "public sports" and named "football" specifically. Presumably baseball was included in "other games, exercises, sports, or pastimes."

South Dakota not only named admission-charging baseball to the forbidden list but also implicated any citizen that advertised the game or made the ball park available. If a Texas ball park open on Sunday could be classed as a "place of public amusement," the owner exposed himself to fine. Utah exempted ball parks. And finally, Vermont, like many others, permitted baseball if it was approved by local voters and if the game "shall not commence until two o'clock in the afternoon."

The "worldly pleasure" aggregate list which became the subject of legislative dispute was not limited to the Doubleday phenomenon. And the corresponding list of rules and regulations shackling this awesome array of Sunday "pleasures" was no more likely to put the recreation-loving citizen's mind at ease.

Various state Sunday laws on the books or being contemplated in the 1930's and 1940's usually regulated, and often prohibited in varying degrees, the following items: shooting, hunting, gaming, card playing, racing, football, tennis, golf, boxing, brag, bluff, poker, seven-up, three-up, twenty-one, vingtun, thirteen cards, odd trick, forty-five, whist, shooting for amusement, horse racing, tippling, theater performances, circuses, shows, basketball, hockey, skating, field contests, miniature golf, ski racing, ski jumping, bowling, billiards, rifle practice, motion pictures, dog racing, playhouse, merry-go-round, concert saloon, pool, wrestling, cockfighting, swimming, opera, lacrosse, soccer, auto racing, interludes, farces, plays, tricks, juggling,

64

sleight of hand, bearbaiting, bullfighting, fiddling, music for sake of merriment, fives, ninepins, long bullets, quoits, exercises or shows, tragedy, comedy, ballet, negro minstrelsy, sparring contests, trials of strength, acrobatic feats, club performances, rope dancing, street carnivals, polo, chasing game, gaming tables, and the carrying of an uncased gun in the woods.

The statutory language naturally creates interpretation problems for law-enforcement officials.

For example, the Ohio Sunday law permits trapshooting on Sunday afternoon "under the auspices of a recognized hunt, trapshooting, rifle or game club of this state"; but it warns, "Whoever, in the open air on Sunday, has implements for hunting or shooting with intention to use them for that purpose, shall be fined."[4] The gun bearer could present a rousing defense on the "intention" issue.

Then there is the innholder of Maine faced with the threat of punishment for the "crimes" of his guests who spend Sunday "drinking or spending their time idly, at play, or doing any secular business"[5] What is the innkeeper to do if he observes two guests playing a game of chess in the lounge? To act is to risk loss of business; not to act is to risk infraction of the law.

Georgia police officials face an unusual enforcement dilemma because of the statute which makes it a misdemeanor to "bathe in a stream or pond of water on the Sabbath day, in view of a road or passway leading to or from a house of religious worship."[6]

The recreations prohibited by these blue laws are not necessarily wrong or immoral in themselves, although some of them do run counter to prevailing religious mores. The majority of the statutes still bear the stamp of religious establishment.

Statutory expressions still on the lawbooks in the thirties and forties were reminiscent of Cotton Mather and associates. Arkansas talked of "Sabbath breaking" and "Christian Sabbath"; Colorado, "Sabbath day"; Delaware, "worldly activity"; Florida, "proper observance of Sunday"; Maryland, "Sabbath day"; Massachusetts, "Lord's day" and "secular business"; Michigan, "secular business"; Minnesota, "breaks the Sabbath"; New York, "Sabbath breaking"; North Carolina, "Lord's day"; North Dakota, "Sabbath breaking"; Oklahoma, "Sabbath breaking"; Pennsylvania, "worldly employment"; Rhode Island, "breakers of the Sabbath"; South Carolina, "Sabbath day" and "worldly labor"; South Dakota, "Sabbath breaking" and "worldly uses"; Tennessee, "work on the Sabbath"; Vermont, "secular business"; Washington, "observance of the Sabbath"; West Virginia, "on a Sabbath day"; and Wyoming, "desecration of the Sabbath day."

But in seeking to establish a government-sponsored religious observance, the "Sabbath" Unionists still largely failed to gain the sympathy of the public. A case in point was the reaction of a Catholic minority in Kansas. The Catholics appreciated the relative freedom of the "Continental Sunday," which contrasted sharply with Puritan restraints. Editors of the *Catholic Advance* commented tartly in 1910 on the observation of a Methodist bishop that Kansas was "the greatest Methodist state in the Union." It was acknowledged that since "the preachers of that denomination seem to have things their own way in Kansas . . . the only thing the few other people who don't ride in Wesley's boat can do is to watch and pray."

The *Advance* had more to say:

> We will let them preach the prohibition law until they pound their pulpits to pieces, . . . but we are strenuously opposed to any legislations that will deprive our young people of health-giving outdoor sport on Sunday afternoon. The Sunday is a day of rest from servile work but is not a day of inactivity or laziness. The Catholic Church established the Sunday anyhow and ought to know best how it is to be observed. She demands, under pain of sin, that all her faithful be present at the holy sacrifice of the mass on Sundays and hear the word of God preached from the pulpits. She requires some considerable time for prayer. This obligation being satisfied, she does not prohibit or interfere in

any way with those innocent amusements which serve for rest or recreation on any day. If our Methodist brethren choose to make laws for a more restricted observance of the Sunday among their own people, that is certainly within their right, and it is no business of ours; but when the same Methodist brethren put their heads together and decide as a church that they will have the State enforce their own church laws upon other churches who do not believe with them, then this is time to call a halt. If they will have the State legislature to enact laws forbidding Methodist children from playing baseball on Sunday afternoon, well, if they haven't religious spunk enough to keep them in the beaten Wesleyan track, we have no objection if they call in the policeman, but we won't allow them to send a policeman over to us, as we get along beautifully without.[7]

In the nineteenth and early twentieth centuries there had been little to discourage Sunday-law promoters. Colonial blue laws had survived disestablishment in the states. Religious-observance objectives had been perpetuated in statutory language. Minorities had felt the sting of arbitrary and discriminatory enforcement.

Late in the nineteenth century the Sunday-law advocates felt strong enough to move on to even bigger things. Despite the language of the first amendment of the Federal Constitution, highly organized religious interests renewed their efforts to secure a national Sunday law.

REFERENCES

1. See "Sunday Baseball Games in New Jersey," *Signs of the Times*, Vol. 39 (1912), No. 21, pp. 11, 12.
2. *American State Papers and Related Documents* (Washington, D.C.: Review and Herald Publishing Association, 1949), page 85.
3. "The Sabbath Breakers," *Liberty*, Vol. 58 (1963), No. 1, p. 36.
4. *Throckmorton's Ohio Code*, annotated 1940, Baldwin's Certified Revision, Section 13053. In *American State Papers*, Third Revised Edition (Washington, D.C.: Review and Herald Publishing Association, 1943), page 492.
5. *Revised Statutes of the State of Maine*, Chapter 255, Section 40. In *American State Papers*, page 467.
6. *Code of Georgia*, Annotated 1936, Section 26-6910.
7. "Church and State," *Catholic Advance*, November 5, 1910. In *American State Papers*, pages 585, 586.

Church leaders demanded that the Government use Federal troops to keep Chicago's Columbian Exposition closed on Sundays.

7.

"THOSE WHO OPPOSE... MUST ABIDE THE CONSEQUENCES"

Delegates to the 1887 National Reform Association Convention stood tall and determined. Aroused by the oratory of their spokesman, David McAllister, they agreed with him that "those who oppose this work now will discover, when the religious amendment is made to the Constitution, that if they do not see fit to fall in with the majority, they must abide the consequences, or seek some more congenial clime."[1]

Just a century before, Ben Franklin had commented: "When a Religion is good, I conceive that it will support itself; and, when it cannot support itself, and God does not take care to support, so that its Professors are oblig'd to call for the help of the Civil Power, it is a sign, I apprehend, of its being a bad one."[2]

But a lot could happen in 100 years. Men can forget.

Early in 1863, when the Civil War and the crisis of national survival were the overpowering issues of the day, representatives of eleven Protestant denominations met in Xenia, Ohio, to create a national Christian theocracy. The National Reform Association made no effort to conceal its avowed intent to destroy Jefferson's wall of separation between church and state.

The association's constitution warned of "subtle and persevering attempts . . . to overthrow our Sabbath laws" and pledged itself "to promote needed reforms in the action of the government touching the Sabbath" and "to secure such an amendment to the Constitution of the United States as will declare the nation's allegiance to Jesus Christ and its acceptance of the moral laws of the Christian religion, and so indicate that this is a Christian nation, and place all the Christian laws, institutions, and usages of our government on an undeniably legal basis in the fundamental laws of the land."[3]

But Lincoln and his Congress appeared to be more concerned with finding a means to penetrate the Confederate defense in Virginia. Pressure from the "reformers" continued, however, and a Reconstruction Congress finally formulated a response to the petitions. The House Committee on the Judiciary reported it "inexpedient to legislate upon the subject," since the fathers of the republic had considered the matter and laid the foundation of a government which "was to be the home of the oppressed of all nations of the earth, whether Christian or pagan."

The committee pointed out that the founders of our nation had reasoned "with great unanimity that it was inexpedient to put anything into the Constitution or frame of government which might be construed to be a reference to any religious creed or doctrine."[4]

When, in 1892, Congress heard demands to attach a Sunday-closing rider to the bill appropriating funds to the Columbian Exposition, New York Senator Hiscock counseled, "If I had charge of this amendment in the interest of the Columbian Exposition, I would write the provision for the closure in any form that the religious sentiment of the country demands."[5]

Connecticut Senator Hawley dared his associates to put in writing a denial that the United States was a Christian nation. "Word it, if you dare; advocate it, if you dare. How many who voted for it would ever come back here again? None, I hope."[6]

A Chicago newspaper reported the reaction of a House committee member on the World's Fair to the clamor for the Sunday-closing rider. He allegedly admitted, "The reason we shall vote for it is, I will confess to you, a fear that, unless we do so, the church folks will get together and knife us at the polls next; and—well, you know we all want to come back, and we can't afford to take any risks."[7]

New Hampshire's Senator Blair sponsored a "Lord's Day" measure "To Promote Its Observance as a Day of Religious Worship," a measure vigorously promoted by the National Reform Association, the Women's Christian Temperance Union, the American Sabbath Union, and other organizations.

In addition to proposing a ban on "secular work, labor, or business" the bill sought to restrain interstate commerce, transportation of the mails, military musters and drills, as well as "transportation . . . by land or water in such way as to interfere with or disturb the people in the enjoyment of the first day of the week, . . . or its observance as a day of religious worship."[8] It also condemned "any play, game, or amusement, or recreation" that could disturb others.

The hearings on the proposal before the Senate Committee on Education and Labor produced a long line of clergy testimonials urging passage. On the afternoon of December 13, 1888, a spirited exchange between Senator Blair and Alonzo T. Jones took place. Jones, a professor of history at the Seventh-day Adventist Battle Creek College in Michigan, took the offensive against the bill:

> It is the religious observance of the day that its promoters, from one end of the land to the other, have in view. In the convention, now in session in this city, working in behalf of this bill, only yesterday Dr. Crafts said: "Taking religion out of the day takes the rest out."
> In the "Boston Monday Lectures," 1887, Joseph Cook, lecturing on the subject of Sunday laws, said: "The experience of centuries shows, however, that you will in vain endeavor to preserve Sunday as a day of rest, unless you preserve it as a day of worship. Unless Sabbath observance be founded upon religious reasons, you will not long

71

maintain it at a high standard on the basis of economic and physiological and political considerations only."

And in the Illinois State Sunday convention held in Elgin, November 8, 1887, Dr. W. W. Everts declared Sunday to be "the test of all religion."[9]

The Elgin convention had pronounced:

> That we look with shame and sorrow on the nonobservance of the Sabbath by many Christian people, in that custom prevails with them of purchasing Sabbath newspapers, engaging in and patronizing Sabbath business and travel, and in many instances giving themselves to pleasure and self-indulgence, setting aside by neglect and indifference the great duties and privileges which God's day brings them.
>
> *Resolved,* that we give our votes and support to those candidates or political officers who will pledge themselves to vote for the enactment and enforcing of statutes in favor of the civil Sabbath.[10]

The Blair bill died in committee. Later, the Senator stripped the bill of the more obvious religious implications and on December 9, 1889, introduced another Federal Sunday-closing measure. Again it failed to gain adequate support and expired.

Sunday-law proponents learned from these skirmishes. They learned that the stronger the religious rationale advanced for creating the establishment, the stronger were the constitutional arguments available to opponents. Consequently the reformers made an effort to cultivate the support of labor on the basis that a Federal blue law would serve a public-welfare purpose and promote the interests of the laboring man.

The industrial revolution, they argued, had worked hardships on the dignity and economic independence of the individual. Exorbitant profits were reaped at the expense of adequate working conditions and wages. The workingman deserved better. Sunday-law proponents sought to exploit this need by linking their cause to public welfare and the individual.

When W. C. P. Breckinridge of Kentucky offered a "Bill to

Prevent Persons From Being Forced to Labor on Sunday," it was channeled to a subcommittee of the House Committee on the District of Columbia for study. Sharp contrasts of opinion were aired in open hearings on February 18, 1890. The cast of characters mirrored the earlier hearings on the Blair bill. Ministerial proponents W. F. Crafts, J. H. Elliott, and George Elliott were joined by representatives of the W.C.T.U. Alonzo T. Jones, J. O. Corliss, and W. H. McKee, representing the Seventh-day Adventist Church, and a representative of the District Knights of Labor opposed the bill.

"No one is being forced to labor on Sunday in the District of Columbia," Jones reported. "Sunday legislation is, in reality, not in behalf of the laboring man at all. It is only a pretense to cover the real purpose—to enforce by law the religious observance of the day."[11]

In view of efforts to enlist labor support for the Sunday-law movement, the testimony of Millard F. Hobbs, chief officer of the District Knights of Labor, was significant. Although he acknowledged the diversity of opinion relative to the Breckinridge bill within his organization, he stated that "the Knights of Labor, as a whole, have refused to have anything to do with it." Every Knight, he said, was in favor of a day of rest, some of two days, but because of the "religious side of the question," they opposed the bill. "What benefits the Knights of Labor wish to obtain, we think, can be better secured by our own efforts through our own organization than by the efforts of others, through the church."[12]

The subcommittee listened, and the bill was never brought to a vote. But Congress was not to escape easily the pressure for Federal action for enforced Sunday closing. When a rider was attached to the bill appropriating funds to the 1893 Columbian Exposition in Chicago, a flurry of Congressional debate ensued. In order to obtain Federal funds, the bill stipulated, the fair had to close each Sunday.

DATELINE SUNDAY, U.S.A.

The American Sabbath Union maintained that this measure "will honor God and preserve the faith of the nation. . . . The nation's faith in God and His laws will be put to the test by the action of its Congress on this subject." The Wisconsin Sunday Rest Association urged that Sunday opening "would tend to break down the Christianity of our country." In October, 1891, a convention of Massachusetts Protestants went on record favoring the Sunday closing of the fair out of "respect to the religious convictions of the millions of Christian people in this great nation who believe that the Sabbath is one of the chief bulwarks of Christianity."[13]

Congressmen felt severe pressure to support the rider. Comments in the *Congressional Record* as well as off-the-cuff remarks revealed concern for voter reaction. Remarked Senator Hawley, "Everybody knows what the foundation is. It is founded in religious belief."[14] Senator Peffer observed, "We are engaged in a theological discussion concerning the observance of the first day of the week."[15]

After days of spirited debate and revision, Sunday-closing advocates scored a victory as President Harrison, on August 5, 1892, signed the measure into law.

Citizens who earlier had not bothered to join in a petition protesting "against the Congress of the United States committing the United States Government to a union of religion and state, in the passage of any bill or resolution to close the World's Columbian Exposition on Sunday," suddenly reacted. Moves to open the fair on Sunday were initiated in Chicago, backed by the city council, the mayor, the press, and the management of the fair. Ironically, they gave religious reasons in support of Sunday opening. The *Tribune* talked loftily of religious services at the fair which would make "Sunday at the World's Fair . . . one of the grandest recognitions of the Sabbath known to modern history."[16]

Religious leaders threatened boycott if the fair opened on

74

Sunday. One excited group telegraphed the President, urging him to "suppress Chicago nullification with Jacksonian firmness and to guard the gates next Sabbath with troops if necessary."[17] Another church organization demanded, in a wire to the attorney general, to know why Federal troops could not be "used, if necessary, to maintain inviolate the national authority, and keep the fair closed on the Lord's day."[18]

A Western newspaper editor found it contradictory to "appeal to the President to enforce closing, if need be, by military force" in order to show the world " 'that we are a Christian nation.' "[19]

Sentiment for Sunday opening was given another opportunity for Congressional exposure following the introduction of a joint resolution in December, 1892, which would have left "the matter of Sunday observance entirely within the power of the regularly constituted authorities of the World's Columbian Exposition."

Samuel Gompers was the voice of the American Federation of Labor at Congressional hearings that followed. He deplored the Sunday closing of the Philadelphia Centennial Exhibition in 1876, which prevented him and thousands of others from attending: "I deny the right of any man or number of men to speak in the name of the wage earners of America, and to say that they favor the closing of the World's Fair on Sunday."[20]

Another labor representative blamed the Protestant evangelical churches for the Sunday closing and accused them of assuming to be guardians of the economic and moral affairs of the working people. He branded this conduct as willfully and ignorantly fraudulent and repudiated the right "of these churches or their representatives to speak or act for us in this matter."[21]

Susan B. Anthony spoke for an open fair. She recalled when Sunday streetcars were banned in Philadelphia, the struggle to open the Philadelphia Art Gallery and New York's Central Park on Sunday, and the "big, long fight before there was any

75

music allowed in the park on Sunday." She classed the Sunday closing of the fair as a "tyranny that should not be practiced by the Congress of the United States."[22]

Predicting that the resolution would die a natural death, the Chicago *Herald* of January 13, 1893, disclosed that the publicity given the issue "brought down upon Congress an avalanche of protests and appeals, from religious people and church organizations all over the country." The newspaper observed that organized opposition from churches and their ministers made some committee members timid to express their convictions by vote, since those demanding Sunday closing could "lose their tempers, and at the next election, make trouble for those who vote against them."

Senator Quay of Pennsylvania had, the previous July, laid before the Senate suggested wording for "the closing of the exposition on the Sabbath day." "Congress will not reverse its action," because if it did, he reasoned, "it could have no other meaning than that the United States, the greatest and most prosperous nation on this earth, had declared officially through its chosen representatives in favor of desecrating the Sabbath and thus breaking one of the commandments."[23] Two weeks later, after the hearings, Quay insisted the Senate would kill the reversal even if it got through the House. "The people of Chicago may as well give up this fight. They can't win it."[24]

Quay was right. Congress did not reverse itself. However, through a series of intricate legal maneuvers the fair found a way to open its gates in a limited way on Sunday, and then repented almost immediately when Sunday attendance declined! Still, Congress had capitulated to religious pressure in 1892 and had given its authority to religious establishment. Although Senator Quay's "Sabbath day" nomenclature was amended out in the final form of the measure, the original intent and spirit could not be masked.

While Congress had acted to close the gates of a world's fair on Sunday, it had simultaneously opened doors to a flood of demands for future sessions of the Federal legislature to give legal recognition to religious practices. During the next half century Congress considered almost a hundred measures designed to honor Sunday.

Thanks to the clerical lobbyists of the American Sabbath Union, the $5,000,000 appropriation to the Louisiana Purchase Exposition (Saint Louis, 1904) carried the condition that fair directors "close the gates to visitors on Sunday."[25] In 1906, the American Sabbath Union chalked up "another grand victory for the Sabbath cause" by persuading Congress to condition its appropriation to the 1907 Jamestown Exposition on the assurance that "the grounds of the exposition shall be closed on Sundays."[26]

When Alabama Congressman Heflin sent to the Sixtieth Congress in 1907 a bill to prohibit certain types of work in the District of Columbia "on the Sabbath day," a host of religiously oriented proposals followed in its wake. The flurry of pressure was so intense that the General Conference of Seventh-day Adventists through its president, A. G. Daniells, and its secretary, W. A. Spicer, sent "A Memorial to Congress" on January 29, 1908, reminding the legislators of the "wise builders of state" who had created a separation of church and state, and urging them "not to enact any religious legislation of any kind."[27]

In 1912, the Federal Government did agree to eliminate Sunday delivery of all but special-delivery mail in "post offices of the first and second classes"; but it has yet to capitulate to demands for a national Sunday law.

REFERENCES

1. Dr. David McAllister, in National Reform Convention at Lakeside, Ohio, August, 1887. In *American State Papers,* Third Revised Edition (Washington, D.C.: Review and Herald Publishing Association, 1943), page 234.
2. Benjamin Franklin, Letter to Dr. Price, October 9, 1780, *Writings of Benjamin Franklin,* Albert Henry Smyth, ed. (New York: The Macmillan Company, 1906), Vol. 8, p. 154.
3. "Constitution of the National Reform Association." In *American State Papers,* pages 235, 236.

4. *House Reports,* Vol. 1, 43d Congress, 1st Session, Report No. 143. In *American State Papers,* page 237.
5. *Congressional Record,* July 13, 1892, page 6755. In *American State Papers,* page 280.
6. *Congressional Record,* July 13, 1892, page 6759.
7. Chicago *Daily Post,* April 9, 1892. In *American State Papers,* page 280.
8. Senate Bill No. 2983 (1888). In *Ibid.,* pp. 243, 244.
9. Alonzo T. Jones, "The National Sunday Law," *American Sentinel,* 1892.
10. *Ibid.,* p. 117.
11. "Arguments on the Breckinridge Sunday Bill," *The Sentinel Library,* No. 29, pages 28-30.
12. *American Sentinel,* February 27, 1890. In *American State Papers,* pages 276, 277.
13. "Arguments on the Breckinridge Sunday Bill," *Op. cit.,* pp. 23-24.
14. *Congressional Record,* July 12, 1892. In *American State Papers,* page 279.
15. *Ibid.*
16. Chicago *Tribune,* December 3, 1892.
17. Chicago *Herald,* May 19, 1893. In *American State Papers,* page 280.
18. *Ibid.* (May 16).
19. Webster City *Graphic-Herald,* quoted in the Des Moines *Leader,* June 1, 1893. In *American State Papers,* page 281.
20. Alonzo T. Jones, *Sunday Closing of the World's Fair* (International Religious Liberty Association, 1893), pages 118, 119.
21. *Ibid.,* p. 31.
22. *Ibid.,* p. 122.
23. Pittsburgh *Leader,* January 2, 1893.
24. Chicago *Herald,* January 19, 1893.
25. *American State Papers,* page 246.
26. *Ibid.,* p. 282.
27. *Congressional Record,* January 29, 1908, Vol. 12, part 2, pp. 1264, 1265.

8. GOLD RUSH, SUNDAY STYLE

Conflict and violent personality clashes served to alienate David S. Terry and Stephen J. Field, California legal pioneers and mutual antagonists.

Kentucky-born Terry joined the Texas Rangers and fought in the Mexican War before coming west, where he was named Chief Justice of the California Supreme Court.

Field, son of a Connecticut clergyman, crossed the borders of the Golden State in time to experience the rip-roaring saga of the gold rush. Like Terry, his legal skills were put to work in the California Supreme Court, where he was designated an associate justice.

When Terry resigned from the court in 1859 to duel on a San Francisco sand dune with David C. Broderick, United States Senator from California, Field was promoted to chief justice. Senator Broderick, a friend of Field, gambled his life on a foolhardy gesture and lost. Antagonism between Terry and Field flared with the death of Broderick. Flames of searing hatred burst into the open thirty years later. The drama of the Field-Terry confrontations was like something out of a dime novel except that both were almost bigger-than-life people, and in the midst of their personal turmoils they crossed swords on the matter of coerced Sunday observance.

David S. Terry, a former Texas Ranger, engineered a religious-liberty plank in the California Democratic party platform.

Field's legal skill took him to the bench of the United States Supreme Court as an associate justice. Terry became a political power in California's Democratic party.

In 1882, Terry engineered a religious-liberty plank in the platform of the California Democratic Party which was credited with wresting political control from the grasp of the Republicans in November of that year. By the summer of 1884 Terry was making headlines in San Francisco as one of several attorneys representing Sarah Althea Hill in her divorce action against multimillionaire William Sharon—a sensational case that rocked Bay Area society with spicy rumors.

Sharon made his millions in Virginia City silver under the auspices of San Francisco's brilliant financier-banker, William Ralston. Remarkably successful in staking out his fortune, William Sharon enjoyed only minor success in creating enduring friendships. The public was less than sympathetic to Sharon's legal dilemma.

Prime issue in the case was whether William had ever entered into a valid and legal marriage with Sarah Althea Hill. If she could prove it, she had a sporting chance of digging into some of that Virginia City silver herself through community property division and alimony award. But Sharon was not about to admit a marriage that would expose his bullion to legal evaporation.

The court waded through wildly contrasting evidence and, to Sharon's chagrin, decided in favor of Sarah. In desperation Sharon raced to the Federal court for help. The United States Circuit Court later declared that the alleged marriage agreement was something less than legal, but the frustrated Sharon was not around to savor his victory. He had died a few weeks earlier.

Two weeks later, on January 7, 1886, David Terry married Sarah at his home in Stockton.

For two years Terry worked indefatigably in the California State Supreme Court, where the Sharon estate was suing for a reversal, and on January 31, 1888, the Supreme Court upheld the Superior Court, declaring the marriage contract legal and valid.

In this contest, which had now lasted over five years, the Terrys were leading by two victories in the state court over one defeat in the Federal court. Sharon's heirs now went back into the Federal Circuit Court asking that, with Sharon's death, the original verdict of fraud be revived.

Assigned to sit with two federal judges on the Circuit Court to rehear the evidence was United States Supreme Court Justice Stephen J. Field.*

Trouble was in the wind, and it didn't take long for the breeze to blow through the Federal courtroom.

When it appeared that the prior Federal court reasoning would be confirmed, Sarah shattered courtroom decorum and launched an outraged verbal blast at Field, accusing him of selling out to the opposition. Field promptly ordered Sarah evicted from the room, and Terry, now a man in his sixties, objected vehemently, with fists flying.

When the dust had settled, David S. Terry found himself confined to a jail cell for six months. Sarah was awarded a shorter term behind bars—thanks to a contempt of court sentence pronounced by Field. It seemed an exorbitant penalty and something less than pure impartiality, at least in the minds of Mr. and Mrs. Terry.

The next confrontation between the Terrys and Justice Field reared up like something out of a bad dream.

In the summer of 1889, Stephen Field returned to California to sit again on the United States Circuit Court. Humiliated by prison confinement at the hands of Field, the Terrys had stepped back into the California sunshine only to find that the California Supreme Court had reversed the prior holding of the state court and ruled that no valid marriage had existed as between

---

*From *Men to Match My Mountains*, by Irving Stone. Copyright © 1956 by Irving Stone. Reprinted by permission of Doubleday & Company, Inc.

GOLD RUSH, SUNDAY STYLE

Sarah Althea Hill and William Sharon. The air was heavy with trouble when Field boarded the San Francisco-bound passenger train out of Los Angeles accompanied by a bodyguard, Deputy Marshal David Naegle.

It might have been just another routine train ride, except that the Terrys came aboard in Fresno. When the entourage stopped for breakfast at a town called Lathrop, the Terrys and Justice Field met face to face in the dining room.

Stephen J. Field, bitter foe of Terry, defended Sunday laws by treating them as civil rather than religious legislation.

CALIFORNIA HISTORICAL SOCIETY, SAN FRANCISCO

DATELINE SUNDAY, U.S.A.

Mrs. Terry slipped quickly into the background, and icy glares melted to physical action as the elderly but agile Terry turned on Field with fists of frustration. When Naegle thought Terry might be reaching for his bowie knife, he reacted by pumping two pistol shots into Terry's chest.

Bitter rivalry between formidable opponents ended tragically with Terry lying face up at Field's feet, unseeing eyes staring blankly into space. Sarah said it was murder! Both David Naegle and Stephen Field had to face the charge, but both successfully pleaded self-defense and were cleared of criminal conduct.

However, the Terry versus Field feud was more than a physical struggle. The two men cherished contrasting intellectual ideologies, as is shown by their opposing views on Sunday legislation more than thirty years before Terry's death.

Field's spiritual antecedents could be traced to Puritanoriented New England Congregationalism, spawning ground for North American blue laws. Terry represented frontier stock from Kentucky and Texas.

In 1858, Field and Terry had sat side by side on the California Supreme Court. When a case arose which challenged the constitutionality of a California "Sabbath" act, the two men took opposing sides. In a sense, they were both pioneers and made legal history by their statements. At a time when most state supreme courts nonchalantly accepted enforced Sunday observance as realistic religious establishment, Terry had the audacity to rule that the California Sunday law was not only an unjustifiable intrusion upon legitimate property interests, but also constituted a denial of religious freedom. This was the first time in history that a state supreme court had been bold enough to break with tradition.

Field rose to the occasion and displayed some audacity of his own. Aware that Sunday laws rested on shaky grounds if justification was tied to religious purposes, Field dissented from the

Terry opinion and refined a creative approach to enforced Sunday observance. The Field doctrine offered constitutional refuge to blue laws by treating them as civil rather than religious legislation. A couple of other state courts had previously tried this plan, but Field was the architect of its refinement and perpetuation.

The first "Sabbath" act in California had been accompanied by spirited legislative debate in the 1850 California legislature. The gold rush atmosphere of early California was brash and bawdy. Certain conscientious political leaders determined to legislate religion into an irreligious society. They sensed, however, that the public would greet such coercion with ridicule rather than enthusiasm. Therefore they characterized the statute as "An Act to Provide for the Better Observance of the Sabbath."

A Jewish merchant living in Sacramento, preferring a Sabbath observed on the seventh day of the week, made no effort to conceal the peddling of his wares on Sunday. An early victim of the long fingers of the California "moralists," Newman spent thirty-five days in jail for his disobedience.

California court dockets were not crowded in those days, and it was not long before Newman had occasion to lay his troubles before the supreme court. He thought the "Sabbath" act violated the California State Constitution on at least two points. Chief Justice Terry and Associate Justice Burnett agreed.

Terry[1] frowned on the act both as a religious establishment and as a violation of the "inalienable" right to acquire property.

Reminiscent of James Madison's recognition of time as property, Terry saw time as an opportunity to acquire property. Since this right was inalienable by constitutional declaration, the legislature had no right to tamper.

David Terry warned that legislative usurpation of a nonexistent power, once allowed, "is without limit." Once the legislature arbitrarily designated a specific "time of compulsory rest," there would be no barrier to further legislation which, left to its wildest whim, could lead to a "prohibition of all occupations at all times." He scoffed at the implication that citizens needed the state to take them by the hand and force them to "seek the necessary repose which their exhausted natures demand," any more than they needed to be fed, ordered to sleep, or compelled to find relief from pain. The chief justice declared that any citizen of California had personal "instincts and necessities" which could meet these needs without the aid of government's long arm.

The "Sabbath" act, like the "laws of the ancients, which prescribed the mode and texture of people's clothing, or similar laws which might prescribe and limit our food and drink, must be regarded as an invasion, without reason or necessity, of the natural rights of the citizen" enacted by government beyond its legitimate sphere of power.

Although the state could legitimately exercise police power to regulate tanneries, slaughterhouses, and the sale of drugs and poisons, the Terry opinion disputed the "civil aspect" arguments of Sabbath-law proponents who sought the same cloak of respectability for enforced Sunday observance. He sliced through the civil regulation assertions and exposed the act as "a purely religious idea" where the "aid of the law to enforce its observance has been given, under the pretense of a civil, municipal, or police regulation."

Terry believed that the act intended "to enforce, as a religious institution, the observance of a day held sacred by the followers of one faith." Other state high courts took a similar view, but where other courts accepted Sunday laws as acceptable religious establishments, Terry took a new tack, declaring the "Sabbath" act to be at cross purposes with California's constitutional guarantee of "free exercise and enjoyment of religious professions and worship, without discrimination or preference."

The constitutional mandate was not met by bland assurances to the Jew or seventh-day Christian that after all, "your conscience is not constrained, you are not compelled to worship or

86

to perform religious rites on that day, nor forbidden to keep holy the day which you esteem as a Sabbath."

Such an approach, however, indicates mere toleration and revocable privilege in contrast to the inalienable rights inherent in complete religious liberty. The achievement of that ideal requires "a complete separation between church and state, and a perfect equality without distinction between all religious sects."

The chief justice pooh-poohed attempts to wink at the "Sabbath" act as a civil rule and, in a slap at the Field dissent, discarded such attempts as mere judicial assertion.

Associate Justice Burnett,[2] a Roman Catholic, concurred with Terry in a separate statement of opinion. Like Terry, he objected to the act because it established "a compulsory religious observance."

To Burnett, religious freedom encompassed a broad principle for all—the believer and unbeliever alike. The Sunday law violated "as much the religious freedom of the Christian as the Jew. Because the conscientious views of the Christian compel him to keep Sunday as a Sabbath, he has the right to object, when the Legislature invades his freedom of religious worship, and assumes the power to compel him to that which he has the right to omit if he pleases." Burnett saw the California Constitution as a barrier to legislative enforcement of any religious observance whatever.

The associate justice hammered away at the lack of legislative power to toy with inalienable rights. In his analysis, compulsory power did not exist for the State of California to "compel the citizen to do that which the constitution leaves him free to do or omit, at his election. . . . The Legislature cannot pass any act, the legitimate effect of which is *forcibly* to establish any merely religious truth, or enforce any merely religious observance."

And even if enforced, Sunday observance could be labeled "civil" only by way of judicial semantics. Burnett rejected this

87

approach. It was definitely beyond the scope of even legitimate police power. "If the Legislature could prescribe the days of rest" for Californians, "it would seem that the same power could prescribe the hours to work, rest, and eat."

And after all, said Burnett, "It is the individual that is intended to be protected. The principle is the same, whether the many or the few are concerned."

Writing on a day when the ugly stain of human slavery was about to split a nation from one end of the Mason-Dixon line to the other, Burnett observed that compulsory Sunday rest in a slave state might make sense as a civil measure to protect "the slave against the inhumanity of the master in not allowing sufficient rest" or if "confined to infants or persons bound by law to obey others."

But in California's golden hills "every man is a free agent, competent and able to protect himself, and no one is bound by law to labor for any particular person. Free agents must be left free, as to themselves. . . . If we cannot trust free agents to regulate their own labor, its times and quantity, it is difficult to trust them to make their own contracts."

The free agent argument, coupled with the declaration that the legislature "cannot prohibit the proper use of the means of acquiring property, except the peace and safety of the State require it," was used by the court majority to strike down the California "Sabbath" act even as a purely civil regulation. The right to acquire property was inalienable, and the blue law had trampled that right. On this both Burnett and Chief Justice Terry agreed. If the act was outside the scope of the legitimate peace and safety interests of the state, it certainly was, as a purely religious issue, outside constitutional limits.

The third member of the court, Associate Justice Stephen J. Field, dissented vehemently. While admitting the possible religious motivation of some legislators in adopting the "Sabbath" act, Field searched for some possible secular purpose that would validate the measure under the police power of the state. This he found in the health and welfare benefits that might come through regular weekly rest, despite the fact that the choice of the day was not left to the individual. Encouraged by a similar innovation used by the Pennsylvania Court in 1848 and the Ohio Court in 1853, Field rejected the "free agent" and "right to acquire property" arguments. Although Field was a minority of one in 1858, he had the last word with Terry in this split of judicial theory.

When Terry left the California Supreme Court in 1859, Stephen J. Field was elevated to the vacated chair of the chief justice. And from that spot in 1861, Field had the satisfaction of seeing the Terry holding in *Ex Parte Newman* repudiated, and his own theories elevated to the majority status in the case of *Ex Parte Andrews*.[3] More than that, Field lived to see the day when he could write his "civil regulation" and "police power" belief into an opinion of the United States Supreme Court.

But the Terry opinion in *Ex Parte Newman* was right for the horde of migrants who invaded the Sierras, leaving a trail of gold and silver dust from San Francisco to Virginia City. America was a melting pot of world nationalities; cosmopolitan California became a melting pot of America. The Terry opinion pioneered a new dimension in human liberty and shook off the shackles of a tradition which was obsolete where church and state were separate.

California adventurers welcomed this new dimension. Men and women who had scrambled through narrow Sierra trails, fought the fevers of the Panama jungle, and sailed the rough waters of the Cape needed no paternalistic hand to lead them to their day of rest. The numbing cold and backaches from labor in the Mother Lode country provided adequate incentive.

Merchants like Newman of Sacramento didn't need to be told when to rest. A miner or rancher in quest of supplies was as likely to arrive in town on Sunday as on any other day. Free enterprisers felt individually capable of determining how best to serve the need of the customer—and how to rest.

The public accepted Field's medicine for a time. But when the "Sabbath" act was succeeded by similar legislative experiments and the Field theory achieved high court acceptance, public resentment boiled over into the political arena in 1882.

Fired by legislative and judicial triumphs, religious forces pushed fanatically for more rigid enforcement of these legal achievements. The Ministerial Union of San Francisco pressured public officials to crack down on those who disobeyed the demands of the blue law. Police Chief Crowley obliged by promising arrests "of persons who may violate this law next Sunday."[4]

Crowley and his force moved in with strong arms, and in less than a month's time the San Francisco dragnet flushed out nearly 1,600 lawbreakers and flooded the court dockets. Rigid enforcement created such a bottleneck in the courts that San Francisco police were forced to ease up.[5]

Most Californians disliked the looks of blue laws on paper, but the effect of enforcement aroused them to real action. With the statewide election scheduled for November, politicians in 1882 had their ears to the ground. What they heard was the ominous sound of resentment. The Democrats responded to the voice of a League of Freedom that was out to destroy the blue laws.

The Republicans listened to church representatives who warned political parties to "be careful of their platform in this direction. Any yielding or temporizing on this and kindred subjects will be resented by the better class of our citizens, who, in all cases, are the power in the land."[6] Republicans had carried California by a 20,319 vote majority in 1878 and had no intention of losing four years later.

Accordingly, when the GOP convention met in 1882, they

90

proposed a platform plank supporting Sunday laws. J. W. Shaeffer of the League of Freedom and Mr. Wagner of the Religious Liberty Association publicly opposed its adoption. But plank number five endorsed "preserving one day in seven as a day of rest from labor" to protect the laboring classes. The Republicans announced: "We are in favor of observing Sunday as a day of rest and recreation, and while we expressly disavow the right or the wish to place any class of citizens [under compulsion] to spend that day in a particular manner, we do favor the maintenance of the present Sunday laws, or similar laws, providing for the suspension of all unnecessary business on that day."[7]

Democrats in San Jose the previous June had also faced up to the Sunday-law issue. Sitting at the head chair of the convention committee considering the blue law was David S. Terry. When the smoke cleared, the committee voted eight to one to include the following plank in the Democratic platform:

> That the Democratic Party, inheriting the doctrine of Jefferson and Jackson, hereby declares its unqualified enmity to all sumptuary legislation, regarding all such exercise of the law-making power as against the just objects of free government, and that all laws intended to restrain or direct a free and full exercise by any citizen of his own religious and political opinion, so long as he leaves others to enjoy their rights unmolested, are antidemocratic and hostile to the principles and traditions of the party, create unnecessary antagonism, cannot be enforced, and are a violation of the spirit of the republican government; and we will oppose the enactment of all such laws and demand the repeal of those now existing.[8]

A few delegates expressed apprehension and suggested that the plank might rob them of the church vote, warning "that its adoption would result in the party's defeat in November."

But Delegate Brady of Fresno urged "that a man ought to be

allowed to worship God according to his dictates of conscience.
. . . We cannot drive people to the worship of God, and it
ought not to be done in that way."

The voice of David Terry came through loud and clear when
he described the disputed matter as a "living issue." He appealed
to all the delegates, declaring it was time to put at rest the
charges which accused the Democratic Party of being too cow-
ardly to meet the issue openly. He believed that the Sunday law
violated both state and Federal principles and that the notion of
"religious holiday" and "police regulation" foisted upon a free-
dom-loving public in an attempt to rationalize Sunday laws was
a "parcel of nonsense put up by the judges."

David S. Terry no doubt recalled the words of his former
colleague, Stephen J. Field, in making this homespun characterization.

A majority of delegates acclaimed the Terry view and adopted
it as plank number five in the Democratic platform. The lines
had been drawn for the political settlement of a religious
issue.

The Methodist Conference of California met in San Francisco in September and resolved to throw its support behind a
"civil Sabbath" and to reflect this dedication in a free ballot.
Without naming the Republicans or Democrats specifically, the
resolution suggested that "any attempt to abolish or change the
day is an attempt to destroy the national life; that the civil Sabbath in the republican state depends upon the ballots of the
citizens; that it is the duty of the Christian citizen to cast his free
ballot where it will best promote the highest interests of the
Christian Sabbath."[9]

The stage was set in November, 1882, for a political test
unique in the history of blue laws. The people could speak. And
they did—with a sweeping Democratic majority of 21,050, in
a sharp reversal of the 1878 voter pattern. The Democrats began
a new year with General George Stoneman in the gover-

nor's mansion and a Democratic majority controlling the legislature.

In a message to the legislature early in 1883, the newly elected governor attacked the California Sunday law and declared it "unwise to cumber the statute books with an enactment which experience has proven cannot be enforced. The result of the late election by an emphatic endorsement of the attitude of the now dominant party on this important subject makes our duty in the premises perfectly clear." "The right to worship free from hindrance or molestation should always be carefully guarded."[10]

True to their platform pledge, the Democratic majority stripped the Sunday law from the California statutes almost as its first order of business in 1883. Shaken Republicans had taken a deep breath of political poison when they inhaled the blue-law atmosphere.

Oddly enough, when Sunday observance was no longer demanded by law, attendance at Sunday worship services in California increased. Sunday-law advocate W. F. Crafts, spokesman for the International Reform Bureau, admitted in an 1885 publication that "both laymen and ministers say that even in California the Sabbath is, on the whole, better observed, and Christian services better attended, than five years ago."[11]

Thus when an aroused electorate spoke in 1882, it backed the Terry plank in the Democratic platform and spurned the Field declaration. It was the first time in history that a state electorate had been so definitely heard at the polls on Sunday laws, and the voice of rejection sounded loud and clear.

Stephen J. Field seemed not to hear the California electorate speak. He was out of earshot in Washington, D.C., serving as an associate justice of the United States Supreme Court. What the voters in the gold-rush country had thrown out, Field was about to dredge up for the entire nation—the theory that coerced Sunday observance offered sufficient secular health and welfare benefits to justify its being forced on the public by legislative fiat. The case which became the vehicle for this national premiere, like Field, came from California. The appellant was Soon Hing, a Chinese laundryman who had tried his hand at free enterprise in San Francisco.

The city by the Golden Gate acted to prevent labor in laundries after 10 p.m. at night as well as all day Sunday. In February of 1884, Police Chief Crowley, of Sunday-law enforcement fame, charged Soon Hing with working after 10 p.m. In 1885 the case landed in the United States Supreme Court, and Justice Field was there to write an opinion.

The facts of the case concerned night labor and the power of the city to control round-the-clock laundry work. Field couldn't resist extending the dictum of the case to include Sunday closing. For the first time the United States Supreme Court gave judicial recognition to the "civil regulation" premise as a means to justify blue laws.

Field's brilliant mind did more than repudiate Terry's progressive rationale and sidestep the expressed will of a California public! His was a judicial assertion that held the fancy of the United States Supreme Court in a grip that could not be broken even in the liberal climate of 1961.

REFERENCES

1. *Ex Parte Newman,* 9 California 502 (1858).
2. *Ibid.*
3. *Ex Parte Andrews,* 18 California 685 (1861).
4. "The Sunday Law," San Francisco *Chronicle,* March 14, 1882.
5. "The Sunday Law," *Signs of the Times,* Vol. 8 (1882), No. 15.
6. *Pacific Methodist.* In "Religious Notes," *Ibid.,* No. 13.
7. "Republican Convention," San Francisco *Evening Bulletin,* August 31, 1882.
8. "Democratic Convention," *Ibid.,* June 21, 1882.
9. "Methodist Conference," San Francisco *Morning Call,* September 27, 1882.
10. "Stoneman's Address," San Francisco *Evening Bulletin,* January 10, 1883.
11. See "Religious Liberty in California History," *Signs of the Times,* Vol. 39 (1912), No. 20.

9. CHAMELEON SUNDAY

As the Sunday fair-closing controversy approached its peak, a United States Supreme Court justice made a surprising pronouncement. Justice David J. Brewer, who delivered a ruling that a Federal law banning contracts with alien laborers does not affect the right of a church to hire a pastor from a foreign country, also made the statement that "this is a Christian nation." In an effort to fortify this declaration, Brewer displayed a variety of evidence, including "the laws respecting the observance of the Sabbath," coupled with "the general cessation of all secular business . . . on that day."[1] The judges' decision was unanimous.

Justice John M. Harlan spoke for the court four years later, in 1896, branding a Georgia blue law "as an ordinary police regulation established by the state under its general power to protect the health and morals and to promote the welfare of its people" —in apparent contrast to the 1892 "Christian nation" dictum.

Justice Stephen J. Field, Brewer's uncle, had pioneered the new dimension in judicial thought enunciated by Harlan. He described Sunday laws as simple *civil* regulations designed to benefit the public welfare, and reasoned that they could be sustained as a legitimate exercise of the police power of the state. Still, even Field appeared not to object to his nephew's candid 1892 recognition of the *religious* nature of Sunday laws.

DATELINE SUNDAY, U.S.A.

Admittedly, blue laws of the late nineteenth century were religious in origin, development, and contemporary operation. But since the rest feature brought "benefit" to the community, the Sunday law could be viewed by some stretch of the imagination as a civil rather than a religious regulation. Thus the state could, by enforcing such a law, claim the promotion of community welfare.

Sunday laws themselves had not changed. Justice Brewer was willing even to cite them as evidence that the United States is a "Christian nation." If there was any change, it was in judicial theory. And the more sophisticated police-power rationale was a tangible shift from the open acknowledgment of religious establishment traditionally used by state courts.

Rarely did any Sunday law face Federal court review in the nineteenth century. It was individual state governments that were burdened with numerous Sunday laws. On the occasions when state blue laws confronted the Supreme Court of the United States, they came usually as a collateral issue. For example:

The ship *Tangier* had made a valid delivery of cotton by unloading its cargo on a Boston dock—even though it did so on a fast day proclaimed by the governor according to an 1860 court decision.[2] In its dictum the court noted it was not necessary for a fast day to be "observed as a Sabbath."

A Nevada Act for the "Better Observance of the Lord's Day" was held no bar to a valid notification of contract rescission given in Nevada on a Sunday in 1875.[3]

A defendant was prevented from using the Wisconsin prohibition on Sunday business as a defense against the enforcement of a contract signed only by the defendant on Sunday.[4]

Theodore P. Bucher was injured while riding a Sunday train. He heard the judge instruct the jury that "he was traveling upon the Sabbath Day, in violation of the law of the State of Massachusetts." To Bucher's chagrin, the United States Supreme

When Theodore Bucher was injured while
riding a Sunday train, the Supreme Court
held that Bucher could collect no damages.

Court of 1888 felt obligated to repeat the decisions of the state court, which held that this illegal act of the plaintiff was a valid defense available to the defendant.[5]

A murder verdict was reversed by the Supreme Court in 1891. The court indicated that the judgment also would have been void if it had been in fact entered on Sunday in violation of applicable law.[6] Since there was no statute to the contrary, the 1897 court ruled that the receiving and entering of a Sunday verdict where the judgment itself was not entered until the following Friday did not constitute a void Sunday judgment.[7]

None of these cases represented a frontal assault charging either an "establishment of religion" or the "prevention of the free exercise of religion." Even after the Fourteenth Amendment became law, not before the twentieth century did the Supreme Court rule that state and local governments must be guided by Federal First Amendment guarantees. Nevertheless the police-power rationale for support of Sunday legislation was planted before the Civil War and took root while the majority of state courts felt free to uphold blue laws as religious establishments.

A Seventh Day Baptist named Specht had clashed with the Pennsylvania Sabbath law about the time William Lloyd Garrison was jousting with the same problem. The highest tribunal of that state took a big step into judicial history by describing the regulation as "essentially but a civil regulation made for the government of man as a member of society."[8]

Then, as if seeking to harmonize the new civil regulation doctrine with the older accepted "religious establishment" approach, the Pennsylvania Supreme Court of 1853 implicitly admitted a church-state union. The court avoided a purely secular justification for Sunday laws, describing them as a "civil institution," since government is founded on "Divine appointment." "Rest one day in seven was enjoined by the precept and example of the Author of our existence, and government, founding itself on Divine appointment, has made it a civil institution."[9]

In that same year the same Pennsylvania court retreated even farther from its revolutionary "civil regulation" doctrine of 1848, recognizing the religious establishment doctrine at least to a degree. The court felt it far from irrelevant to its decision to sustain the divine authority of the institution. As if to remove any doubt, the court stated, "We have no *right* to give up this institution. It has come down to us with the most solemn sanctions, both of God and man."[10]

Other religious establishment attitudes emerged in subsequent Pennsylvania decisions. In 1855 the court said: "It is perfectly natural . . . that a Christian people should have laws to protect their day of rest from desecration. Regarding it as a day necessarily and divinely set apart for rest from worldly employments, and for the enjoyment of spiritual privileges, it is simply absurd to suppose that they would leave it without any legislative protection."[11]

In 1859 the court was sure that "the Sabbath and its institutions were the prominent means" to the progress of civilization. It asked, "How, then, is it possible for a Christian people to avoid protecting such a day and its institutions?"[12]

In 1867 Justice Strong of the Pennsylvania Supreme Court, in a *nisi prius* hearing, declared that Christianity is part of that state's common law. He stated, "If Christianity is part of the common law, it carries with it a civil obligation to abstain on the Lord's day from all worldly labor and business, except works of necessity and mercy. Christianity without a Sabbath would be no Christianity."[13]

Though speaking of police power, the Pennsylvania court still was reluctant to abandon the religious establishment tradition. At the time, the civil regulation concept had not emerged in its purest form, but the seed had been planted.

DATELINE SUNDAY, U.S.A.

The Ohio Supreme Court in 1853 described the Sunday law of that state as a "mere municipal, or police regulation, whose validity is neither strengthened nor weakened by the fact that the day of rest it enjoins is the Sabbath day."[14]

Pennsylvania and Ohio had done some innovating, but it was a Californian who refined and developed the rationale which ultimately captured the attention of the United States Supreme Court. Two of the three judges sitting on the California Supreme Court in 1858 ruled that the "Act to Provide for the Better Observance of the Sabbath" violated the constitution of that state.[15] Justice Stephen J. Field, a bitter personal antagonist of Chief Justice David Terry, dissented vehemently. While admitting that the law referred to the Christian Sabbath, and that religious convictions could have controlled some of the legislators who voted for the measure, Field refused to see more than a "rule of civil conduct." He claimed that the law did not "even allude to the subject of religious profession or worship."

He argued that there existed only the establishment of a civil regulation and the means "to protect labor." He maintained that "a civil regulation cannot be converted into a religious institution because it is enforced on a day which a particular religious sect regards as sacred." He skillfully framed the basis for law which was embraced by every court that adopted the "police power" philosophy. Said the justice: "The prohibition of secular business on Sunday is advocated on the ground that by it the general welfare is advanced, labor protected, and the moral and physical well-being of society promoted." *He referred to both the Specht and the Bloom cases as instrumental in the formulation of his dissent.*

Three years later, Field had his way in California. When Chief Justice Terry resigned in 1859, Justice Field presided through the October term, 1862. When another Sunday-law case came before the court in 1861, two new justices joined with Field and followed the "police power" of the earlier Field dissent

100

and ruled that the object of the Sunday law "was only to require duties purely civic or secular."[16]

Massachusetts found occasion to term its Lord's-day statute as "essentially a civil regulation" in response to the Field doctrine.[17] This 1877 case of *Commonwealth v. Has* was unique because it contradicted Massachusetts cases, both before and after, that accepted Sunday laws as religious establishments.[18] Still it was to become a pivotal point of reference in future considerations of the constitutionality of the Massachusetts Sunday law.

In 1892 the Georgia court likewise adopted the "police regulation" theory, drawing a fine line between "keeping a day holy as a religious observance, and merely forbearing to labor on that day in one's ordinary vocation or business pursuit."

The case involved a man named Hennington, who worked for a railroad that was at odds with the Georgia Sunday law prohibiting freight trains from moving through Georgia on Sunday, even though the train originated in Tennessee and was routed to Mississippi. The extent of a state's right to regulate interstate commerce was the prime issue that finally reached the United States Supreme Court, but the "police purposes" of Sunday legislation received plenty of exposure along the way.

The Georgia court declared, "The statute can fairly and rationally be treated as a legitimate police regulation." The court held that the Sunday-closing statute is not "vitiated, or in any wise weakened, by the chance, or even the certainty, that in passing it the legislative mind was swayed by the religious rather than by the civil aspect of the measure."[19]

In 1852 the Georgia court had shown an inclination to disapprove "municipal arrangements which overlook and disregard the moral law of the Great Jehovah, who, from the smoking top of Mount Sinai proclaimed to all the world, 'Remember the Sabbath-day to keep it holy; in it thou shalt not do any work.' "[20]

In 1871 the same court declared, "The law fixes the day recognized as the Sabbath day all over Christendom, and that day, by Divine injunction, is to be kept holy." Then it contradicted itself by stating, "The Christian Sabbath is a civil institution" deserving of legislative regulation for "the preservation of good morals and the peace and good order of society."[21]

In 1873 the same court emphasized the sanctity of Sunday which was to be protected from violation because "the Sabbath day is regarded as the Lord's day."[22] In 1879 the court described Sunday as a holy day with "the current of decision by this Court" having been "pro-Sabbatic in full measure."[23]

Although the civil institution dogma had been alluded to in 1871, it was not until the Hennington case in 1892 that the Georgia court appeared willing to tone down the religious aspect of Sunday legislation. Ironically, it picked the year of the Columbian Exposition struggle and the year that Justice Brewer declared his "Christian nation" sentiments.

Before the United States Supreme Court was offered the Hennington matter, the stage was set by a case in San Francisco relating to the regulation of working hours for laundries. The ordinance in question prohibited night work at laundries between 10 p.m. and 6 a.m. and also demanded Sunday closing. A man named Soon Hing was arrested for working after 10 p.m., February 25, 1884.

When the case came to the Supreme Court of the United States in 1885, an expert on "police power" was there to deliver the opinion of the court. Justice Stephen J. Field did more than find that the regulation of the hours of night work was a valid "police regulation." He also touched on the Sunday issue. Reminiscent of his dissenting remarks in *Ex Parte Newman,* Field reasoned that "laws setting aside Sunday as a day of rest are upheld, not from any right of the Government to legislate for the promotion of religious observances, but from its right to protect all persons from the physical and moral debasement which comes from uninterrupted labor." He judged Sunday laws to be "beneficient . . . to the poor and dependent, to the laborers in our factories and workshops and in the heated rooms of our cities."[24]

Although it was one man's expression, it served as a beacon light for subsequent judicial thought. In this sense it was a landmark in the move to recognize blue laws as valid "civil regulations." Sitting with Field on the Soon Hing matter was Justice John M. Harlan. He later adopted and embellished the Field approach in the Hennington case in 1896.

Both Harlan and Field were present to hear the Brewer dictum of 1892 that "laws respecting the observance of the Sabbath" are a part of the evidence that this is a Christian nation. Although temporary lapse from the police power principle was implicit, neither Field nor Harlan saw fit to argue on the record at the time that Sunday laws are not *religious* but *civil* regulations.

Justice Harlan waited until the *Hennington* v. *Georgia* case in 1896 to speak out for the police power approach to Sunday legislation. (Only Justice Horace Gray along with Justices Field and Harlan participated in all three decisions—Soon Hing, Hennington, and the "Christian nation" proposal.)

Chief Justice Melville Fuller and Justice Edward D. White comprised the Hennington case minority which argued that the Federal Congress has exclusive jurisdiction over interstate commerce, and state power must give way to Federal even in a "mere regulation of police."

Justice Harlan was joined by Justices Field, Gray, Brown, Shiras, and Peckham in upholding the right of the state of Georgia to regulate railroad lines running through the state irrespective of the interstate commerce aspect. They extended this ruling to the right of the state "to prohibit all persons, under penalties, from using the Sabbath as a day for labor and for pursuing their ordinary callings." And if the statute forbidding the movement of "freight trains, on the Sabbath day, had been

103

expressly limited to trains laden with domestic freight, it could not be regarded otherwise than as an ordinary police regulation established by the State under its general power to protect the health and morals and to promote the welfare of its people."

For precedent authority in this ruling, the court cited the Bloom case along with the Field view as expressed in *Ex Parte Newman*. Harlan also incorporated the bold language of the Georgia court. His statement was reminiscent of the earlier Field attitude:

> There is nothing in the legislation in question which suggests that it was enacted . . . with any other purpose than to prescribe a rule of civil duty for all who, on the Sabbath day, are within the territorial jurisdiction of the State. It is none the less a civil regulation because the day on which the running of freight trains is prohibited is kept by many under a sense of religious duty. The legislature having, as will not be disputed, power to enact laws to promote the order and to secure the comfort, happiness, and health of the people, it was within its discretion to fix the day when all labor should cease. . . .
>
> Both upon principle and authority the statute of Georgia is, in every substantial sense, a police regulation established under the general authority possessed by the legislature to provide by laws, for the well-being of the people.[25]

This was the same Justice Harlan who, in 1908, spoke to a religious assembly in the nation's capital in open advocacy of the *religious* values of the "Sabbath" establishment.

The year 1896 marked a high point in the history of judicial comment relating to Sunday laws. When a Minnesota Sunday-closing law directed against barbers was subsequently heard, the court would not reverse itself. The court held that the classification of barbers was not so arbitrary as to violate the constitution. "We have uniformly recognized state laws relating to the observance of Sunday as enacted in the legitimate exercise of the police power of the State."[26]

The police power doctrine was in full flower. But the police power contention leaves questions unanswered.

1. Under the police power approach, is there any religious establishment that cannot be validated because of public-welfare benefits? If not, where can the line be drawn with constitutional certainty?

2. When in 1896 the Supreme Court adopted the police power rationale in earnest, there was little evidence of legislative or individual intent that Sunday laws are a civil institution. On the contrary, there is evidence that the "civil" label was exclusively a judicial invention. At what point in history, other than the moment of judicial opinion, can it be said that Sunday laws abandoned their historic religious nature to become harmless civil institutions?

3. Chief proponents of Sunday legislation have been ardent religious groups. Chief victims of Sunday-law enforcement have been religious minorities. Why?

4. If Sunday was intended to be a civil holiday for the public welfare, why the criminal penalties for violation? Fourth of July and Labor Day observances carry no penalties.

5. If the "observance" is structured to protect labor as suggested by Field, why fine the man who works by his own choice on Sunday?

6. When the citizen is given Sunday for rest, why by the same law deny him the pleasure of "worldly amusements" and Sunday sports?

7. If it is a valid civil regulation, why does Sunday legislation arbitrarily establish classes of labor and business that are or are not acceptable? If coerced rest is essential on Sunday, why is it not equally essential for all citizens regardless of occupation?

8. If simultaneous rest is impossible for all citizens, why not enact a simple welfare measure that guarantees one day's rest in

seven to all for each consecutive seven-day period, with the choice of the day left to individual need and convenience?

9. How can a state like Massachusetts which had a "one day in seven" law concurrent with its Sunday-rest law, utilize the "police power" as opposed to the "religious establishment" rationale for sustaining the Sunday law? Where a "one day in seven" law exists, would not the remaining purpose of the Sunday law be "religious establishment"?

10. If blue laws are to promote better health, is there anything inherent in the nature of the day, Sunday, that is more healthful than any other day of the week? In the valid work-hour regulations of state governments, there is no designation as to the days when the work must be performed, nor the hours of the day when work must commence, nor the time of the day or night when men must sleep. What entitles Sunday observance to this restrictive treatment?

11. Why are Sunday-law prohibitions sometimes limited to certain geographic districts or population levels, making crimes contingent not only upon the hour and the day but also upon the size and location of the community where the conduct occurs?

12. If Sunday laws are not religious establishments, why do some statutes carry toleration exemptions for religious minorities that worship on a day other than Sunday?

Whatever the answers, many state courts took no notice of Field's police power approach and continued to cling to religious establishment in support of blue laws even after the United States Supreme Court had spoken in 1896 and 1900.

But what if the First Amendment to the Federal Constitution were made applicable to state and local government and then a state Sunday law was attacked directly as an "establishment of religion" and as a law "preventing the free exercise of religion"?

Twentieth-century judicial development produced the answer.

REFERENCES

1. *Church of the Holy Trinity* v. *United States,* 143 U.S. 457 (1892).
2. *Richardson* v. *Goddard,* 64 U.S. 28 (1860).
3. *Pence* v. *Langdon,* 99 U.S. 578 (1878).
4. *Gibbs & Stenet Mfg. Co.* v. *Bruckey,* 111 U.S. 595 (1884).
5. *Bucher* v. *Cheshire Rail Road Company,* 125 U.S. 555 (1888).
6. *Ball* v. *United States,* 140 U.S. 118 (1891).
7. *Stone* v. *United States,* 167 U.S. 178 (1897).
8. *Specht* v. *Commonwealth,* 8 Pennsylvania 312 (1848).
9. *Omit* v. *Commonwealth,* 21 Pennsylvania 426 (1853).
10. *Johnston* v. *Commonwealth,* 22 Pennsylvania 102, (1853).
11. *Mahoney* v. *Cook,* 26 Pennsylvania 342 (1855).
12. *Commonwealth* v. *Nesbit,* 34 Pennsylvania 398 (1859).
13. *Sparhawk* v. *The Union Passenger Railway Co.,* 54 Pennsylvania 401 (1867).
14. *Bloom* v. *Richards,* 2 Ohio 387 (1853).
15. *Ex Parte Newman,* 9 California 502 (1858).
16. *Ex Parte Andrews,* 18 California 678 (1861).
17. *Commonwealth* v. *Has,* 122 Massachusetts 42 (1887).
18. *Bennett* v. *Brooks,* 91 Massachusetts 118 (1864).
    Commonwealth v. *White,* 190 Massachusetts 578 (1906).
    Commonwealth v. *McCarthy,* 244 Massachusetts 484 (1923).
19. *Hennington* v. *State,* 90 Georgia 396 (1892).
20. *Neal* v. *Crew,* 12 Georgia 93 (1852).
21. *Karwisch* v. *The Mayor and Council of Atlanta,* 44 Georgia 204 (1871).
22. *Bass* v. *Irwin,* 49 Georgia 436, (1873).
23. *Weldon* v. *Colquitt,* 62 Georgia 449, (1879).
24. *Soon Hing* v. *Crowley,* 113 U.S. 703 (1885).
25. *Hennington* v. *Georgia,* 163 U.S. 299 (1896).
26. *Petit* v. *Minnesota,* 177 U.S. 164 (1900).

10. FIRST DAY VERSUS FIRST AMENDMENT

Volleys of hot lead shredded the natural beauty of the Pennsylvania countryside in July, 1863.

The place was Gettysburg, a pivot point in United States history. General Lee had organized an invasion from northern Virginia in an effort to slice up the Union heartland. General Meade and his Federal forces were just as determined to repel the invasion and break the back of the Confederacy. Of the 150,000 Americans committed to the conflict, nearly one third would be dead or wounded when the battle was over. It began on July 1 and raged throughout July 2 and July 3. By July 4, 1863, the course of history had been irrevocably altered.

As the ranks formed for battle, the Union Army entrenched itself along Cemetery Ridge, its left flank guarded by a craggy knoll called Little Round Top. Strewn with rocks, scrubby brush, and trees, Little Round Top provided a commanding view of the Federal line.

Little Round Top was also the key to the Battle of Gettysburg. General Meade had posted two divisions along the southern portion of Cemetery Ridge and the Little and Big Round Tops; but General Sickles, the corps commander, sensed the approach of a Confederate attack on July 2 and determined to improve this position—without benefit of orders from Meade.

108

When Sickles moved his men forward to what he believed to be strategic advantage, Little Round Top was up for grabs.

Shrewd Confederate generals did not wait for an invitation. They assaulted the exposed Union left flank. The two Federal divisions could no longer return to the Round Tops and Cemetery Ridge if they wanted. Blue uniformed infantrymen struggled valiantly in the exposed positions of a peach orchard and a wheat field. The aggressive gray line simply overpowered them.

The Federal left was crumbling, and Confederate skirmishers were preparing to attack the Round Tops when Brigadier General Gouverneur K. Warren rode up and diverted an artillery battery and a couple of infantry brigades to defensive positions on Little Round Top. The ranks were woefully thin, and there was little time to dig in. Already snipers behind the rocks of Devil's Den were zeroing in on the officers with deadly accuracy. A pall of acrid smoke hung heavy. The crack of rifles, the metallic whine of packaged death cutting through the air, the massive explosives, the screams of the dying, and the gutteral cries from onrushing men pitted against one another in a game of death—this raging spectacle engulfed Little Round Top.

In the last analysis, it was a story of men. At the extreme left end of this Federal left flank were some troops from Maine brought to the scene by the desperate command of General Warren. To their left was no more Union Army. Coming at them from the front were gray-clad soldiers from Alabama. South and North, Alabama and Maine—strangers meeting for the first and last time on a Pennsylvania hillside in frantic and agonizing combat. Enemies, not from personal animosities but because history made them so.

Bullets are no respecters of persons. They tore out the hearts of the youth from Maine and Alabama alike, as ugly red blotches marked grotesque monuments on the rocks of Little Round Top. With the enemy so close, there was no time to reload; the bayo-

net, the knife, the sword, and the crunch of a gun butt on a human skull—these were the weapons.

Then it was over! The men from Maine, the living, the dead, and the dying, still clung to the gouged-out crevices of Little Round Top. The men from Alabama, those who could, withdrew to regroup. But General Lee was never to have his guns mounted on Little Round Top, and without Little Round Top, Pickett's charge the next day did not succeed. Gettysburg was lost to the South.

Without Gettysburg, the South could not win the war. And without victory, the Confederacy would die.

110

General Lee failed to mount his guns on Little Round Top, and Pickett's charge the next day also resulted in defeat.

With the passing of the Confederacy in 1865, the United States emerged into a new era. What had been a Federal Government with strong state loyalties and rivalries became a national government with strong central leadership. States rights declined while the scope of individual rights expanded.

The rights and dignities of individual citizens of the United States were protected by law, irrespective of any "prior condition of servitude." Out of the national torture and tumult of Gettysburg came a rebirth, a rebuilding, and the Fourteenth Amendment to the United States Constitution.

This amendment said in part:

111

> No State shall make or enforce any law which shall abridge the privileges or immunities of citizens of the United States; nor shall any State deprive any person of life, liberty, or property, without due process of law; nor deny to any person within its jurisdiction the equal protection of the laws.

Ten years after the close of the war, James G. Blaine urged Congress to adopt a constitutional amendment which would remove religious establishment from the reach of state governments just as certainly as the First Amendment had created a wall of separation between church and state for the Federal Government. The Blaine proposal touched on specifics in addition to general guarantees.

> No State shall make any law respecting an establishment of religion or prohibiting the free exercise thereof; and no money raised by taxation in any State, for the support of public schools, or derived from any public fund therefor, nor any public lands devoted thereto, shall ever be under the control of any religious sect; nor shall any money so raised, or lands so devoted, be divided between religious sects or denominations.[1]

With slight modification, the House overwhelmed opposition to the amendment by a vote of 180 to 7 in favor of Blaine's proposal. On August 14, 1876, ten days after the House vote, a majority of the Senate voted for the measure—28 to 16. (At that time Senators were still chosen by state legislatures rather than by direct vote of the people.)

Since proposed constitutional amendments require a two-thirds vote in Congress before being sent to the states for ratification, the Senate majority was inadequate by the narrowest of margins. The Blaine amendment died in Congress. If it had cleared Congress and been adopted by the states, it is conceivable that state Sunday laws could have been wiped from the books before 1900.

Nevertheless, the Fourteenth Amendment was law. The repercussions from its impact cut a wide swath in judicial history. By 1925 the United State Supreme Court had decreed that First Amendment guarantees were applicable to state and local government through the provisions of the Fourteenth Amendment.[2] By 1943 the court confirmed that the freedom of religion guaranteed by the First Amendment applied to the states through the Fourteenth Amendment.[3]

But while this legal evolution in human rights was in metamorphosis, state Sunday laws were still being used as tools of religious intolerance. In Pennsylvania, where the high court introduced the "civil regulation" doctrine in 1848, the Pittsburgh Sabbath Association arranged for the arrest of members of the Pittsburgh Symphony Society for "furnishing music to the public on Sunday" in 1929. Two years later in a Philadelphia suburb "a policeman arrested a boy for kicking a football on Sunday. When the father protested, the . . . policeman shot and killed the father."[4]

"A deputy sheriff of Washington County arrested two Seventh-day Adventists for Sunday work, one—a crippled mother who walks on crutches—for washing clothes on her own premises, and the other a man who donated and hauled a load of wood to a church to heat it for religious services."[5] The place was Virginia, the year, 1932.

Eight Lincoln, Nebraska, boys were fined $5 each in 1921 for playing horseshoes in a vacant lot on Sunday. A 1930 Sunday football game in New Jersey was stopped, and in 1924 a New Jersey court invoked a 1798 blue law and found it illegal to play a phonograph or listen to the radio on Sunday because this was "music for the sake of merriment."

When a Sunday-law "spy" peered into the privacy of a Baltimore home in 1926 and saw a man pressing his pants on Sunday, the act was reported, and a fine resulted. In Georgia, in 1930, the state where the "police power" doctrine had been aired in the Hennington case, there was arbitrary use of the Sunday law. "The police of Clayton County protected and helped a traveling circus to land in town and put on a show; they also cooperated with airplanes which took people for rides and made much money; yet they arrested a Bible colporteur for delivering a book explaining the Bible, on Sunday, since the person who ordered the book requested that the book be delivered then because it was the only day he was at home."[6]

But the ultimate testing ground for blue laws under the enlightenment of the First Amendment was Massachusetts. This was fitting, for here was a land saturated with the lore of freedom and its conflicts. Here the Pilgrims landed. Here was the residence of Anne Hutchinson and the earlier home of Roger Williams. This was where the tea was unceremoniously dumped into the harbor during a unique Boston party. "The shot heard round the world" was fired at the green in Lexington, and the Sons of Liberty saw the whites of British eyes at Bunker Hill. Massachusetts sons were in the thick of the Gettysburg conflict —as well as every other serious challenge to the national liberty. Garrison held his anti-Sunday-law convention here in 1848.

Home of the deeply religious, Massachusetts was the last of the original thirteen colonies to remove vestigial evidences of original church-state union. And like its sister colonies, colonial blue laws remained on the books in one form or another even after the formal but incomplete disestablishment. The Massachusetts Lord's Day law was amended more than seventy times since its inception.

Here, perhaps, was the best possible laboratory in which to test the dynamics of democratic development and determine the vulnerability of ancient blue laws under the scrutiny of First Amendment guarantees.

In 1877 the Massachusetts court apparently tried to tie into the "police power" justification of Sunday laws by describing its blue law as "essentially a civil regulation," even though the com-

plaint in the case of *Commonwealth* v. *Has* charged the defendant with opening his shop on Sunday "to the great scandal of
religion, against good morals and manners, and against the peace
of said Commonwealth."[7]

But even in the face of the civil regulation language introduced into the Has opinion, subsequent statements of the state
court admitted for the record that the Sunday law "was originally
inserted to secure the observance of the Lord's Day in accordance
with the views of our ancestors, and it ever since has stood and
still stands for the same purpose," and acknowledged that the
law was "enacted to secure the proper observance of the Lord's
Day as understood by our forefathers."[8]

In 1923 the same court ruled against Sunday bread deliver-
ies and explained that the statute which prohibited the perform-
ance of labor, business, or work on Sunday "was enacted to secure
respect and reverence for the Lord's Day," and "that the day
should be not merely a day of rest from labor, but also a day
devoted to public and private worship and to religious meditation
and repose, undisturbed by secular cares or amusements."[9]

That same year in Massachusetts "three Seventh-day Adventists were arrested and fined for painting the interior of a house
on Sunday," despite the fact "they had kept Saturday, and there
was an exemption clause in the law that covered their cases." In
1924, two Worcester men were fined for Sunday violations—one
for shining shoes and the other for transporting a hog.[10]

Then came the decisions of the United States Supreme Court
extending First Amendment guarantees to individual states.
Could the Massachusetts statute entitled "Observance of the
Lord's Day" survive? Was it either an "establishment of religion" or a means of preventing "free exercise of religion"?
This question was asked in Springfield, and it traveled all the
way to the United States Supreme Court for an answer.

The Crown Kosher Super Market of Massachusetts was a
corporation, with a controlling interest owned by an Orthodox

115

Jew. Specializing in kosher food products, the market catered primarily to Jewish patronage and closed weekly from sundown Friday evening through sundown Saturday evening.

On Sundays the market traditionally opened its doors from eight in the morning until six in the evening. One third of the week's business was done on this one day, since Orthodox Jewish patrons would not shop on Saturday even if the store had remained open.

The Massachusetts blue law had by this time acquired a crazy-quilt pattern of amendments and exceptions. Some businesses exempt by statute were allowed to operate, thus enabling an enterprising citizen to engage in one business on six days of the week and another all day Sunday. The law said Yes to the sale of tobacco on Sunday but No to the sale of food. Candy was permissible, but not meat. A barber must close down completely on Sunday, but a bootblack could work until 11 a.m. The wholesale disposition of fish was acceptable, but not retail sale of the identical fish. Professional football could be played on Sunday, during stipulated afternoon hours only.

Further confusion resulted from an exemption which allowed Sunday activity for an observer of the seventh-day Sabbath. The exemption covered those who "believe that the seventh day of the week ought to be observed as the Sabbath and actually refrain from secular business and labor on that day if (they) disturb no other person thereby."[11] The problem here was in the interpretation of the phrase "disturb no other person thereby."

Thus, when the Crown Kosher Super Market was accused of violating the Massachusetts law, the Jewish merchant found no help in the state courts. But with the First Amendment guarantees available through the Fourteenth Amendment, Orthodox Jews took the issue to the Federal court. Here they charged that the Massachusetts "Lord's Day" law established religion and prevented the free exercise of the Jewish faith. Appellants also alleged denial of equal protection of the laws and an invalid exercise of the police power of a state because of capricious classifications and arbitrary exceptions.

Over the vigorous dissent of District Judge William T. McCarthy of Boston, in 1959 Federal Circuit Judges Calvert Magruder and Peter Woodbury made judicial history by granting appellants the injunctive relief sought.

The court noted that the first Massachusetts Sunday law and the modified colonial versions "had the religious purpose to compel a seemly observance of that day of the week celebrated as the Sabbath (Sunday) by the dominant Christian sect."[12] Referring to the massive amendments that created "an almost unbelievable hodgepodge" on the statute books, it rejected any analysis which would show the Sunday law had abandoned its religious character.

The court criticized the finding in the 1877 Has case, charging that "the characterization of the Sunday law as being merely a civil regulation providing for a 'day of rest' seems to have been an *ad hoc* improvisation . . . because of the realization that the Sunday law would be more vulnerable to constitutional attack, under the state constitution, if the religious motivation of the statute were more explicitly avowed." Other Massachusetts state court decisions such as *Bennett* v. *Brooks* in 1864, and *Commonwealth* v. *White* in 1906, were cited as evidence substantiating the religious rather than secular character of the establishment.

Coupled with this was the fact that the appellants were of a minority religious persuasion. Friend-of-the-court briefs supporting the appellants' position were filed by the International Religious Liberty Association and the Southern New England Conference of Seventh-day Adventists.

The Archdiocesan Council of Catholic Men and the Lord's Day League of New England joined in offering an opposing friend-of-the-court opinion. The latter brief referred to the common "purpose of preventing the further secularization and commercialization of the Lord's Day."

DATELINE SUNDAY, U.S.A.

The Federal court majority also commented that the Hennington holding of 1896 was obsolete because the United States Supreme Court of that day had given its decision *"before the modern development of limitations upon the powers of the state implicit in the Fourteenth Amendment."*

Accordingly, the Federal court found in the Crown Kosher case that the Massachusetts Sunday law had furnished special protection to dominant Christian sects which celebrate Sunday as the Lord's Day, without furnishing comparable protection to those Christian sects and to Orthodox and Conservative Jews who observe Saturday as a day of rest. The Federal court unmasked the "police power" sham and found the Massachusetts first-day law to be in conflict with the First Amendment guarantees of the United States Constitution.

It was a blow to blue-law advocates that they would not take lying down. They appealed to the United States Supreme Court. To make it easier for that court to return to the "police power" rationale of the Field era, the Sunday-law protagonists this time refrained from disclosing a common "purpose of preventing the further secularization and commercialization of the Lord's Day."

The stratagem worked.

REFERENCES

1. *Congressional Record,* 44th Congress, 1st Session, December 14, 1875, page 205.
2. See *Gitlow* v. *New York,* 268 U.S. 652 (1925).
3. See *Thornhill* v. *Alabama,* 310 U.S. 88 (1940); *Cantwell* v. *Connecticut,* 310 U.S. 296 (1940); *Douglas* v. *Jeannette,* 319 U.S. 157 (1943); *Murdock* v. *Pennsylvania,* 319 U.S. 105 (1943).
4. *American State Papers* (Washington, D.C.: Review and Herald Publishing Association, 1943), pages 566, 567.
5. *Ibid.,* p. 567.
6. *Ibid.,* p. 563.
7. *Commonwealth* v. *Has,* 122 Massachusetts 42 (1877).
8. *Commonwealth* v. *White,* 190 Massachusetts 578 (1906).
9. *Commonwealth* v. *McCarthy,* 244 Massachusetts 484 (1923).
10. *American State Papers,* page 564.
11. *General Laws of Massachusetts,* Chapter 136, Section 6. In *American State Papers,* page 470.
12. *Crown Kosher Super Market* v. *Gallagher,* 176 U.S. 466 (1959).

11. ESTABLISHMENT— RELIGION OR RECREATION?

A New York local board of education submitted the following prayer to principals for recitation in public schools: "Almighty God, we acknowledge our dependence upon Thee, and we beg Thy blessings upon us, our parents, our teachers, and our Country."

Did this constitute an establishment of religion in violation of the First Amendment of the United States Constitution? The majority of the Supreme Court of the United States said Yes in June, 1962,[1] and a wave of public reaction swept the nation.

Neither Justice Frankfurter nor Justice White participated in the decision, and Justice Stewart registered a strong dissent. Justice Black spoke for the majority that found the act an unconstitutional religious establishment, and Justice Douglas concurred.

The majority opinion reviewed the history of religious establishment. It noted first that the "establishment clause" was designed to avoid a "union of government and religion" which "tends to destroy government and to degrade religion." Second, it noted the "historical fact that governmentally established religions and religious persecutions go hand in hand." It pointed to the sixteenth century Book of Common Prayer, created in

119

England by government authority, with its resultant controversies. This, it explained, is what happens when religion is subjected to the whim of politics. "It is an unfortunate fact of history that when some of the very groups which had most strenuously opposed the established Church of England found themselves sufficiently in control of colonial governments in this country to write their own prayers into law, they passed laws making their own religion the official religion of their respective colonies."

The court saw a threat to free individual worship in a government act which put an "official stamp of approval upon one particular kind of prayer or one particular form of religious services." The prayers are not exempt from the limitations of the "establishment clause," the court decided, merely because the prayer is "denominationally neutral nor the fact that its observance on the part of the students is voluntary." To show "direct governmental compulsion" is not essential, since the "establishment clause" precludes any laws "which establish an official religion whether those laws operate directly to coerce nonobserving individuals or not."

The "prayer" was a mechanical form, not offensive to any religious minority. It was not couched in statutory language but came from administrative governmental authority. Participation in the recitation was voluntary—any student could be excused without undue embarrassment. The procedure did not envelope the population at large, but only schoolchildren under the jurisdiction of the educational agency. Nonparticipants would not be subject to fine or imprisonment for failing to join in the exercise. Apart from any religious implications, the regular morning recitation could point to some secular welfare attributes—respect for family, patriotism for country, and moral training of youth in a society threatened by criminal encroachment. With secular benefits present, conceivably the court could have classed the matter as "civil regulation" within the legitimate "police power," and therefore not in violation of the Constitution. Instead, the court held the prayers to be an establishment of religion.

In sharp contrast to the 1962 regents' prayer case in New York, the Massachusetts Lord's Day observance law, tested in 1961, was a statutory enactment of the state legislature which applied to every citizen in the state. It was offensive to doctrinal concepts of religious minorities. Participation in the "observance" was not subject to the voluntary choice of the individual citizen. "Crimes" were created by statute so that fines or imprisonment awaited violators.

James Madison enunciated a philosophic commitment to a church and a state coexisting separately in an atmosphere of mutual respect. Far from suggesting government hostility to religion, Madison favored executive proclamations of fasts and festivals as long as the language was recommendatory and not injunctive.

Government policy cordial to religious practice but short of "any penal sanction enforcing the worship" fitted Madison's frame of definition for church-state separation. Free exercise was protected, establishment prevented.

Scrutinized within the dimension of Madison's "penal sanction test," the regents' prayer of the Engle case bears constitutional characteristics; whereas the coercive element in legislation enforcing Sunday idleness runs afoul of acceptable government action.

Yet, the Supreme Court of the United States took a position directly opposed to the Madison test. It struck down the non-penal voluntary prayer of the regents in 1962, while the criminal law sanctions were allowed to stand in four 1961 Sunday-law cases.[2]

In one of the 1961 blue-law cases (*McGowan* v. *Maryland*), Chief Justice Earl Warren remarked: "We do not hold that Sunday legislation may not be a violation of the 'Establishment' Clause if it can be demonstrated that its purpose—evidenced either on the face of the legislation, in conjunction with its legislative history, or in its operative effect—is to use the State's coercive power to aid religion."[3] The Massachusetts Sunday law seemed to fit that description. It was frankly religious, making liberal use of Lord's-day terminology. Its legislative history was religious both in origin and in legislative intent. Its operative effect, like Sunday legislation in other states, showed evidence of discriminatory and arbitrary enforcement against religious minorities.

Since the Supreme Court Sunday-law decisions in 1896 and 1900, the First Amendment guarantees had been ruled applicable to state and local governments via the Fourteenth, opening the door to a religious "establishment" and "free exercise" test of blue-law constitutionality.

As recently as 1923 the highest state tribunal in Massachusetts had described the Sunday law as "religious." The Federal court that decided the issue in 1959, found the Massachusetts blue law "religious." The 1962 United States Supreme Court found religious "establishment" in government sponsorship of the regents' prayer.

Barely thirteen months before the controversial *Engle* v. *Vitale* decision, the Supreme Court ruled on the Massachusetts Sunday law as relating to the Crown Kosher case. As in the Engle case, the "establishment clause" question was raised. "Was the Massachusetts Sunday law an establishment of religion?" Eight justices said No! One justice said Yes! The decision came in a flurry of action, with opinions released concurrently relative to the four different Sunday-law cases—one from Massachusetts, one from Maryland, and two from Pennsylvania.

To reach its decision in the Crown Kosher case the court simply resurrected the nineteenth-century Field doctrine of "police power" and "secular" purpose. But, like the preacher who pounded his pulpit and raised his voice the loudest when his argument was weak, the court took a lot of words to say it—reportedly the aggregate total ranked second in quantity to any decision in Supreme Court history.

The same ecclesiastical authoritarianism that had produced the Book of Common Prayer had established rigid Sunday observance. And while the Massachusetts Lord's Day law of 1961 did not collar the citizen and place him directly in the church pews, it did barricade avenues to most secular activity. The citizen rash enough to go to the park to play a baseball game at 11:30 Sunday morning would have to skirt a statutory roadblock and risk fine and imprisonment.

Said the chief justice, "We agree with the court below that, like the Sunday laws of other States, the Massachusetts statutes have an unmistakably religious origin." But he was able to detect a change that "came about in 1782" where the statutory language declared that "the Observance of the Lord's Day" promotes the "Welfare of a Community" and provides "Seasons for Relaxation from Labor and the Cares of Business." Hence, Earl Warren observed, "the statute's announced purpose was no longer solely religious."

In examining the specific laws challenged in the Crown Kosher case, Chief Justice Warren admitted that "the statutes still contain references to the Lord's Day"; but he found that "for the most part, they have been divorced from the religious orientation of their predecessors." To fortify this contention, the opinion pointed to an expanded scheme of permitted activities which now allows dancing, concerts, and "sports of almost all kinds," while "church attendance is no longer required." The court was content to consider "the objectionable language" as "merely a relic."[4]

Despite the fact that the sharp curtailment of the "worldly amusements" traditionally attacked by Sunday laws remained to confuse and complicate the Sunday "rest," "relaxation," "repose," and "recreation" allegedly available to the citizen, the majority view was that "the present scheme is one to provide an atmosphere of recreation rather than religion," and that "the 'character' of the day would appear more likely to be

123

intended to be one of repose and recreation" than of a religious nature.

The 1923 Massachusetts case of *Commonwealth* v. *McCarthy* which had characterized the state Sunday law as "religious" was relegated to footnote status in the Warren opinion. That state court had confirmed that the Massachusetts Sunday law "was enacted to secure respect and reverence for the Lord's day" and "that the day should be not merely a day of rest from labor, but also a day devoted to public and private worship and to religious meditation and repose, undisturbed by secular cares or amusements."[5] In 1961, the chief justice chose instead to quote from the *Commonwealth* v. *Has* decision of 1877, which, following

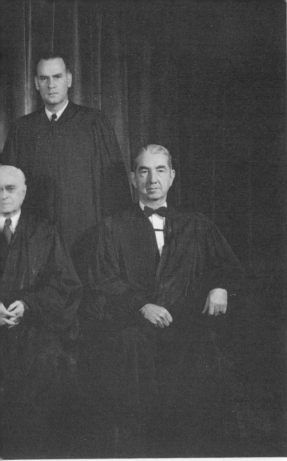

The Supreme Court of the United States considered the Field tradition persuasive and found secular purposes in the nation's Sunday laws.

Field doctrine, describes the Lord's Day statute as "essentially a civil regulation."[6]

In sidestepping the use of the specific language of the "several cases, between 1877 and 1923, which gave a religious characterization to the statute," the court argued in the 1961 Crown Kosher case that "in none of these cases was there a contention regarding religious freedom, and none of the cases stated the statute's purpose to be exclusively religious." To bolster the conclusion that "the relevant factors having been most carefully considered, we do not find that the present statute's purpose or effect is religious," the majority referred to a report from the Massachusetts Legislative Research Council relative to legal holidays and their observance. That report had talked generally of protection to the public offered by Sunday laws which provided a "period of rest and quiet," the promotion of "health, peace, and good order" and a statutory structure "essentially civil in character." This report bore a date of 1960—the year *after* the lower Federal court had characterized the statute "religious."

As to arguments that the state could "accomplish its secular purpose by alternative means that would not even remotely or incidentally aid religion," the court announced its rejection based upon reasons stated in the case of *McGowan* v. *Maryland,* and cited that case as additional authority for its reversal of the 1959 decision of the lower Federal court in the Crown Kosher case.[7]

The "crimes" of the appellants in the McGowan case consisted of Sunday sales of a toy submarine, a stapler and staples, a can of floor wax, and a three-ring loose-leaf binder. The sales occurred in an Anne Arundel County, Maryland, discount store. In that county, permitted sales extended to foodstuffs, auto and boat accessories, flowers, toilet goods, hospital supplies, and souvenirs.

Although "the taking of oysters and the hunting or killing of game is generally forbidden," other sports were allowed, providing they had a niche in the statutory list of exceptions and took place in geographically acceptable locations. And, before proceeding with his Sunday "rest" and "recreation" with confidence, the Maryland citizen had to consider the time of day. An act could be illegal one moment of the day and legitimate the next. No wonder the statutory exactions required the skill of a Supreme Court to interpret!

The "establishment clause" issue was raised in *McGowan* v. *Maryland,* appellants contending "that the purpose of the enforced stoppage of labor on that day is to facilitate and encourage church attendance, . . . to induce people with no religion or people with marginal religious belief to join the predominant

126

Christian sects," and "to aid the conduct of church services and religious observance of the sacred day."

Speaking for the majority decision, Chief Justice Warren acknowledged that "there is no dispute that the original laws which dealt with Sunday labor were motivated by religious forces." And he recited evidence that many years ago "nonreligious arguments for Sunday closing began to be heard more distinctly and the statutes began to lose some of their totally religious flavor." Then the chief justice embraced the "police power" philosophy of the Californian, Justice Stephen J. Field. Warren quoted from Field's dissent in *Ex Parte Newman;* Field's words in the Soon Hing decision of 1885; the "civil regulation" language enunciated by Harlan in the Hennington case; and the full acceptance of this dogma in *Petit* v. *Minnesota* at the turn of the century.

These decisions were in each case written in an era before First Amendment guarantees had been held applicable to state and local government and placed upon a judicial pedestal of protection. These decisions came from an era that was also the scene of religious agitation for Federal Sunday legislation and of arbitrary enforcement of Sunday laws against religious minorities.

Nevertheless, in the McGowan case the Supreme Court found the Field tradition persuasive, and the majority rejected the lower Federal court ruling in favor of "the state supreme court's determination that the statute's present purpose and effect is not to aid religion but to set aside a day of rest and recreation."

The court saw no problem in the coexistence of "secular" and "religious" purposes in civil regulations. It ignored Roger Williams's distinction between the first four and the last six of the Ten Commandments and compared blue laws to laws prohibiting theft, murder, and adultery.

As to alternative means for the achievement of "secular" purpose, the chief justice wrote that a "one-day-in-seven" rest law requiring rest from labor for an unspecified twenty-four-hour period during each consecutive seven days was inadequate to meet the state's secular goal to set aside "a day of rest, repose, recreation, and tranquillity." He used the "family day" argument in justifying the state's quest for "a special atmosphere of tranquillity, a day which all members of the family or friends and relatives might spend together."

Determined to preserve the Sunday institution irrespective of religious overtones, the court concluded, "Sunday is a day apart from all others. The cause is irrelevant; the fact exists."[8]

The Pennsylvania blue law attacked in the *Two Guys From Harrison* v. *McGinley* case also received the blessing of the Supreme Court. Looking to the "relevant judicial characterizations and, particularly, the legislative history leading to the passage of the 1959 Act immediately before us, we hold that neither the statute's purpose nor its effect is religious."[9]

Justice Felix Frankfurter wrote an opinion concurring with the majority decision on both the McGowan and the Two Guys cases, in which he was joined by Justice John M. Harlan, namesake of the justice Harlan who wrote for the court in the Hennington case.

Frankfurter launched into a detailed analysis of the history and development of Sunday legislation. His views were supplemented by a charted outline of state Sunday-law classifications as extant in 1961.

Frankfurter also acknowledged that "the earlier among the colonial Sunday statutes were unquestionably religious in purpose. . . . But even the seventeenth century legislation does not show an exclusively religious preoccupation." He pointed to a 1792 Massachusetts Sunday law preamble as early evidence that such legislation began to "display a duplicity of purpose."

The "seventeenth century" language in the laws before the court, Frankfurter argued, "does not of itself prove the continuation of the purposes for which the colonial governments enacted these laws, or that these are the purposes for which their successors of the twentieth [century] have retained them and modified them." He rejected "one-day-a-week laws" as inadequate substitutes because they "do not accomplish all that is accomplished by Sunday laws. They provided only a periodic physical rest, not that atmosphere of entire community repose which Sunday has traditionally brought." Like the Warren statement, Frankfurter's concluded that "the statutes of Maryland, Massachusetts, and Pennsylvania which we here examine are not constitutionally forbidden fusions of church and state."[10]

Thus the majority of the court found a legitimate secular purpose in Sunday legislation which justified its existence under the "police power" of the state. Classed as a "civil regulation," the court said, it was not an establishment of religion.

Thirteen months later, in the board of regents' prayer case, it was essentially the same court that declared: "When the power, prestige and financial support of government is placed behind a particular religious belief, the indirect coercive pressure upon religious minorities to conform to the prevailing officially approved religion is plain."[11]

Justice William O. Douglas in the 1961 cases took issue with the majority and in a dissenting opinion characterized the Sunday laws before the court as an establishment of religion.

The landmark decisions of the court were greeted with mixed reactions. The Lord's Day Alliance and other religious proponents of Sunday laws breathed a sigh of relief that the blue laws could remain on the books, regardless of the rationale employed by the court. Religious minorities who observe the seventh day had hoped for a continuation of the trend of the decade of the forties, during which court majorities spoke through the pens of Justices Douglas, Black, and Frank Murphy for complete religious liberty. These religious groups were disappointed in 1961.

Citizens without religious preferences, and with no bias toward

DATELINE SUNDAY, U.S.A.

Sunday observance, still preferred to create their own "atmosphere of recreation" without the threat of fine for playing baseball at the wrong hour of the day on Sunday.

For generations, Sunday-law boosters had preached of "family day," "health and welfare," "rest from labor," "recreation," and "community benefit." Now the majority of the court adopted this line of argument.

The court majority made it clear that the "secular" purpose it looked to in Sunday legislation was, in addition to physical "rest," the creation of an "atmosphere of recreation." Admittedly the religious purpose of blue laws requires the observance of a specific day in a specific manner. Did the secular purpose of an "atmosphere of recreation" lend itself to any other statutory possibility, such as "one-day-in-seven" legislation? No, said the court.

"One-day-in-seven" laws require that an individual be given twenty-four hours of rest in each consecutive seven-day period —without designating the day but guaranteeing rest from uninterrupted labor for the individual. If the "one-day-in-seven" statute also gave the individual the free choice as to which day he would rest, presumably all members of the family would select the same day to create an "atmosphere of recreation." They would also be good judges of the recreation they personally enjoyed, be it baseball on the front lawn, hunting in the woods, or even the reading of blue laws on the front porch.

The Fourth of July and Labor Day are annual holidays that create an "atmosphere of recreation." There are no criminal penalties attached to the observances. Participation is voluntary. Each family seems to know how to use the time without looking to a law book for information as to what is or is not legal. If a legislature objectively sought a secular objective of "rest, relaxation, repose, and recreation" for all its constituents, it is conceivable that the holiday atmosphere could be created without exposure to charges of "religious establishment," and without the

130

coercion that characterizes blue laws with their threats of fines and prison penalties.

It is questionable whether legislatures had "secular" purposes in mind as they amended blue laws. The prevailing theology of Sunday observance had undergone major metamorphosis since colonial days. What had once been considered "worldly" had evolved into accepted Sunday conduct in twentieth-century America. Legislative amendments added to colonial-era blue laws reflected that theological evolution. It is conceivable that legislatures unwittingly endeavored to keep pace with theological change rather than presenting a planned statutory scheme designed to achieve "secular" ends.

And if there ever was a legitimate "secular" legislative intent, when did it materialize? The 1923 Massachusetts state court could see only "religious" purpose thirty-eight years before the United States Supreme Court said "recreation." And was the "secular" purpose pointed to by the court in 1961 *exclusive; dominant; equal;* or was it merely *incidental* to the "religious" purpose in the blue laws?

Little more than a year later, the Supreme Court read "establishment" into the regents' prayer. Here was a relatively innocuous school exercise that suggested some "secular" benefits to the family, the community, and the nation. Admittedly concurrent with a "religious" purpose, was the "secular" ingredient in the prayer exercise of lesser significance than in the weekly Sunday observance that had been a symbol of religious allegiance for centuries, and had carried criminal sanctions to prove it?

Under the Field doctrine of "civil regulation," could there be any religious holy day, ceremony, practice, or educational function that would not have at least some concurrent incidental "secular" benefit to the "welfare of the community"? Now that the 1961 interpretation has the force of law, is the state or the citizen left with any standard to determine when if ever blue laws can be construed as religious establishments?

DATELINE SUNDAY, U.S.A.

Roger Williams had talked of two tables of the Decalogue. The last six commands, he said, dealt with man's duty to man, whereas the first four dealt exclusively with man's duty to God. Williams saw valid "secular" purpose in the last six, but not in the first four.

In addition to the fourth commandment, "Remember the Sabbath," duty to God included abstention from idol worship and reverence in the use of the name of God. Observance of a day has been interpreted as a symbol of allegiance to a religious cause. Could the other commands of the first table of the Decalogue carry sufficient secular benefit to remove them also from the prohibitions of the First Amendment?

The answers are left for another day. Meanwhile, the 1961 Supreme Court had something to say on the subject of the "free exercise clause" of the First Amendment.

REFERENCES

1. *Engle* v. *Vitale*, 370 U.S. 421 (1962).
2. See *McGowan* v. *Maryland*, 366 U.S. 420 (1961); *Gallagher* v. *Crown Kosher Super Market*, 366 U.S. 617 (1961); *Braunfeld* v. *Brown*, 366 U.S. 599 (1961); *Two Guys From Harrison* v. *McGinley*, 366 U.S. 582 (1961).
3. *McGowan* v. *Maryland, Op cit.*
4. *Gallagher* v. *Crown Kosher Super Market, Op. cit.*
5. *Commonwealth* v. *McCarthy*, 244 Massachusetts 484 (1923).
6. *Commonwealth* v. *Has*, 122 Massachusetts 40 (1877).
7. *Gallagher* v. *Crown Kosher Super Market, Op. cit.*
8. *McGowan* v. *Maryland, Op. cit.*
9. *Two Guys From Harrison* v. *McGinley, Op. cit.*
10. *McGowan* v. *Maryland, Op. cit.*
11. *Engle* v. *Vitale, Op. cit.*

12. FREE EXERCISE— CONSCIENCE OR COMMERCE?

In 1961, Sunday-law opponents hoped that the Supreme Court would strike down blue laws either as an "establishment" of religion or as an unconstitutional infringement on the "free exercise" of religion. The court rejected a contention that the legislative classifications and irregular system of Sunday prohibitions constituted a denial of "equal protection" of the law. It also denied that "the laws are so vague as to fail to give reasonable notice of the forbidden conduct and therefore violate 'due process.'"

This left the "free exercise" question—the other side of the two-edged constitutional sword for the protection of religious liberty.

The "establishment clause" is a broadly based issue that can be raised by any citizen acting in good faith. In *McGowan* v. *Maryland* and *Two Guys From Harrison* v. *McGinley,* where the injury alleged by the parties was economic rather than an infringement of personal religious belief, the parties still could attack Sunday laws as an establishment of religion.

The right of a citizen to raise the "free exercise" issue is more narrowly construed by the majority of the court. Thus, in the Crown Kosher case as well as in *Braunfeld* v. *Brown,* the court extended its consideration to the "free exercise" as well as the

133

"establishment" clause of the First Amendment, since the parties challenging Sunday laws in these two cases were Orthodox Jews alleging infringement of personal religious freedom.

Did applicable Sunday laws "prevent the free exercise of religion" of Mr. Braunfeld or the owners of the Crown Kosher market? Six members of the Court said No! Justice Douglas, along with Justices Stewart and Brennan, said Yes!

Where religious establishment could be found, it would logically follow that there was a resultant infringement of free exercise of a religious minority. Prevention of "free exercise" of religion could be found, however, without necessarily finding a corresponding religious establishment. Thus, by avoiding impalement on the establishment issue, the majority was not bound to find free-exercise infringement.

In *Braunfeld* v. *Brown,*[1] the charge of infringement of "free exercise" was based on two arguments: first, that the Sunday laws allegedly operated to hinder the "Orthodox Jewish faith in gaining new adherents"; and second, that economic pressure on Braunfeld required him either to give up seventh-day Sabbath observance as a tenet of his faith, or to continue to operate at competitive disadvantage economically.

Chief Justice Warren in writing the majority decision conceded that Braunfeld and "all other persons who wish to work on Sunday will be burdened economically by the State's day-of-rest mandate" but drew a line of distinction between what he pictured as an "indirect burden" and a law that would make a religious practice unlawful. "The statute before us does not make criminal the holding of any religious belief or opinion, nor does it force anyone to embrace any religious belief or to say or believe anything in conflict with his religious tenets," said the court.

The opinion acknowledged that Sunday law "operates so as to make the practice of their religious beliefs more expensive" and that the religious minority may well face "some financial

134

sacrifice in order to observe their religious beliefs," but maintained that "the option is wholly different than when the legislation attempts to make a religious practice itself unlawful."

The majority implied that before it would find infringement of free exercise, there would have to be evidence of *direct* prohibition rather than mere *indirect* hardship. And "even though the burden may be characterized as being only indirect," infringement could still be found "if the purpose or effect of a law is to impede the observance of one or all religions." Braunfeld believed his case met that test, but the court majority disagreed.

The Warren opinion declared that a statute designed to advance the secular goals of the state "is valid despite its indirect burden on religious observance, unless the state may accomplish its purpose by means which do not impose a burden." It then closed the door on the "one-day-in-seven" law, as an alternative, by citing the rationale in the McGowan opinion.

The court also rejected the alternative means which offered a statutory exemption for minority religions that worshiped on another day. For backing, Warren talked of the enforcement problems that could be created as well as the threat to the entire statutory framework which sought to eliminate "the atmosphere of commercial noise and activity." Then there was the threat that Sunday opening by the minority "might well provide these people with an economic advantage over their competitors who must remain closed on that day," paradoxically the same problem confronting the minority before the court, which the opinion had described as an acceptable "indirect burden" under the circumstances.

Here the chief justice toyed with a dangerous bit of contradictory logic. Speaking to the objectionable features of an exemption for those who closed their businesses from sundown Friday evening to sundown Saturday evening, he warned: "With this competitive advantage existing, there could well be the temptation for some, in order to keep their businesses open

135

on Sunday, to assert that they have religious convictions which compel them to close their business on what had formerly been their least profitable day."

Here was the irony. In this very case, Orthodox Jews had claimed that the Sunday laws "operate so as to hinder the Orthodox Jewish faith in gaining new adherents" because of the privileged sanctuary extended to first-day observance. The law operated to make Sunday observance more economically attractive than worship on the seventh day of the week, according to Braunfeld. But the court shrugged this off as an "indirect burden" on Braunfeld's faith. Then the court itself, through the Warren statement, utilized the essential heart of this rationale in its effort to show that a Sunday law "exemption" for a minority conscience would not be fair since it might encourage some to join a minority religious cause for a commercial purpose!

If in fact an exemption clause would operate to encourage some to join a minority faith for sheer commercial advantage, why would not the Sunday law itself operate to encourage some to join a majority faith for the same reason? And if it did, would there not be new ammunition that Sunday laws constituted an establishment of religion? After all, the existence of the state-enforced Sunday-rest observances gave a competitive edge to religious majorities that were enabled to attract members without fear of any "indirect burden" or penalties accompanying membership. In that sense, the operative effect of the statute would be religious, to say nothing of its purpose. While Braunfeld was denied recognition of the ingredients of this logic in his assault on the Sunday law itself, the court incorporated these ingredients in its own assault on the exemption!

An earlier Supreme Court had thrown out a license tax for the distribution of religious literature as an unconstitutional tax on religion.[2] Now the 1961 majority frankly acknowledged "financial sacrifice" and religious beliefs that were "more expensive," but did not admit that this "indirect burden" was a tax on

136

religion or religious belief or an infringement of religious free exercise.

The court left Braunfeld no other alternatve but to give up his conscientious belief and sell clothing and home furnishings in Philadelphia on Saturday, or else to continue to close down on Saturday by conscience and on Sunday by coercion, with "financial sacrifice."

The owners and patrons of the Crown Kosher Super Market in Springfield, Massachusetts, were also told by the court, through the holding in the Braunfeld decision, that being saddled with an "indirect burden" and competitive disadvantage did not infringe their free exercise of religion.

Justice Frankfurter, concurring with the majority in both *Braunfeld* v. *Brown* and *McGowan* v. *Maryland,* wrote an opinion[3] attached to the latter case to cover both. He introduced his remarks with an attack on Sunday-law exemptions for the benefit of citizens that worship on another day. His thinking overlapped with the Warren opinion by citing the problems of maintaining "the atmosphere of general repose" for a single day; problems of policing; the possible competitive disadvantage to a Sunday keeper if the Orthodox Jew could open for business on the first day of the week; and the danger "that administration of such a provision may require judicial inquiry into religious belief."

Like Warren, Frankfurter recognized that blue laws "do create an undeniable financial burden upon the observers of one of the fundamental tenets of certain religious creeds, a burden which does not fall equally upon other forms of observance." But he rejected the comparison to the cases where previous courts had found an unconstitutional tax on religion, because "the burden which the Sunday statutes impose is an incident of the only feasible means of achievement of their particular goal" and "the measure of the burden is not fixed by legislative decree."

Justice Felix Frankfurter decided that "community interest" outweighed religious freedom in the Sunday-law controversy.

The associate justice gave the legislature credit for reasoning that the competitive disadvantage of the Orthodox Jew might be offset "by the industry and commercial initiative of the individual merchant," and that after all, if there were no Sunday law at all, he would still be at a disadvantage from the nonobserving merchant that opened seven days a week as compared with his six. Indirect comfort for an "indirect burden"!

Frankfurter was a scholar known for balancing competing interests. Here he chose to balance religious freedom versus what he chose to describe as "community interest." Was the need for an "atmosphere of general repose" of sufficient importance to the public in order "to outweigh the restraint upon the religious exercise of Orthodox Jewish practicants?" Yes, said the associate justice. And "in view of the importance of the community interests which must be weighed in the balance, is the disadvantage wrought by the nonexempting Sunday statutes an impermissible imposition upon the Sabbatarian's religious freedom?" To this, his response was No.

Speaking only for himself and not for Justice Harlan, who had joined in his concurring opinion, Frankfurter did favor remanding the Braunfeld case to the district court, but only because he felt there had been "too summary a disposition" of the case.

Potter Stewart, newest and youngest member of the court, agreed with the dissent of Justice Brennan in the Braunfeld case and added some remarks of his own. In a concurring dissent as marked for its brevity as Justice Frankfurter's concurrence with the majority had been for its comprehensive detail, Justice Stewart expressed his conviction that "Pennsylvania has passed the law which compels an Orthodox Jew to choose between his religious faith and his economic survival. That is a cruel choice. It is a choice which I think no State can constitutionally demand. For me this is not something that can be swept under the rug and forgotten in the interest of enforced Sunday togetherness.

I think the impact of this law upon these appellants grossly violates their constitutional right to the free exercise of their religion."[4]

Both Justice Stewart and Justice William J. Brennan agreed with the majority on the "establishment clause" and "equal protection clause" issues, but were convinced, like Justice William O. Douglas, that Braunfeld's free exercise of religion had been infringed.

The Brennan dissent[5] rejected the exposure of First Amendment guarantees to any balancing act. In his view, "personal liberty" was enshrined on a pedestal which reached above mere social convenience. In words reminiscent of the religious freedom cases of the 1940's, Brennan stated that "the values of the First Amendment, as embodied in the Fourteenth, look primarily towards the preservation of personal liberty, rather than towards the fulfillment of collective goals."

Brennan summarized the issue as "whether a State may put an individual to a choice between his business and his religion." In his view, a law requiring such a choice prohibited "the free exercise of religion."

He cited, as a precedent, a 1943 decision on *West Virginia State Board of Education* v. *Barnette,* written by Justice Jackson, indicating that the mere existence of a state interest which is "substantial and important, as well as rationally justifiable" was not sufficient in itself to trample individual conscience. He quoted Jackson as saying: "Freedoms of speech and of press, of assembly, and of worship may not be infringed on such slender grounds. They are susceptible of restriction only to prevent grave and immediate danger to interests which the State may lawfully protect." Brennan could find no such "grave and immediate danger" to the interests of the state that could justify the blue-law encroachment on Braunfeld.

He interpreted the majority opinion as repudiation of the Jackson language because, "without so much as a deferential nod towards the high place which we have accorded religious freedom in the past," the court now seemed to say "that any substantial state interest will justify encroachments on religious practice, at least if those encroachments are cloaked in the guise of some nonreligious public purpose." It appeared to Brennan that "this clog upon the exercise of religion, this state-imposed burden on Orthodox Judaism, has exactly the same economic effect as a tax levied upon the sale of religious literature," which the Supreme Court had previously forbidden as unconstitutional.

He eyed the constitutional scale in a vain search for the weighty "overbalancing need" and "compelling state interest" that led the majority to allocate a subordinate role to conscience. It was not the interest of seeing that "everyone rest one day a week," since the appellant rested as a matter of religious conviction. It was "not the desire to stamp out a practice deeply abhorred by society, such as polygamy," as in a nineteenth century case that had come before the court. Nor was "it the state's traditional protection of children." Rather, "it is the mere convenience of having everyone rest on the same day."

The associate justice disputed the majority argument that "mere convenience" could constitutionally justify the denial of "an exemption for those who in good faith observe a day of rest other than Sunday." The difficulties that the "Court conjures" in the granting of such an exemption Brennan viewed as "more fanciful than real." As a result, "administrative convenience" had been exalted to a level so as to "justify making one religion economically disadvantageous." This result he did not accept.

Neither did he accept the court's claim that a substantial burden on religion could be justified by its being only indirect. He concluded by reminding his associates of the words of Maryland Representative Daniel Carroll, spoken August 15, 1789, during Congressional debates on the First Amendment, that "'the rights of conscience are, in their nature, of peculiar delicacy, and will little bear the gentlest touch of government.' "

The year 1961 became a landmark in Sunday-law history. A traditional religious symbolism emerged relatively unscathed from a massive legal confrontation, despite persuasive arguments presented by a minority of the court. Unmoved by evidence of at least concurrent religious purpose present in blue laws, the United States Supreme Court chose to emphasize "atmosphere of recreation." The court resurrected the "police power" and "civil regulation" rationale that Stephen Field had pioneered and refined.

Associate Justice William O. Douglas, a member of the court since 1939, also made legal history in a resounding dissent which protested the majority findings on both issues.

REFERENCES

1. *Braunfeld* v. *Brown,* 366 U.S. 599 (1961).
2. See *Murdock* v. *Commonwealth of Pennsylvania,* 319 U.S. 105 (1943). Also *Follett* v. *Town of McCormick,* 321 U.S. 573 (1944).
3. *McGowan* v. *Maryland,* 366 U.S. 459 (1961).
4. See Stewart Dissent, *Braunfeld* v. *Brown,* 366 U.S. 616 (1961).
5. See Brennan Dissent, *Ibid.,* 610.

13.

THE DOUGLAS DISSENT

by JUSTICE WILLIAM O. DOUGLAS

(United States Supreme Court Justice William O. Douglas dissented from the majority in the 1961 Sunday-law cases. He believed that the blue laws before the court constituted a violation of both the "establishment clause" and the "free exercise clause" of the First Amendment. Except for footnotes, Justice Douglas's statement is here reproduced in full, as recorded in *McGowan* v. *Maryland,* 366 U.S. 561-581 [1961].)

The question is not whether one day out of seven can be imposed by a State as a day of rest. The question is not whether Sunday can by force of custom and habit be retained as a day of rest. The question is whether a State can impose criminal sanctions on those who, unlike the Christian majority that makes up our society, worship on a different day or do not share the religious scruples of the majority.

If the "free exercise" of religion were subject to reasonable regulations, as it is under some constitutions, or if all laws "respecting the establishment of religion" were not proscribed, I could understand how rational men, representing a predominantly Christian civilization, might think these Sunday laws did not unreasonably interfere with anyone's free exercise of religion and took no step toward a burdensome establishment of any religion. .

But that is not the premise from which we start, as there is agreement that the fact that a State, and not the Federal Government, has promulgated these Sunday laws does not change the

143

scope of the power asserted. For the classic view is that the First Amendment should be applied to the States with the same firmness as it is enforced against the Federal Government. See *Lovell v. City of Griffin*, 303 U.S. 444, 450; *Minersville School District v. Gobitis*, 310 U.S. 586, 593; *Murdock v. Pennsylvania*, 319 U.S. 105, 108; *Board of Education v. Barnette*, 319 U.S. 624, 639; *Staub v. City of Baxley*, 355 U.S. 313, 321; *Talley v. California*, 362 U.S. 60. The most explicit statement perhaps was in *Board of Education v. Barnette, supra*, 639.

> "In weighing arguments of the parties it is important to distinguish between the due process clause of the Fourteenth Amendment as an instrument for transmitting the principles of the First Amendment and those cases in which it is applied for its own sake. The test of legislation which collides with the Fourteenth Amendment, because it also collides with the principles of the First, is much more definite than the test when only the Fourteenth is involved. Much of the vagueness of the due process clause disappears when the specific prohibitions of the First become its standard. The right of a State to regulate, for example, a public utility may well include, so far as the due process test is concerned, power to impose all of the restrictions which a legislature may have a 'rational basis' for adopting. But freedoms of speech and of press, of assembly, and of worship may not be infringed on such slender grounds. *They are susceptible of restriction only to prevent grave and immediate danger to interests which the State may lawfully protect.* It is important to note that while it is the Fourteenth Amendment which bears directly upon the State it is the more specific limiting principles of the First Amendment that finally govern this case."

With that as my starting point I do not see how a State can make protesting citizens refrain from doing innocent acts on Sunday because the doing of those acts offends sentiments of their Christian neighbors.

The institutions of our society are founded on the belief that

Sunday laws, said Justice Douglas, make a sharp break with the American ideal of liberty as enshrined in the First Amendment.

there is an authority higher than the authority of the State; that there is a moral law which the State is powerless to alter; that the individual possesses rights, conferred by the Creator, which government must respect. The Declaration of Independence stated the now familiar theme:

> "We hold these Truths to be self-evident, that all Men are created equal, that they are endowed by their Creator with certain unalienable Rights, that among these are Life, Liberty and the Pursuit of Happiness."

And the body of the Constitution as well as the Bill of Rights enshrined those principles.

The Puritan influence helped shape our constitutional law and our common law as Dean Pound has said: The Puritan "put individual conscience and individual judgment in the first place." The Spirit of the Common Law (1921), p. 42. For those reasons we stated in *Zorach* v. *Clauson*, 343 U.S. 306, 313, "We are a religious people whose institutions presuppose a Supreme Being."

But those who fashioned the First Amendment decided that if and when God is to be served, His service will not be motivated by coercive measures of government. "Congress shall make no law respecting an establishment of religion, or prohibiting the free exercise thereof"—such is the command of the First Amendment made applicable to the State by reason of the Due Process Clause of the Fourteenth. This means, as I understand it, that if a religious leaven is to be worked into the affairs of our people, it is to be done by individuals and groups, not by the Government. This necessarily means, *first* that the dogma, creed, scruples, or practices of no religious group or sect are to be preferred over those of any others; *second,* that no one shall be interfered with by government for practicing the religion of his choice; *third,* that the State may not require anyone to practice a religion or even any religion; and *fourth,* that the State cannot compel

146

one so to conduct himself as not to offend the religious scruples of another. The idea, as I understand it, was to limit the power of government to act in religious matters (*Board of Education* v. *Barnette, supra; McCollum* v. *Board of Education,* 333 U.S. 203), not to limit the freedom of religious men to act religiously nor to restrict the freedom of atheists or agnostics.

The First Amendment commands government to have no interest in theology or ritual; it admonishes government to be interested in allowing religious freedom to flourish—whether the result is to produce Catholics, Jews, or Protestants, or to turn the people toward the path of Buddha, or to end in a predominantly Moslem nation, or to produce in the long run atheists or agnostics. On matters of this kind government must be neutral. This freedom plainly includes freedom from religion with the right to believe, speak, write, publish and advocate antireligious programs. *Board of Education* v. *Barnette, supra,* 641. Certainly the "free exercise" clause does not require that everyone embrace the theology of some church or of some faith, or observe the religious practices of any majority or minority sect. The First Amendment by its "establishment" clause prevents, of course, the selection by government of an "official" church. Yet the ban plainly extends farther than that. We said in *Everson* v. *Board of Education,* 330 U.S. 1, 16, that it would be an "establishment" of a religion if the Government financed one church or several churches. For what better way to "establish" an institution than to find the fund that will support it? The "establishment" clause protects citizens also against any law which selects any religious custom, practice, or ritual, puts the force of government behind it, and fines, imprisons, or otherwise penalizes a person for not observing it. The Government plainly could not join forces with one religious group and decree a universal and symbolic circumcision. Nor could it require all children to be baptized or give tax exemptions only to those whose children were baptized.

Could it require a fast from sunrise to sunset throughout the

Moslem month of Ramadan? I should think not. Yet why then can it make criminal the doing of other acts, as innocent as eating, during the day that Christians revere?

Sunday is a word heavily overlaid with connotations and traditions deriving from the Christian roots of our civilization that color all judgments concerning it. This is what the philosophers call "word magic."

> "For most judges, for most lawyers, for most human beings, we are as unconscious of our value patterns as we are of the oxygen that we breathe."—Cohen, *Legal Conscience* (1960), p. 169.

The issue of these cases would therefore be in better focus if we imagined that a state legislature, controlled by orthodox Jews and Seventh-Day Adventists, passed a law making it a crime to keep a shop open on Saturdays. Would a Baptist, Catholic, Methodist, or Presbyterian be compelled to obey that law or go to jail or pay a fine? Or suppose Moslems grew in political strength here and got a law through a state legislature making it a crime to keep a shop open on Fridays. Would the rest of us have to submit under the fear of criminal sanctions?

Dr. John Cogley recently summed up the dominance of the three-religion influence in our affairs:

> "For the foreseeable future, it seems, the United States is going to be a three-religion nation. At the present time all three are characteristically 'American,' some think flavorlessly so. For religion in America is almost uniformly 'respectable,' bourgeois, and prosperous. In the Protestant world the 'church' mentality has triumphed over the more venturesome spirit of the 'sect.' In the Catholic world, the mystical is muted in favor of booming organization and efficiently administered good works. And in the Jewish world the prophet is too frequently without honor, while the synagogue emphasis is focused on suburban togetherness. There are exceptions to these rules, of course; each of the religious communities continues to cast up its prophets, its

rebels and radicals. But a Jeremiah, one fears, would be positively embarrassing to the present position of the Jews; a Francis of Assisi upsetting the complacency of American Catholics would be rudely dismissed as a fanatic; and a Kierkegaard, speaking with an American accent, would be considerably less welcome than Norman Vincent Peale in most Protestant pulpits."

This religious influence has extended far, far back of the First and Fourteenth Amendments. Every Sunday School student knows the Fourth Commandment:

> "Remember the sabbath day to keep it holy.
> "Six days shalt thou labour, and do all thy work:
> "But the seventh day is the sabbath of the LORD thy God: in it thou shalt not do any work, thou, nor thy son, nor thy daughter, thy manservant, nor thy maidservant, nor thy stranger that is within thy gates:
> "For in six days the LORD made heaven and earth, the sea, and all that in them is, and rested the seventh day: wherefore the LORD blessed the sabbath day, and hallowed it." Exodus 20:8-11.

This religious mandate for observance of the Seventh Day became, under Emperor Constantine, a mandate for observance of the First Day "in conformity with the practice of the Christian Church." See *Richardson* v. *Goddard,* 23 How. 28, 41. This religious mandate has had a checkered history; but in general its command, enforced now by the ecclesiastical authorities, now by the civil authorities, and now by both, has held good down through the centuries. The general pattern of these laws in the United States was set in the eighteenth century and derives, most directly, from the seventeeth century English statute. 29 Charles II, c. 7. Judicial comment on the Sunday laws has always been a mixed bag. Some judges have asserted that the statutes have a "purely" civil aim, *i.e.,* limitation of work time and provision for a common and universal leisure. But other judges have recognized the religious significance of Sunday and that the laws existed to enforce the maintenance of that significance. In general, both threads of argument have continued to interweave in the case law on the subject. Prior to the time when the First Amendment was held applicable to the States by reason of the Due Process Clause of the Fourteenth, the Court at least by *obiter dictum* approved State Sunday laws on three occasions: *Soon Hing* v. *Crowley,* 113 U.S. 703, in 1885; *Hennington* v. *Georgia,* 163 U.S. 299, in 1896; *Petit* v. *Minnesota,* 177 U.S. 164, in 1900. And in *Friedman* v. *New York,* 341 U.S. 907, the Court, by a divided vote, dismissed "for the want of a substantial federal question" an appeal from a New York decision upholding the validity of a Sunday law against an attack based on the First Amendment.

The *Soon Hing, Hennington,* and *Petit* cases all rested on the police power of the State—the right to safeguard the health of the people by requiring the cessation of normal activities one day out of seven. The Court in the *Soon Hing* case rejected the idea that Sunday laws rested on the power of government "to legislate for the promotion of religious observances." 113 U.S. 710. The New York Court of Appeals in the *Friedman* case followed the reasoning of the earlier cases, 302 N.Y. 75, 80, 96 N. E. 2d 184, 186.

The Massachusetts Sunday law involved in one of these appeals was once characterized by the Massachusetts court as merely a civil regulation providing for a "fixed period of rest." *Commonwealth* v. *Has,* 122 Mass. 40, 42. That decision was, according to the District Court in the *Gallagher* case, "an *ad hoc* improvisation" made "because of the realization that the Sunday law would be more vulnerable to constitutional attack under the state Constitution if the religious motivation of the statute were more explicitly avowed." 176 F. Supp. 466, 473. Certainly prior to the *Has* case, the Massachusetts courts had indicated that the aim of the Sunday law was religious. See *Pearce* v. *Atwood,* 13 Mass. 324, 345-346; *Bennett* v. *Brooks,* 91 Mass.

150

118, 121. After the *Has* case the Massachusetts court construed the Sunday law as a religious measure. In *Davis* v. *Somerville*, 128 Mass. 594, 596, 35 Am. Rep. 399, 400, it was said:

> "Our Puritan ancestors intended that the day should be not merely a day of rest from labor, but also a day devoted to public and private worship and to religious meditation and repose, undisturbed by secular cares or amusements. They saw fit to enforce the observance of the day by penal legislation, and the statute regulations which they devised for that purpose have continued in force, without any substantial modification, to the present time."

And see *Commonwealth* v. *Dextra*, 143 Mass. 28, 8 N. E. 756. In *Commonwealth* v. *White*, 190 Mass. 578, 581, 77 N. E. 636, 637, the court refused to liberalize its construction of an exception in its Sunday law for works of "necessity." That word, it said, "was originally inserted to secure the observance of the Lord's day in accordance with the views of our ancestors, and it ever since has stood and still stands for the same purpose." In *Commonwealth* v. *McCarthy*, 244 Mass. 484, 486, 138 N.E. 835, 836, the court reiterated that the aim of the law was "to secure respect and reverence for the Lord's day."

The Pennsylvania Sunday laws before us in Nos. 36 and 67 have received the same construction. "Rest and quiet, on the Sabbath day, with the right and privilege of public and private worship, undisturbed by any mere worldly employment, are exactly what the statute was passed to protect." *Sparhawk* v. *Union Passenger R. Co.*, 54 Pa. 401, 423. And see *Commonwealth* v. *Nesbit*, 34 Pa. 398, 405, 406-408. A recent pronouncement by the Pennsylvania Supreme Court is found in *Commonwealth* v. *American Baseball Club*, 290 Pa. 136, 143, 138 A. 497, 499: "Christianity is part of the common law of Pennsylvania . . . and its people are christian people. Sunday is the holy day among christians."

The Maryland court, in sustaining the challenged law in No.

151

8, relied on *Judefind* v. *State,* 78 Md. 510, 28 A. 405, and *Levering* v. *Park Commissioner,* 134 Md. 48, 106 A. 176. In the former the court said:

> "It is undoubtedly true that rest from secular employment on Sunday does have a tendency to foster and encourage the Christian religion, of all sects and denominations that observe that day, as rest from work and ordinary occupation enables many to engage in public worship who probably would not otherwise do so. But it would scarcely be asked of a court, in what professed to be a Christian land, to declare a law unconstitutional because it requires rest from bodily labor on Sunday, except works of necessity and charity, and thereby promotes the cause of Christianity. If the Christian religion is, incidentally or otherwise, benefited or fostered by having this day of rest, (as it undoubtedly is,) there is all the more reason for the enforcement of laws that help to preserve it." 78 Md., at pages 515-516, 28 A. at page 407.

In the Levering case the court relied on the excerpt from the Judefind decision just quoted. 134 Md. at 54-55, 106 A. at 178.

We have then in each of the four cases Sunday laws that find their source in Exodus, that were brought here by the Virginians and by the Puritans, and that are today maintained, construed, and justified because they respect the views of our dominant religious groups and provide a needed day of rest.

The history was accurately summarized a century ago by Chief Justice Terry of the Supreme Court of California in *Ex Parte Newman,* 9 Cal. 502, 509:

> "The truth is, however much it may be disguised, that this one day of rest is a purely religious idea. Derived from the Sabbatical institutions of the ancient Hebrew, it has been adopted into all the creeds of succeeding religious sects throughout the civilized world; and whether it be the Friday of the Mohammedan, the Saturday of the Israelite, or the Sunday of the Christian, it is alike fixed in the affections of its followers, beyond the power of eradication, and in most

of the States of our Confederacy, the aid of the law to enforce its observance has been given under the pretense of a civil, municipal, or police regulation."

That case involved the validity of a Sunday law under a provision of the California Constitution guaranteeing the "free exercise" of religion. Calif. Const., 1849, Art. I, § 4. Justice Burnett stated why he concluded that the Sunday law, there sought to be enforced against a man selling clothing on Sunday, infringed California's constitution:

> "Had the act made Monday, instead of Sunday, a day of compulsory rest, the constitutional question would have been the same. The fact that the Christian voluntarily keeps holy the first day of the week, does not authorize the Legislature to make that observance compulsory. The Legislature can not compel the citizen to do that which the Constitution leaves him free to do or omit, at his election. The act violates as much the religious freedom of the Christian as of the Jew. Because the conscientious views of the Christian compel him to keep Sunday as a Sabbath, he has the right to object, when the Legislature invades his freedom of religious worship, and assumes the power to compel him to do that which he has the right to omit if he pleases. The principle is the same, whether the act of the Legislature compels us to do that which we wish to do, or not to do. . . .
>
> "Under the Constitution of this State, the Legislature cannot pass any act, the legitimate effect of which is forcibly to establish any merely religious truth, or enforce any merely religious observances. The Legislature has no power over such a subject. When, therefore, the citizen is sought to be compelled by the Legislature to do any affirmative religious act, or to refrain from doing anything, because it violates simply a religious principle or observance, the act is unconstitutional." *Id.*, at 513-515.

The Court picks and chooses language from various decisions to bolster its conclusion that these Sunday laws in the modern setting are "civil regulations." No matter how much is written, no matter what is said, the parentage of these laws is the Fourth

Commandment; and they serve and satisfy the religious predispositions of our Christian communities. After all, the labels a State places on its laws are not binding on us when we are confronted with a constitutional decision. We reach our own conclusion as to the character, effect, and practical operation of the regulation in determining its constitutionality. *Carpenter* v. *Shaw,* 280 U.S. 363, 367-368; *Dyer* v. *Sims,* 341 U.S. 22, 29; *Memphis Steam Laundry* v. *Stone,* 342, U.S. 389, 392; *Society for Savings* v. *Bowers,* 349 U.S. 143, 151; *Gomillion* v. *Lightfoot,* 364 U.S. 339, 341-342.

It seems to me plain that by these laws the States compel one, under sanction of law, to refrain from work or recreation on Sunday because of the majority's religious views about that day. The State by law makes Sunday a symbol of respect or adherence. Refraining from work or recreation in deference to the majority's religious feelings about Sunday is within every person's choice. By what authority can government compel it?

Cases are put where acts that are immoral by our standards but not by the standards of other religious groups are made criminal. That category of cases, until today, has been a very restricted one confined to polygamy (*Reynolds* v. *United States,* 98 U.S. 145) and other extreme situations. The latest example is *Prince* v. *Massachusetts,* 321 U.S. 158, which upheld a statute making it criminal for a child under twelve to sell papers, periodicals, or merchandise on a street or in any public place. It was sustained in spite of the finding that the child thought it was her religious duty to perform the act. But that was a narrow holding which turned on the effect which street solicitation might have on the child-solicitor:

> "The state's authority over children's activities is broader than over like actions of adults. This is peculiarly true of public activities and in matters of employment. A democratic society rests, for its continuance, upon the healthy, well-rounded growth of young people into full maturity as

citizens, with all that implies. It may secure this against impeding restraints and dangers within a broad range of selection. Among evils most appropriate for such action are the crippling effects of child employment, more especially in public places, and the possible harms arising from other activities subject to all the diverse influences of the street. It is too late now to doubt that legislation appropriately designed to reach such evils is within the state's police power, whether against the parent's claim to control of the child or one that religious scruples dictate contrary action." *Id.*, 168-169.

None of the acts involved here implicates minors. None of the actions made constitutionally criminal today involves the doing of any act that any society has deemed to be immoral.

The conduct held constitutionally criminal today embraces the selling of pure, not impure, food; wholesome, not noxious, articles. Adults, not minors, are involved. The innocent acts, now constitutionally classified as criminal, emphasize the drastic break we make with tradition.

These laws are sustained because, it is said, the First Amendment is concerned with religious convictions or opinion, not with conduct. But it is a strange Bill of Rights that makes it possible for the dominant religious group to bring the minority to heel because the minority, in the doing of acts which intrinsically are wholesome and not antisocial, does not defer to the majority's religious beliefs. Some have religious scruples against eating pork. Those scruples, no matter how bizarre they might seem to some, are within the ambit of the First Amendment. See *United States* v. *Ballard,* 322 U.S. 78, 87. Is it possible that a majority of a state legislature having those religious scruples could make it criminal for the nonbeliever to sell pork? Some have religious scruples against slaughtering cattle. Could a state legislature, dominated by that group, make it criminal to run an abattoir?

The Court balances the need of the people for rest, recreation, late sleeping, family visiting, and the like against the command of the First Amendment that no one need bow to the religious beliefs of another. There is in this realm no room for balancing. I see no place for it in the constitutional scheme. A legislature of Christians can no more make minorities conform to their weekly regime than a legislature of Moslems, or a legislature of Hindus. The religious regime of every group must be respected—unless it crosses the line of criminal conduct. But no one can be forced to come to a halt before it, or refrain from doing things that would offend it. That is my reading of the Establishment Clause and the Free Exercise Clause. Any other reading imports, I fear, an element common in other societies but foreign to us. Thus Nigeria in Article 23 of her Constitution, after guaranteeing religious freedom, adds, "Nothing in this section shall invalidate any law that is reasonably justified in a democratic society in the interest of defence, public safety, public order, public morality, or public health." And see Article 25 of the Indian Constitution. That may be a desirable provision. But when the Court adds it to our First Amendment, as it does today, we make a sharp break with the American ideal of religious liberty as enshrined in the First Amendment.

The State can, of course, require one day of rest a week: one day when every shop or factory is closed. Quite a few States make that requirement. Then the "day of rest" becomes purely and simply a health measure. But the Sunday laws operate differently. They force minorities to obey the majority's religious feelings of what is due and proper for a Christian community; they provide a coercive spur to the "weaker brethren," to those who are indifferent to the claims of a Sabbath through apathy or scruple. Can there be any doubt that Christians, now aligned vigorously in favor of these laws, would be as strongly opposed if they were prosecuted under a Moslem law that forbade them from engaging in secular activities on days that violated Moslem scruples?

156

There is an "establishment" of religion in the constitutional sense if any practice of any religious group has the sanction of law behind it. There is an interference with the "free exercise" of religion if what in conscience one can do or omit doing is required because of the religious scruples of the community. Hence I would declare each of those laws unconstitutional as applied to the complaining parties, whether or not they are members of a sect which observes as its Sabbath a day other than Sunday.

When these laws are applied to Orthodox Jews, as they are in No. 11 and No. 67, or to Sabbatarians their vice is accentuated. If the Sunday laws are constitutional, kosher markets are on a five-day week. Thus those laws put an economic penalty on those who observe Saturday rather than Sunday as the Sabbath. For the economic pressures on these minorities, created by the fact that our communities are predominantly Sunday-minded, there is no recourse. When, however, the State uses its coercive powers—here the criminal law—to compel minorities to observe a second Sabbath, not their own, the State undertakes to aid and "prefer one religion over another"—contrary to the command of the Constitution. See Everson v. Board of Education, supra, 15.

In large measure the history of the religious clause of the First Amendment was a struggle to be free of economic sanctions for adherence to one's religion. Everson v. Board of Education, supra, 330 U.S. 11-14. A small tax was imposed in Virginia for religious education. Jefferson and Madison led the fight against the tax, Madison writing his famous Memorial and Remonstrance against that law. Id., 12. As a result, the tax measure was defeated and instead Virginia's famous "Bill for Religious Liberty," written by Jefferson, was enacted. Id., 12. That Act provided:

> "That no man shall be compelled to frequent or support any religious worship, place, or ministry whatsoever, nor shall be enforced, restrained, molested, or burthened in his

157

body or goods, nor shall otherwise suffer on account of his
religious opinions or belief. . . ."

The reverse side of an "establishment" is a burden on the "free
exercise" of religion. Receipt of funds from the State benefits
the established church directly; laying an extra tax on nonmem-
bers benefits the established church indirectly. Certainly the
present Sunday laws place Orthodox Jews and Sabbatarians
under extra burdens because of their religious opinions or beliefs.
Requiring them to abstain from their trade or business on Sunday
reduces their workweek to five days, unless they violate their
religious scruples. This places them at a competitive disadvantage
and penalizes them for adhering to their religious beliefs.

"The sanction imposed by the state for observing a day other
than Sunday as holy time is certainly more serious economically
than the imposition of a license tax for preaching," which we
struck down in *Murdock* v. *Pennsylvania*, 319 U.S. 105, and in
Follett v. *McCormick*, 321 U.S. 573. The special protection
which Sunday laws give the dominant religious groups and the
penalty they place on minorities whose holy day is Saturday
constitute, in my view, state interference with the "free exercise" of religion.

I dissent from applying criminal sanctions against any of
these complainants since to do so implicates the States in religious matters contrary to the constitutional mandate. Reverend
Allan C. Parker, Jr., Pastor of the South Park Presbyterian
Church, Seattle, Washington, has stated my views:

> "We forget that, though Sunday-worshiping Christians
> are in the majority in this country among religious people,
> we do not have the right to force our practice upon the
> minority. Only a church which deems itself without error
> and intolerant of error can justify its intolerance of the
> minority.
> "A Jewish friend of mine runs a small business establish-
> ment. Because my friend is a Jew his business is closed each

158

Saturday. He respects my right to worship on Sunday and I respect his right to worship on Saturday. But there is a difference. As a Jew he closes his store voluntarily so that he will be able to worship his God in his fashion. Fine! But, as a Jew living under Christian inspired Sunday closing laws, he is required to close his store on Sunday so that I will be able to worship my God in my fashion.

"Around the corner from my church there is a small Seventh Day Baptist church. I disagree with the Seventh Day Baptists on many points of doctrine. Among the tenets of their faith with which I disagree is the 'seventh-day worship.' But they are good neighbors and fellow Christians, and while we disagree we respect one another. The good people of my congregation set aside their jobs on the first of the week and gather in God's house for worship. Of course, it is easy for them to set aside their jobs since Sunday-closing laws—inspired by the Church—keep them from their work. At the Seventh Day Baptist church the people set aside their jobs on Saturday to worship God. This takes real sacrifice because Saturday is a good day for business. But that is not all—they are required by law to set aside their jobs on Sunday while more orthodox Christians worship.

". . . I do not believe that because I have set aside Sunday as a holy day I have the right to force all men to set aside that day also. Why should my faith be favored by the state over any other man's faith?"

With all deference, none of the opinions filed today in support of the Sunday laws has answered that question.

Pope John XXIII pleaded for "proper observance everywhere of Sunday as a day of rest" based on a "change of mind in society."

14. BLUE-LAW GREEN LIGHT

"Seldom has an issue of liberty been argued on flabbier grounds,"[1] declared *Time* magazine of the 1961 blue-law decisions. The magazine took issue with Chief Justice Warren's conclusion that "most [Sunday laws] at least, are of a secular rather than a religious character" and reviewed his feeling that coerced observance had evolved into an innocent and innocuous "time for family activity, for late sleeping, for passive and active entertainments, for dining out and the like."

The *Time* criticism pointed out:

U.S. blue laws are riddled with erratic contradictions. In Pennsylvania it is legal to sell a bicycle on Sunday, but not a tricycle; in Massachusetts it is against the law to dredge for oysters, but not to dig for clams; in Connecticut genuine antiques may lawfully be sold, but not reproductions. The New York blue law code is particularly messy. Bars may open at 1 p.m., but baseball games may not begin until 2 p.m. It is legal to sell fruits but not vegetables, an automobile tire but not a tire jack, tobacco but not a pipe. It is unlawful to sell butter or cooked meat after 10 a.m., except that delicatessens may sell these foods between 4 p.m. and 7:30 p.m.[2]

Less than a month after the landmark decisions of May 29,

1961, the court compounded the confusion about the meaning of "atmosphere of recreation" by refusing to hear a South Carolina case which challenged the statutory prohibition of Sunday movies.

Years before commercial motion pictures flashed on theater screens in Hometown, America, the state of South Carolina had acted to block all commercial amusements on Sunday. Now there were those who felt that Sunday movies could fit the "atmosphere of recreation" definition advanced by the Supreme Court. Seven court members, however, rejected a petition for hearing in an unsigned *per curiam* order, while Justice Brennan and Justice Douglas argued that the issue should be heard.[3]

Right or wrong, the Sunday-law pronouncements of the Supreme Court in 1961 proved controversial. In the storm of action and reaction which followed, the editorial comment in the nation's press was mixed, while religious interests showed their hand with renewed confidence and vigor.

The Detroit *Free Press* took a dim view of the decision, noting, "The machinations of great minds are frequently fascinating, and not easily understood by those who rely on common sense instead of technicalities." The editor expressed amazement at the court's finding that "the laws against doing business on Sunday have nothing to do with religion," and he observed that "even the justices must have known this is ridiculous." Then he added:

> How, when the words are written into the law, the justices can pretend they aren't is beyond our comprehension. . . . The clear wording and all past practices indicate that blue laws are intended to enforce religious concepts. Even when providing exceptions such as Michigan's, they can interfere with the right of a minority to a different belief.
>
> As of this week, they may be considered constitutional, but that does not mean they are reasonable. The court has ruled for the majority and totally ignored the religious rights of minorities.[4]

The Washington *Post* also criticized the decision and predicted new constitutional tests. "If, as we fear, the decision spawns a spate of such blue laws, the religious motivation will become so clear that the court will no longer be able to ignore it."[5]

The Washington *Evening Star* expressed approval of the decision, and urged state legislatures to revise blue laws and to "begin cleaning them up to rid them of the inconsistencies and contradictions."[6] The *Star* reminded the states that "secular, rather than religious considerations, have now become controlling and will continue to shape their future."

Editors of *Christian Century* recognized that certain religious considerations lurked on the scene and predicted that the opinion "does not speak the last word on the constitutionality of Sunday laws." The necessity for a review would result from "the excesses of overly zealous Christians who mistakenly see in the Supreme Court decisions sanction for the extension of old Sunday laws and the establishment of new ones." It noted that "already a flurry of activity for the passage of additional legislation prohibiting business on Sunday" was obvious, and warned that "such programs, vigorously promoted by Christians, will refute the court's definition of Sunday as primarily a secular holiday in our time and culture and will clearly establish the relationship between Sunday as a legal day of rest and the religious practice of the Christian community."[7]

This predicted reaction of overly zealous Christians was already making news. In Detroit, Michigan, the Thursday following the release of the court opinion, the Detroit Council of Churches declared war on Sunday commerce. It went on record "supporting legislation, if necessary, to force the closing of department stores on Sunday."[8] However, a Roman Catholic spokesman expressed hope "that individual conscience, more than legislation, will return Sunday as a day of prayerful observance and well-ordered rest and relaxation."

Vetoing a legislative decision to permit Sunday liquor sales in Maine, Governor Read explained that he objected to a law which would militate against "Lord's Day" observance. Possibly he had not read the text surrounding the Supreme Court's opinion. "Christian principles are strongly ingrained in the character of Maine people," he said. "Respect for the Lord's Day is one of the basic attitudes. The change contemplated by this bill could be, unwittingly, the first step in the erosion of our heritage."[9]

Massachusetts also seemed unaware of the secular nature of Sunday. Earlier in the year, while the Supreme Court still deliberated, the Lord's Day League of New England hosted a meeting of labor and merchant leaders calculated "to see that the present Sunday laws are enforced in Massachusetts and that the 1961 state legislature passes no measures to allow any more secular activities on the Sabbath."[10]

Less than five months after the most active blue-law proponents in Massachusetts went on record opposing "secular activities on the Sabbath," the Supreme Court found a secular purpose in the Massachusetts blue law!

When the May 29 decision hit the headlines, G. Vaughn Shedd, spokesman for the Lord's Day League of New England, exuberantly declared:

> After many months of cooperative effort between the office of the Massachusetts attorney general and other concerned groups, the Sunday laws have been held constitutional. . . .
>
> This decision announced by the U.S. Supreme Court on May 29 culminated much dedicated work of numerous legislators, church groups of many beliefs, and the Lord's Day League. The preservation of Sunday as a day of rest and relaxation from secular business is a welcome assurance to the entire community."[11]

With the "secular" pronouncement locked firmly in the lawbooks, Mr. Shedd felt secure in exposing the leadership role church groups had played in the controversy. He might have been a bit less secure in his assumption that the decision was welcomed by the entire community if he could have known the results of a grass-roots poll the following summer. Massachusetts citizens were asked, "Do you favor repealing or retaining Sunday laws?" Pollsters were startled to receive 25,799 answers for repeal and 2,036 for retention.

The ink had barely dried on the May 29 decision before Massachusetts Attorney General Edward J. McCormack, Jr., "issued an order instructing all police officials to begin rigid enforcement of blue laws in their localities."[12] Hours later the crackdown began. Police started out by canceling a Memorial Day dance in Dedham sponsored by the Columban Fathers to benefit a Korean missionary. A crowd of 1,000 was turned away.[13] The Memorial Day enforcement was a foretaste of what was to follow.

The Boston *American* reported that the Massachusetts Police Chiefs Association planned to map out a definite blueprint for police action in the crisis.

> The sky was blue, some of the blood and a few noses, but mostly the air was blue—the last because of the Sunday Blue Laws.
>
> The U.S. Supreme Court's decision upholding their constitutionality meant a lot of plans went bluey, especially when bluecoats in Dedham and Danvers moved to enforce them.
>
> But the Memorial Day enforcement was only partial; the big test comes Sunday. Memorial Day is one of several holidays blanketed by the Blue Laws which apply every Sunday of the year.[14]

The following week, confusion reigned. With tongue in cheek, the Boston *Traveler* viewed the blue-law haze as a dilemma "to start us grabbing at our thumbs." Then the writer queried: "What's right and what isn't? Is the sale of gasoline OK, but not the sale of spark plugs? Is it all right to buy a magazine in a drugstore, but not in a book shop? Who's on first?

165

DATELINE SUNDAY, U.S.A.

Until the muddle clears, we nominate Sundays and holidays for sleeping."[15]

While summer simmered long and hot that year in Massachusetts, a commission directed by Professor Arthur Sutherland of Harvard University was selected to study the conflicting Sunday laws and make recommendations for a solution to the problem. Commission members included G. Vaughn Shedd of the Lord's Day League, a voice which had been heard before; and Msgr. Francis J. Lally, editor of the Roman Catholic newsweekly, *The Pilot*, a voice which was about to be heard. Both men, with a majority of the commission members, saw wisdom in scratching the "Lord's Day" title in favor of "Common Day of Rest Law," but otherwise they favored stricter enforcement. A minority, including Sutherland and Rabbi Moses Shienkopf, pushed for "greater liberalization of the law and extensive local option."[16]

By the spring of 1962, the legislature was considering a formula which would allow about forty activities formerly banned on Sunday. Real-estate dealers could show property but not sell it. Bathhouses at beaches would stay open, along with libraries, art galleries, drugstores, bakeries, and auto supply stores selling tires and parts. Cultivating land was permitted, also harvesting crops and running pet shops and certain other businesses.[17] And, since hundreds of merchants had remained open during the enforcement in the summer of 1961, "taking the attitude that it is cheaper to keep paying fines than lose all Sunday trade," the new proposal called for enforcement by injunction if necessary.

Despite careful efforts to rewrite the law to specify a secular purpose, a sensational religious issue erupted in June, 1962. Senator Frank Foster of Boston proposed an exemption clause for minorities who observe a day of worship other than Sunday. This was adopted by the state senate, twenty-one votes to fourteen. It would have granted "Sabbatarians complete exemption from the provisions of the state's Sunday laws."[18]

166

Then the ceiling caved in. In its June 9 issue, *The Pilot,* a Roman Catholic newsweekly, lashed out in an editorial attack against the amendment as "both unjust and offensive." The statement from the office of Msgr. Lally branded Foster's proposal as "bad legislation, passed under pressure." It said that if enacted into law the amendment would give "commercial advantage to one minority in the community while it penalizes others, and it strikes at the heart of the day of rest which Sunday has been in our society for centuries." The editorial noted that the Massachusetts house had on May 22 killed the amendment passed by the senate. House rejection of the plan was a "wise" decision, *The Pilot* stated, and it called on senators to reconsider their action. "There is no need of destroying Sunday for the rest of the community to relieve the religious necessities of Sabbatarians."[19]

The editorial listed the names of the senators who had backed the amendment, and copies of the document were distributed to parishioners at services the following day, Sunday, June 10. Churchleaders urged members to contact their senators and representatives to register opposition to the amendment.

On Monday, June 11, the senate agreed to reopen the issue with some reference being made to statements in *The Pilot* the previous Saturday.

The exemption amendment was subjected to a new vote in the senate. Sharply reversing the previous tally, the amendment was defeated by a margin of thirty-one votes to eight.

This was more than merely coincidental. The character of Massachusetts Sunday law had been shaped with the help of religious influence, more than a year *after* the Supreme Court had whitewashed the previous blue law as "secular."

Orthodox Jews and Seventh-day Adventists, as well as the general public which had disapproved of enforced Sunday observance, could find little comfort in the modernized statute. But at least it was then legal to engage in some form of "do-it-yourself" home construction on Sunday, which is more than Roger Williams could have done safely.

"Democracy and freedom of conscience took a stinging blow on Beacon Hill this week,"[20] announced *The Jewish Advocate* following the senate action. The *Advocate* charged *The Pilot* with exerting a "naked display of pressure on civil law." As to the senate, the Jewish editorial expressed a fear that it had "surrendered its objectivity and autonomy with overtones frightening to contemplate."

A disappointed Rabbi Samuel J. Fox of the Massachusetts Council of Rabbis observed, "There is no question but that religious prejudice is evident and the rights of minorities are denied."[21]

Red-faced legislators later discovered that a loophole in the much-revised law opened the door to possible Sunday dancing after 1 p.m., subject to certain conditions. When the Boston city council voted to exercise its local option and allow Sunday dancing, religious leaders stormed city hall in a demonstration of opposition. In the procession was Dr. G. Vaughn Shedd, who appeared on behalf of the Massachusetts Council of Churches, along with Dr. Alfred B. Minyard of the Lord's Day League and Msgr. Joseph P. Donlan for the Catholic Council of Men and Women. But the Boston Musician's Union managed to win council approval by arguing that "dancing was basically a religious act and was started as a form of prayer. If it's a sin to dance on Sunday, it's a sin to allow dancing any day."[22]

As clamor for further loosening of Sunday restrictions continued, the Massachusetts house approved further revision in the spring of 1963. But again *The Pilot* raised its voice in protest as it warned, "Those who persist in raising these questions must be aware that their assaults on the day of rest merely create community division and bitterness."[23] *The Pilot* called for defeat of the measure in the Massachusetts senate, and, reminiscent of the result the previous year, the proposal passed into oblivion.[24]

The religion-inspired backwash of the 1961 decision was not confined to Massachusetts, Pennsylvania, and Maryland, states with laws which had been subjected to court scrutiny. The green light flashed "go" for blue-law crusaders from coast to coast.

For example, early in 1961, "Minnesota churches and clergymen were urged at the annual meeting of the Minnesota Council of Churches to help defeat a bill to permit sale of liquor on Sundays in Minneapolis and Saint Paul."[25] By March, a Pastor's Action committee had sent letters to 500 pastors in the Minneapolis area urging them to advise their parishioners to "do your shopping on weekdays and give your patronage to stores that remain closed on Sunday."[26] Backing the "Let's Save Sunday" campaign were representatives of the Methodist, Presbyterian, Lutheran, Evangelical and Reformed, and Evangelical United Brethren churches. The group received the approval of Archbishop William O. Brady, Roman Catholic leader in Saint Paul, the following month: "We need a fully united Christian front to defend our Christian Sunday."[27]

Early in 1962 the Minneapolis city council went on record in favor of deleting a Saturday exemption clause in a local city ordinance over the vigorous protests of three local Seventh-day Adventist pastors.[28] The "Save Our Sunday" campaign had produced legislative dividends in the Twin Cities and many suburbs. Pressure mounted for statewide tightening of control on Sunday activity.

The Minneapolis *Tribune* put the question to the public. Did they want to decide for themselves without legislative mandate, on the issue of Sunday closing? Sixty-five percent answered Yes, while "three out of every ten persons think laws are needed to keep Sunday business in bounds."[29] Despite this clear lack of public support, proponents pushed for tighter statewide restrictions and managed to obtain legislative approval in 1963, only to see their efforts vetoed by Governor Karl F. Rolvaag. Although the governor did not think the bill was designed "to encourage religious observance," he vetoed it because he believed it sought "to enlist the power of the state to protect narrow commercial interests." To this he added, "Even if this bill did forbid all secular activity on Sunday, I would still oppose it because I believe the state should never interfere in matters of private conscience."[30]

Church groups were among the supporters of a revised South Carolina Sunday-closing law in 1962.[31] The North Little Rock Ministerial Alliance in Arkansas appeared before the city council of North Little Rock to support a proposed Sunday-closing ordinance.[32] The Ohio Catholic Welfare Conference spoke out against a proposed amendment that would weaken the Ohio Sunday law: "Americans who are a 'religious people' with a traditional Sunday observance would deplore any change in the present laws which would be conducive to the secularization of Sunday and making it a day of business as usual."[33]

The Allentown Area Council of Churches in Pennsylvania urged churchgoers to "boycott those stores that defy the Sunday laws barring retail sales."[34] A Maine priest, C. Martin O'Toole, advised his parishioners to boycott Portland area merchants who engaged in Sunday business.[35]

The Kansas City Council of Churches energetically opposed a Missouri house proposal that would allow Sunday liquor sales. The churchmen described the proposal as "incompatible with a Christian observance of that day."[36]

Colorado formed its own "Save Our Sunday" committee, headed by a former president of the Pueblo Council of Churches. In an open effort to "promote a more spiritual observance of the Sabbath," the Colorado Sunday-closing advocates drew support from Roman Catholic leadership as well as local merchant and labor organizations.[37]

Evangelical Protestantism, traditional champion of blue laws, had succeeded by this time in garnering support from other segments of Protestantism as well as more than occasional support of Roman Catholics. An esteemed American cardinal had given his personal blessing to the Sunday-observance cause in 1888. His approving hand had been grasped eagerly. But not until later did Roman Catholics display the zeal for legislative action that Evangelicals had inherited from the Puritans.

The most impressive Roman Catholic comment came from Pope John XXIII in September, 1961, three months after the United States Supreme Court had spoken. Appearing before convention delegates of the International Union of Master Bakers, the pontiff pleaded "for the proper observance everywhere of Sunday as a day of rest. He said this 'presupposes a change of mind in society and intervention of the powers of the state.' 'Sunday,' he added, 'will really be the day of God when this comes about. It will be recognized as a social right to be enjoyed by all classes of society for the exercise of their religious duties and the practicing of works of charity. The Church will be happy when this takes place, and all society will reap the benefits.' "[38]

Not only had interchurch cooperation strengthened support for Sunday legislation; labor organizations and commercial enterprises joined with them. Church leaders remained at the vanguard, while business was welcomed to the ranks for united action. Downtown merchants, feeling the competitive pinch of the suburban discount stores which could attract the patrons' dollars seven days a week, joined the churches in their crusade. This move attracted the attention of the *Wall Street Journal*:

> Pressed by competition from discount houses that open on Sunday, retailers pick up the Sabbath-closing cry of religious groups. Texas, Michigan, South Carolina, Massachusetts, and Louisiana recently passed laws restricting selling on Sunday. California department stores push for a similar crackdown, although a trade group there found that 90 percent of persons polled in a survey favored stores being open on Sunday.

171

DATELINE SUNDAY, U.S.A.

Blue laws continue under heavy legal bombardment from Sunday-opening adherents. North Carolina's supreme court killed that state's Sunday-closing law because it was "vague and indefinite." Some states adopt compromise laws. In Texas and Michigan, stores may open Sunday if they close on Saturday. However, Sunday-closing laws go unenforced in many cities as state and local officers wrangle over who's responsible for their enforcement.

A few big department and variety chains muffle their attacks on Sunday selling because they contemplate opening discount stores which, to compete with other discounters, may have to open Sundays.[89]

The contest had its humorous side. Oklahoma lawmakers laughed to death a "principal holiday" proposal which would have banned ordinary labor on Sunday. Waggish amendments proposed ranged from exemptions for "chicken picking, neck wringing, and bathing in public with or without bathing suits,"[40] to bans on "cotton chopping, fish bait digging, cow milking, and bowling." One proposal would have wiped out Sunday activities on golf courses, in pool halls, at swimming pools, in domino parlors, and in beer taverns as well as television broadcasting.

"Since this is a moral issue we should go all the way," said one senator. "We'll have the people at home on Sunday with their families reading the Scripture."[41]

Elsewhere the clamor for tighter enforcement and expanded legislation crescendoed in 1963, reaching from the decorous East across the plains and deserts to the Wild West.

REFERENCES

1. *Time* magazine, October 25, 1963, page 56.
2. *Ibid.*
3. *Religious News Service,* June 19, 1961.
4. "As We See It," Detroit *Free Press,* June 1, 1961.
5. *Religious News Service,* June 2, 1961.
6. *Ibid.*
7. "Blue Laws and the Court," *The Christian Century,* July 19, 1961, pages 867, 868.
8. Detroit *Free Press,* June 2, 1961.
9. *Religious News Service,* June 9, 1961.

10. *Ibid.,* January 13, 1961.
11. "Love Blue Laws," Springfield, Massachusetts *Free Press,* June 3, 1961.
12. Boston, Massachusetts, *Record,* May 30, 1961.
13. Boston, Massachusetts, *Globe,* May 31, 1961.
14. Boston, Massachusetts, *American,* May 31, 1961.
15. Boston, Massachusetts, *Traveler,* June 7, 1961.
16. *Religious News Service,* November 16, 1961.
17. *Ibid.,* May 3, 1962.
18. *Ibid.,* June 7, 1962.
19. *Ibid.*
20. *Ibid.,* June 15, 1962.
21. *Ibid.,* July 5, 1962.
22. *Ibid.,* November 1, 1962.
23. *Ibid.,* April 5, 1963.
24. *Ibid.,* April 11, 1961.
25. *Ibid.,* February 10, 1961.
26. *Ibid.,* March 14, 1961.
27. *Ibid.,* April 10, 1961.
28. *Ibid.,* February 7, 1962.
29. *Ibid.,* March 7, 1962.
30. *Ibid.,* May 5, 1963.
31. *Ibid.,* March 30, 1962.
32. *Ibid.,* October 13, 1961.
33. *Ibid.,* September 24, 1962.
34. *Ibid.,* November 3, 1961.
35. *Ibid.,* December 14, 1961.
36. *Ibid.,* February 14, 1963.
37. *Ibid.,* December 12, 1961, and December 14, 1961.
38. *Ibid.,* September 21, 1961.
39. "Business Bulletin," *Wall Street Journal,* August 9, 1962.
40. *Religious News Service,* July 14, 1961.
41. *Ibid.,* June 16, 1961.

Peopled from its earliest years by hardy individualists, the Golden State has repeatedly repulsed coercive Sunday laws.

LAMBERT

15. SUNDAY AND THE GOLDEN STATE

California's sons played key roles in the Sunday conflict in the nineteenth century. In 1858 David S. Terry was instrumental in creating the first state supreme court finding that Sunday laws violated religious liberty. His antagonist, Stephen J. Field, fostered the dissenting view that Sunday laws had a valid secular purpose which justified their existence under the police power of the state. Field successfully planted this philosophy in opinions of the United States Supreme Court.

By the year 1887 the Sunday-law issue was being contested again, with the American Sabbath Union and the Lord's Day Alliance confidently predicting victory for a state Sunday-law measure. Edward Thompson, Pacific Coast spokesman, boasted, "The American Sabbath Union has never lost a campaign yet, and we are not going to lose this one. We have given ourselves three years to conquer California."[1]

That year the legislature was flooded with petitions inspired by the union and their Prohibitionist allies demanding restraint of "Sunday traffic and work, as well as all coarse and noisy amusements."[2]

Petitioners carefully emphasized the civil-regulation phrases which Stephen J. Field, in his legal opinions, had suggested. A blue-law spokesman writing on February 19, 1890, acknowledged "how cautious we have to be in wording of this petition, for as we have no state law recognizing the Sabbath day, we have no hope of closing the saloon on that day except as a municipal and police arrangement in the interest of sobriety, morality, law, and order." He candidly admitted:

> If we would undertake to close the saloons because the Sabbath is a day sacred by divine authority, we would be met at once, both by the council and by the courts, with the declaration: The state of California knows no religious Sabbath—no Sunday except a holiday. Thus we would be defeated at the very beginning.[3]

The legislature ignored the petitions and pressures. However, in 1893 it did act to protect the laboring man through a measure guaranteeing one day's rest in seven for employees, with the choice of the day left to the discretion of the employer. A "civil regulation" designed to protect the health and welfare of an individual rather than a day, the revolutionary concept cleared the assembly by a vote of 56 to 4 and the senate 29 to 0.[4]

But Sunday-law enthusiasts could not cheerfully accept mere health and welfare measures. In a thinly veiled warning to the 1895 legislature, they suggested that "legislators who make good laws in favor of Sabbath observance are the best friends of the state."[5] But the most they could wheedle from the California government was a Sunday-closing law which singled out barbers.

Why barbers? Perhaps it was the "nose of the camel" approach. Whatever the cause, the statute was too weak to survive. The next year, the California supreme court junked it as unconstitutional "class" legislation:

> When any one such class is singled out and put under the criminal ban of a law such as this, the law not only is special, unjust, and unreasonable in its operation, but it works an invasion of individual liberty, the liberty of the free labor which it pretends to protect.[6]

Sunday-law promoters lost, but they also learned! They bounced back in 1909 with a proposal to incorporate coerced Sunday observance into the California constitution, beyond the reach of the legislature. C. L. Tufts, one of the active spokesmen for the proposal, met with Northern California clergymen to map a new strategy. He urged formation of an organization which would allow ministers to pull the strings from the background, while business leaders, "not necessarily members of the church," would front to the public. He feared that otherwise citizens "would recognize at once the ministerial aspect, and the object for which we are laboring would be defeated."[7] The Tufts plan called for cooperation of Catholic priests wherever possible. In a concerted effort, proponents would initiate an attack on gambling followed by a push for midnight closing of saloons, then on to a Sunday ban on bars, and finally the blue-law amendment to the constitution.

These ambitious maneuvers were met head on by J. O. Corliss of the Seventh-day Adventist Religious Liberty Association. The association had gathered 38,000 signatures of voters opposed to the "criminal-for-a-day" law.

Noting that the most spirited resistance came from the small Adventist denomination, W. H. G. Temple offered some intemperate remarks to one legislative committee: "This is a Christian nation," and "we have the right to demand that the alien in religion shall conform outwardly to our customs. When one branch of the Christian church, so small it is insignificant, takes another day for Sunday, we have a right to make that sect conform to our practice."[8]

However, the legislature voted down the Sunday law, and its defeated advocates were bitter. In 1912, one of them, the California State Superintendent of the Sunday Rest Proposition, suggested to a San Jose audience that the minority opposition be banished to some never-never land outside the United States: "Those who are not loyal enough to the American Government

177

to observe its American sabbath should find a spot in some other part of the world where they can go and spend their time as they wish."[9]

This utterance came on the heels of a 1911 brush with the Religious Liberty Association. "Having been creditably informed that preparation for a strong effort to secure a Sunday-rest law at the forthcoming legislature of 1911 was being made by religious leaders, the Pacific Religious Liberty Association secured in a month's time more than sixty-eight thousand signatures of voters to petitions against any religious legislation."[10]

The association needn't have worried. Blue-law advocates failed to find a legislator willing to sponsor their measure.

Faced with an unfriendly legislature, Sunday proponents next tried the initiative to give the choice to California voters in 1914. The language of the 1893 "one-day-in-seven" rest law was lifted, and the specific designation of Sunday slipped in as the mandatory rest period. The Los Angeles Chamber of Commerce branded it "discriminatory," but Senator William Kehoe threw his political prestige on the line behind the proposal. He insisted that Sunday laws were not enforced as religious measures by any state: "None has been so bold, as to claim" that in the enforcement of Sunday observance in other states "religious or blue laws are being forced upon the people."[11]

The Kehoe message failed to get through to the people. Initiative measure No. 45 went down to oblivion by a margin of 457,890 to 290,679.

Sunday-law lobbyists turned back to the California legislature in 1917 and again in 1919. They brought along some labor-union support, hoping to impress the state representatives. But the legislature again turned them down.

Rebuffed by an adamant legislature, the Sabbath Union dropped out of sight for a decade and then reappeared in 1929. A zealot by the name of Harold P. Malcolm, president of the American Sabbath Day Enforcement League, toured the state, boasting of plans "to ask Congress at its next session to enact Sunday-enforcement laws with teeth in them." He talked confidently of plans to clear the state's highways of Sunday traffic "as part of a nationwide campaign to compel Sunday observance."[12]

Sunday laws "savor too much of unwarranted interference with personal liberty," groaned a representative of the California Oil and Gasoline Association. He challenged the proposal as an effort "to impose religious ideas upon the citizenry . . . in the guise of public welfare or economic progress."[13]

Warned the Palo Alto *Times:*

> Out here in liberal-minded California, we laugh at those funny states "back East," that have Sunday blue laws. But if we don't watch out we will be making a beginning in blue legislation ourselves. . . .
>
> [This] will be giving the grandest sort of encouragement to the professional blue law promoters to try at the next election to put over laws forbidding Sunday baseball, Sunday movies, Sunday motoring, Sunday cigar selling, and everything else except Sunday church attendance.[14]

The Sacramento *Union* declared:

> The churches cannot legislate themselves into popularity by closing everything else on the Sabbath. . . . When we try to shove religious differences into politics, into fraternal life, and into things where they have no place, we get into trouble.[15]

Quipped a Los Angeles *Record* column:

> If this idiotic law is ever passed, "Yours truly" would just as soon spend every Sunday in the county jail as under all the blue restrictions of this puritanical proposal.[16]

In the November, 1930, election, 214,533 Californians voted for coerced Sunday closing, but more than a million voted No! Initiative measure No. 26 went the way of other California blue-law proposals.

DATELINE SUNDAY, U.S.A.

Three more decades passed, while diverse religious cultures and persuasions continued to enjoy unparalleled prosperity in the Golden State, despite the lack of a general Sunday-observance law on the books for nearly a century. Then the shock wave emanating from the 1961 United States Supreme Court decision reached westward to California, about to become the most populous state in the Union.

On Monday, March 4, 1963, State Senator Joseph Rattigan of Sonoma, California, launched an attack against the alleged "moral, social, and economic damage caused by Sunday selling." The antidote, he urged, was Senate Bill 845, a general Sunday-closing law for the state.

Malcolm in 1929 had tried to make it a crime to drive a car on the public highway on Sunday. Assemblyman Tom Carrell, San Fernando Valley auto dealer, suggested to a new generation in 1959 and 1961 that it should be a crime to *sell* a car on Sunday. Twice his proposal cleared the assembly but died in the senate. Three decades had passed since the 1930 debacle, and Carrell's Sunday-law proposals fared no better.

The Religious Liberty Association again went to bat and opposed both the 1959 and 1961 proposals as a vestige of Puritan-inspired blue laws. A brief sent to the legislature in 1961 questioned:

> If the state can force a store to *close* on Sunday, conversely can the state force a store to *open* on Sunday or Saturday? If the state can tell *when* to sell can it also tell *what* to sell, *where* to sell, and *who* to sell to?
> The problem of classifying what can or cannot be sold on Sunday results in an acutely arbitrary result. . . . While some merchants would be denied the privilege of selling automobiles on Sunday, neighboring merchants would still be free to sell auto accessories and parts such as seat covers, fan belts, tires, batteries, headlights, [and] floor mats, [as well as] gasoline, and oil. While a father would not be free to buy an automobile for use on the highway, he

180

would still be allowed to purchase a motor-driven midget-sized auto for his son's use in the backyard.

A dealer denied the right to sell an automobile on Sunday might nevertheless be free to sell a bicycle, boat, airplane, or service to cars previously sold. . . .

Although AB 289 would prevent the *sale* of automobiles on Sunday, it would presumably leave the door open to Sunday *rental* or leasing of cars. . . . Except in a legal sense, is a *rental* any more or less a commercial transaction than a sale of a motor vehicle?[17]

Californians still liked the smell of free air in the 1960's. With their votes they subscribed to the views of an editorial in the Pasadena *Star-News:*

Sunday blue laws, in general, prevent the operation of stores and sometimes of amusement enterprises. . . . This procedure might be explainable under an authoritarian government having an established church, but it hardly accords with principles of democracy or of protection of the rights of minorities. . . . The observance, if any, of a religious holiday is a question for the individual to decide.[18]

The century-old San Rafael *Independent-Journal* remarked that AB 289 "strikes us as a step backward. . . . A blue law is in effect a kind of infringement on a person's religious freedom. . . . A law prohibiting the Sunday operation of one business seems to us poor legislation."

According to the Garden Grove *News:*

Many will share the high aim of the bill as a means of implementing the Fourth Commandment, [but] we have general misgivings about legislation to enforce a religious edict on which public opinion has not arrived at a consensus.

Even from the viewpoint of those who prefer businesses to close on Sunday, the legislation is unnecessary. Our American heritage is that the form of society originates from moral conviction in the hearts of individual men, not the other way around.[19]

DATELINE SUNDAY, U.S.A.

Henry C. MacArthur, Sacramento columnist, writing on the "Affairs of State," saw the issue as commercial rather than religious, and said, "Once again, the California state legislature is twiddling its fingers in private business, and voting to enact laws which violate the rights of citizens and businessmen to operate their business as they choose."

Small-volume auto dealers felt the threat of large-volume sales organizations which offered a night-and-day seven-days-a-week sales pitch. They saw AB 289 as a means to stifle the competition.

Though the 1959 bill failed to get through the senate, Assemblyman Carrell successfully enlisted the support of many of his colleagues as cosponsors of his 1961 efforts. In California's eighty-member assembly, forty-one votes were needed to pass a bill; on April 6, 1961, Carrell got exactly forty-one.

It was a nonpartisan verdict. Assemblymen from both sides of the aisle gave support, and the members voting "no" represented both Democrats and Republicans.

Assemblyman Howard J. Thelin hit hard at the proposal: "It is easy to condemn religious and racial discrimination when a vandal scrawls swastikas on a synagogue, but here we see it in more subtle form. If we believe in a free economy, how can we say one group of businessmen must close on Sunday?"[20]

"This little gem has been with us before," added Assemblyman Walter Dahl, who eyed it as "only a starter."[21]

Tom Carrell was either unaware of the facts or he was misquoted, when he claimed he did not know "of any Jew or Seventh-day Adventist who closes his business on Saturday."[22] Earlier in the year, when he had introduced AB 289, Carrell was quoted as saying, "The Adventists say that if we have this type of legislation, they want us to include Saturday."[23] The Adventists had, in fact, made it plain that their church opposed coerced observance of any day.

With the slim assembly majority on record in support of

182

his measure, Carrell then faced the formidable senate hurdle. Kern County Senator Walter W. Stiern asked some point-blank questions:

> Is it morally justifiable to make a man a criminal for keeping his business open on Sunday? . . . Suppose a dealer doesn't sell cars on Sunday, but demonstrates them and keeps his business open for the public to look at cars on Sunday. If this is not a violation of the law, has the bill accomplished anything? . . . Why should the legislature select the automobile dealer as the object of a Sunday-closing law? Why not other businesses? . . . Why close the dealers on Sunday rather than on some other day of the week? . . . If it is the purpose of the bill to give people a holiday on their religious holy day, why not pass a law which does that rather than pass this bill?[24]

Proponents failed to answer these and other questions to the satisfaction of the senate committee studying the measure, and AB 289 joined the growing discard heap of California blue-law proposals.

No sooner had Tom Carrell's effort met with senate rebuff than a "Citizens Advisory Committee" in Los Angeles began to raise a million-dollar war chest to put Sunday closing back on the ballot in initiative form. Committee coordinator Haskel N. Grubbs admitted that a survey showed 90 percent of Californians interviewed said they would not support a Sunday-closing law. However, he said he hoped citizen interest in the possibility of saving money through Sunday closing might be the key to victory.[25]

Grubbs had reason to fear public sentiment. In a privately sponsored interview program, 2,600 Californians were given a list of typical Sunday activities and asked if they favored making these activities illegal on the first day of the week. Only 14 percent approved the criminal-for-a-day concept even for the most patently "secular" activity. Thus a plurality of six to one opposed coerced Sunday observance.[26]

183

13—D.S.

DATELINE SUNDAY, U.S.A.

The Field Research Company released a survey in March, 1963, which showed that 60 percent of the public opposed Sunday-closing laws and 35 percent favored them.[27]

The widely heralded initiative did not appear on the California ballot in 1962, but "Californians Against Commercializing Sunday" picked up the banner and carried it to the 1963 legislature on the wings of Senator Rattigan's SB 845.

Encouraged by the green light flashed to "secular" blue laws by the United States Supreme Court, some California retailers pooled their resources and tried to sell their employees on a massive letter-writing campaign directed to the legislature. Dire warnings, bordered in black, of threats to community economy and family welfare were printed in a brochure headlined "Sunday Blight."

Senator Rattigan and his backers sought to avoid the religious implication by arguing that the bill did not "affect religion."

Retorted the Religious Liberty Association:

> While arguments are heard that "this is not a 'Blue Law' " and that "it does not affect religion," proponents warn of "moral" damage stemming from Sunday business and that unless Sunday selling is restricted "a sizable percentage of our citizenry will be observing Sunday, not as a day of rest but as just another working day." An introductory statement within the bill itself refers to the "preservation of Sunday as a day free from work" to permit, among other things specified, "religious worship if and as desired by any person."[28]

Cree Sandefur, spokesman for 20,000 Seventh-day Adventists in the Los Angeles area, asked, "What possible 'moral' damage could result from selling on Sunday an item which on six days of the week it is considered perfectly moral to sell, unless a purely religious factor is attached?"[29]

As proposed, SB 845 would have made Sunday sales of clothing, furniture, appliances, television sets, radios, cameras, jew-

184

elry, and, of course, automobiles a crime. So-called "essential" items which could be sold as usual without penal sanctions were drugs, gasoline, auto supplies, food, real estate, newspapers, souvenirs, and novelty items.

The legal status of the nonessential sales would also depend on the scene of the action. Area classifications based upon population size and geographic location were incorporated, creating what opponents charged was an enforcement crazy quilt with which an already harassed and undermanned police force would be left to cope.

The Los Angeles *Times* asked in amazement, "How is purchase of real property rated essential, and a car purchase nonessential?" The "premise that retail sales personnel are deprived of a day of rest by Sunday selling doesn't stand examination. Virtually all retailing help gets two days a week off. Many prefer weekdays off, to avoid resort crowds and Sunday traffic on their rest days." With reference to allegations of Senator Rattigan, the bill's sponsor, the *Times* continued:

> Despite his statement that this is not a "blue" law, and does not affect religion, the moral issue is injected. The scare word "wide-open" is applied to Sunday selling, to conjure up visions of profligacy and debauch associated with the "wide-open" towns of the frontier.
>
> Advocates of the measure carefully avoid the key issue, which is public convenience. For hundreds of thousands of families, with husband and wife both working, the weekend is the only period available for joint shopping.[30]

Los Angeles Mayor Sam Yorty expressed concern for minorities. Said the mayor, "I cannot see that it's fair to say that everybody must close on Sunday when everybody does not observe Sunday as the Sabbath."[31]

Robert D. Wood, speaking for television station KNXT, asked:

> Why is the sale of a house and lot on Sunday essential

to public health and welfare, but not the sale of a new or used automobile? Where is the logic to the sale of a bottle of whiskey on Sunday, but not the sale of a lawn mower?

And what about the supermarkets under the provisions of this proposed Sunday-selling Law? They could sell you a loaf of bread, a jar of pickles, or a can of corn, but on Sunday they would be required to hide the kitchen knives, the flashlight batteries, the electric light bulbs, and the fly swatters.

And the super drugstores. . . . They could fill your prescription or sell you a bottle of aspirin on Sunday, but to escape being arrested, they would make you put back a pocket comb, a bottle of nail polish, or a toy balloon and tell you to come back on Monday. . . .

KNXT feels strongly the free enterprise system should not be subjected to excessive restrictions by government. KNXT also feels very strongly that under our free-enterprise system, the police power of the state is used properly to enforce competition, not to restrain it.[32]

In reviewing the argument of SB 845 backers that "it ensures a leisurely Sunday for store clerks and 'protects' people of the state from 'moral, social, and economic damage,'" columnist Ridgeley Cummings suggested it "will be news to policemen, firemen, newspaper reporters, restaurant workers, hotel clerks, filling station operators, soda jerkers, and thousands of others who work on Sunday that they need this 'moral protection.'"[33] The proposal had not extended its "protective" mantle to these working groups.

The Glendale Chamber of Commerce lent its official backing to the Rattigan proposal, but Glendale *News Press* Editor Carroll N. Parcher took a dim view of the bill, as to the issues of both religious freedom and free enterprise. Said he, "Dangers of regulating business by legislation should be especially apparent to retailers already faced with a myriad of regulatory decrees. And once the door is opened on this type of legislation, there is no end in sight.[34]

186

Blue-law opponents stumbled on a new ally in 1963. When the California Retailers Association backed Sunday closing to control competition, discount-house competitors bristled in reaction. In a biting attack published in its monthly advertiser circulated to customers, one of the large discount houses, Unimart, chided:

> Californians are now witnessing the sorry spectacle of a group of frightened department-store owners milling around Sacramento attempting to pass legislation which would force competition—the membership store or discount store—to close Sundays. . . . The same men who attend service clubs and public meetings to preach free enterprise, risk capital, and rugged individualism, are now in Sacramento trying to injure competition by passing an obviously vague and unconstitutional law which would close certain parts of certain stores in certain towns on certain days— namely Sundays. As it stands now, if the law passes you can buy a six-pack at our store on Sundays but you can't buy an opener."[35]

The Religious Liberty Association of the Seventh-day Adventists distributed newspaper advertising attacking the incongruity of a "one-day-criminal" law; and State Chairman Philip Corvin, of "Californians Against Commercializing Sunday" immediately countered with a seventeen-page mimeographed throwaway accusing, "It is an economic interest, not one of religion, which motivates their opposition to this bill."[36] Ignoring the moral arguments advanced by Senator Rattigan, Corvin declared, "The bill is not morality-oriented."

But the tide of California opinion which had been mounting for eighty years could not be washed away by a last-minute attack against a religious minority. In April, Senator Rattigan himself announced that he was withdrawing the measure from further consideration for lack of support, explaining that support on the senate floor for SB 845, the Sunday-selling bill, while substantial, was not sufficient to gain its passage. In his announcement he hopefully predicted that someday a reasonable regulation of Sunday selling in California might become a reality.

Since SB 845 had included a ban on Sunday auto sales, those concerned with this special interest had not bothered to introduce the customary blue law applicable only to cars. But when SB 845 was discarded, auto-closing proponents resorted to desperate strategems. On January 10, Tom Carrell had offered the assembly a simple seven-line proposal which would revise the speed limit for passenger cars pulling trailers on state highways. It was printed as Assembly Bill 82, and in its original form had nothing to do with Sunday laws.

No sooner had Senator Rattigan dropped Senate Bill 845 than Tom Carrell threw Assembly Bill 2893 into the hopper, the Sunday-closing measure applicable to auto dealers. But the problem with AB 2893 was its number. Introduced long after the legislature had opened for business, it lacked priority. Stuck with an April birthday and high number, there was little chance that a packed legislative schedule would give way to the attention essential for passage.

Then came some sensational legislative surgery! On April 29, 1963, Tom Carrell offered an amendment to AB 82, in which the original wording was discarded, with the exception of the desired high-priority number, AB 82. In place of the original speed-law language, the complete contents of what had been AB 2893 appeared, lock, stock, and—blue law.

The new SB 82, the automobile sales prohibition bill for 1963, was diluted by a May 9 amendment which limited its application to specific counties. And in that form the assembly gave its blessing, but not before there was considerable flurry in the legislative hallways in an effort to corral enough "aye" votes to send it on to the senate.

The procedure did not slip by unnoticed!

"This measure, according to information received, was amended from a proposal dealing with auto speeds to the closing of auto dealers on Sunday in such a way that it could slip onto the assembly floor with little or no public scrutiny," chided Cree Sandefur, Southern California Adventist leader, in a message to the press May 13. "When the measure came to the assembly floor it lacked enough votes to assure its passage. Its proponents had to beat the legislative bushes for additional assemblymen and then call a roll-call vote to finally see it pass the lower house."

However, the senate ignored the patched-up AB 82, and the 1963 legislative session ended without a Sunday blue law on the books. No one bothered to come back with any more "one-day-criminal" offering during the next general session of the legislature in 1965.

The voice of a free California public had been heard!

REFERENCES

1. Edward Thompson, quoted by W. N. Green, "The Sunday-law Program," *Signs of the Times,* Vol. 16 (1890), No. 46, p. 565.
2. *Ibid.*
3. *Christian Statesman,* March 13, 1930.
4. *California Assembly, 1893,* 30th Session, page 481; and *California Senate, 1893,* 30th Session, page 365.
5. *Journal of California Senate, 1895,* 31st Session, page 548.
6. *Ex Parte Jentzsch,* 112 California 468 (1896).
7. Essence of remarks of C. L. Tufts as reported in "Plans for Sunday Legislation," *Pacific Union Recorder,* September 30, 1909.
8. "Divine Talks to Law Makers," Sacramento *Bee,* January 18, 1909.
9. "California and Religious Liberty," *Signs of the Times,* Vol. 39 (1912), No. 24, p. 390.
10. *Ibid.,* No. 22, p. 358.
11. Frank C. Jordan, Secretary of State, Comp., "Initiative Measure No. 45," *Amendments to Constitution and Proposed Statutes,* November 3, 1914 (State Printing Office, 1914), page 83.
12. Rev. Harold P. Malcolm, D.D., San Diego *Sun,* September 18, 1929.
13. Fred B. Wood, Comp., *Proposed Amendment to Constitution and Proposed Laws,* November 4, 1930, Part I, pages 31, 32.
14. Dallas E. Wood, *"Feature Column"* Palo Alto *Times,* March 15, 1930.
15. "Daily Column," Sacramento *Union,* February 2, 1930.
16. "Yours Truly," Los Angeles *Record,* July 9, 1930.
17. "Implications of Assembly Bill 289," *Liberty Letter* (Religious Liberty Association, Southern California Chapter), February 15, 1961.
18. Editorial, Pasadena *Star-News,* November 30, 1960.
19. Garden Grove *News,* April 27, 1961.
20. Los Angeles *Examiner,* April 7, 1961.
21. *Ibid.*

DATELINE SUNDAY, U.S.A.

22. *Ibid.*
23. "Auto Sales," Huntington Park *Signal,* January 13, 1961.
24. Walter W. Stiern, from letter to Warren L. Johns, April 20, 1961.
25. *Women's Wear Daily,* New York, as quoted in *Liberty News,* January, 1962.
26. Private poll sponsored by Southern California Chapter, Religious Liberty Association, February, 1962.
27. "Majority Opposes Sunday Closing Laws," Field Research Co., as reported by Los Angeles *Times,* March 21, 1963.
28. "Dangers of the 'One-day Criminal' Concept Set Forth in SB 845," Religious Liberty Association, Southern California Chapter, March 21, 1963.
29. Cree Sandefur, statement released to press March 5, 1963.
30. "The 'Moral' Issue of Sunday Selling," Los Angeles *Times,* March 6, 1963.
31. "Yorty Opposes Sunday Closing Laws as Unfair," Los Angeles *Times,* March 22, 1963.
32. Robert D. Woods, "Eighty Years Without a Sunday Closing Law," KNXT, March 18, 1963.
33. Ridgeley Cummings, "Blue Law Legislation Raises Its Ugly Head in California," March, 1963.
34. Carroll N. Parcher, "In My Opinion," Glendale *News Press,* March 4, 1963.
35. "A Word About Sunday Selling," *Unimart,* April, 1963, page 32.
36. Philip Corvin, "Commentary on Vital Aspects of SB 845 The Sunday Selling Bill" (Californians Against Commercializing Sunday).

16. THE RIGHT TO REST

Suppose every Christian seventh-day-Sabbath worshiper in the United States pulled up stakes, moved to Wyoming, and there became a religious majority. And suppose a realization of political power whetted the settlers' appetites, so that they proceeded to impose their convictions on the local public through civil law. Would you want to live there?

A hitherto religious minority would suddenly possess political power. The hypothetical "new majority" could eye with interest the *McGowan v. Maryland* decision handed down by the Supreme Court of the United States in 1961. Using identical language, it could enact a "Sabbath" law making it a crime not to observe the seventh-day Sabbath and paraphrase the words of the chief justice to make them read, "Saturday is a day apart from all others. The cause is irrelevant; the fact exists."

The author who framed this question about life under a "new majority" continued:

Inasmuch as Sabbath keepers believe that Sabbath keeping is one of the requirements of the Ten-Commandment law and that society itself would be greatly blessed if all people kept the Sabbath that Jesus kept, they could violate the God-given principle of individual choice and,

a. Sponsor and pass by majority legislative vote a strict

191

Saturday-rest law. They could pattern this law after some of the blue laws already on the statute books of certain states by substituting the word "Saturday" for the word "Sunday."

b. There might be a vigorous protest against such an un-American law by those who believe in our Bill of Rights and the essential rightness of the First Amendment to the Constitution, but the political-minded Sabbath keepers could easily ignore this protest by calling this a health-and-welfare law. Surely the laboring man needs rest from toil and protection from those who would exploit him!

c. When some would say: "Give us a one-day-in-seven rest law but do not discriminate against us and our religious beliefs by enforcing a Saturday law," the Sabbath keepers could justify their designation of a particular day by declaring that this is merely a police measure, that there must be uniformity, and that the majority need not respect the rights of the minority on such questions.[1]

Christian keepers of the seventh day will never colonize Wyoming or any other state. Hopefully, if given the taste of political strength, they would never abandon an historic commitment to separation of church and state and resort to civil law to enforce observance of their day of worship. Ideally, concern would rather be directed to protecting the right of an individual to rest one day each week.

The Christian who is committed to voluntary seventh-day Sabbath observance acts without government compulsion. On the contrary, he often endures direct economic hardship because of his inner compulsion to "keep holy" the seventh day.

The 1961 Supreme Court Sunday-law decisions acknowledged the indirect economic disadvantage which confronted a Sabbath keeper forced to surrender his time on Sunday. The price the government demanded was 14.28 percent of his time—a high rate of interest to pay because personal religious practice did not conform to majority custom. But this was not all. Hundreds have seen careers evaporate and lifelong security swept away, all because of a decision to unite with a religious persuasion which puts a premium on the literal observance of the fourth commandment.

Consider, for instance, the church elder relieved of his job with a railroad only a few years before retirement benefits were available, solely because he determined to honor a commitment to conscience. Add the aircraft industry executive; the telephone lineman; the oil company employee; and the maintenance man. Unavailable for work on Saturday, they lost their jobs. Emergencies, along with works of necessity and charity, yes. "It is lawful to do well on the Sabbath days." Matthew 12:12. Routine commerce or labor on the seventh day—no, regardless of damage to the pocketbook.

Remarkably, personal hardship and economic loss have been minimized because many employers have taken pains to respect conscientious convictions. Acting without compulsion of the state, employers often have adjusted schedules to honor individual need. But sometimes, through no fault of the employer, the very character of the job prevents such accommodation. Then the Sabbath keeper may find himself out of a job.

Adell Sherbert had to make this kind of decision in 1959. She had worked in the Spartan Mills in Spartanburg, South Carolina, for thirty-five years. In 1957 she joined the Seventh-day Adventist Church. At the time, the mill was operating five days a week, and there was no problem. But in 1959, all three shifts were pushed to a six-day week. Management asked Miss Sherbert to work Saturdays, and she respectfully declined.[2]

What about her right to rest? If Miss Sherbert had been a majority Christian who worshiped on Sunday, she would have had no problem. Not only did South Carolina have an ancient blue law restricting normal commercial activity on the first day of the week, which the United States Supreme Court let live unchallenged in 1961, but statutory protection guaranteed Sunday rest as a matter of conscience. In the event the state authorized the mills to run on Sunday during "national emergencies," there was the assurance:

> No employee shall be required to work on Sunday . . . who is conscientiously opposed to Sunday work; and if any employee should refuse to work on Sunday on account of conscientious . . . objections, he or she shall not jeopardize his or her seniority by such refusal or be discriminated against in any other manner.[3]

Miss Sherbert worshiped on Saturday and was thus excluded from this statutory protection. She was a sober, capable employee available for work six days a week. She lost her job at Spartan Mills. She tried to find employment in three other mills but failed.

At last she went to the state for unemployment compensation. She indicated a willingness to work in another mill, or even in another industry, as long as Saturday work was not required.

But the South Carolina Employment Security Commission refused her request for compensation. The state supreme court agreed with the commission and ruled against her, four to one. The lone dissenting voice, Justice Bussey, argued that it was "morally injurious" to require a strict Sabbath observer to work on the seventh day against religious principle.

If the state has a constitutional right as a matter of police power to force a citizen to rest on Sunday, what about the right of the individual to choose a day of religious worship for himself as a matter of free exercise of conscience? Did the denial of unemployment compensation to Miss Sherbert by the State of South Carolina constitute an infringement upon her free exercise of religion, in violation of the First Amendment?

The United States Supreme Court tackled the issue in 1963. State administrative agencies as well as state supreme courts had split on results time after time as individuals pursued claims for unemployment compensation when they lost their jobs for refusal to engage in "secular" activity on Saturday. Denial of claims was usually based on the premise that the claimant was not truly "available for work" within the meaning of the compensation statutory scheme.

Did the State of South Carolina have a constitutional right to deny Miss Sherbert unemployment compensation when her conscience told her on what day of the week to rest? A seven-man majority of the United States Supreme Court decided that there had been an infringement of Miss Sherbert's free exercise of religion. Justices Harlan and White dissented, finding no constitutional violation.

Miss Sherbert was "available for work" six out of every seven days. Health and welfare interests of the state would not condone a seven-day work week. The 1961 court majority had gone on record approving an enforced observance of a state-selected day of rest. Still, the dissenting voices in *Sherbert* v. *Verner* took a position which denied the right of an individual to select the day of rest for himself without suffering financial hardship.

In the eyes of Harlan, as stated in his dissent,[4] Miss Sherbert was in fact unavailable for work because of a "purely personal reason" and therefore outside the scope of statutory protection. He was not swayed by the fact that she was available for work six days a week in any industry where a job was available. According to Harlan, "She was denied benefits just as any other claimant would be denied benefits who was not 'available for work' for personal reasons" and not "because she was a Seventh-day Adventist."

He equated "religious conviction" with "personal consideration," declaring, "The fact that these personal considerations spring from her religious convictions was wholly without relevance to the state court's application of the law."

Harlan was troubled with the majority result which he felt "necessarily overrules *Braunfeld* v. *Brown* . . . which held that it did not offend the 'Free Exercise' Clause of the Constitution for a State to forbid a Sabbatarian to do business on Sunday."

For one thing, he believed the secular purpose of the Sherbert case was even clearer than that of the Braunfeld decision. He also declared that "the indirect financial burden of the present law is far less than that involved in Braunfeld."

Two years after Braunfeld, Harlan candidly acknowledged that "forcing a store owner to close his business on Sunday may well have the effect of depriving him of a satisfactory livelihood if his religious convictions require him to close on Saturday as well." But far from backing away from the Braunfeld holding, Justice Harlan simply indicated that the loss to the individual minority was even smaller in the Sherbert case. "Here we are dealing only with temporary benefits, amounting to a fraction of regular weekly wages and running for not more than twenty-two weeks," he said.

Although the associate justice acknowledged that the state could accommodate religious conviction, if it wished, by granting exceptions to eligibility requirements for people like Miss Sherbert, he could not admit that the state was in any way constitutionally compelled to make such an accommodation.

Belittling the economic plight of Miss Sherbert, he saw only an "indirect, remote, and insubstantial effect . . . on the exercise of appellant's religion," and concluded that the compulsion on the state to provide this compensation was inappropriate and in fact threatened to give "direct financial assistance to religion."

Harlan and White ignored the fact that the majority in Braunfeld had subordinated free exercise of religion only under pressure from an alleged public interest which might be upset by a Sabbatarian exemption. In the Sherbert case there was little evidence of comparable pressure of public interest. There was only individual conscience which the Harlan-White view reduced to "purely personal reasons."

The dissenting words contrasted sharply with the echoes of court opinions written in the forties which had exalted religious

196

liberty and placed it on a pedestal along with other First Amendment guarantees—completely out of reach of mere public convenience or administrative whim.

United States Supreme Court Justice Frank Murphy, a Roman Catholic and one-time governor of Michigan, had become known as a leading exponent of ultimate religious liberty. Frequently he spoke for the court, and his words helped to carve a niche of special protection for First Amendment guarantees.

Justice William J. Brennan, a Roman Catholic, came to the Supreme Court in 1956. Like Justice Murphy, he put religious liberty on a pedestal. It was Brennan who enunciated the thinking of the seven-man majority in the 1963 *Sherbert* v. *Verner* decision.[5] He began by quoting from the statute which declared a claimant ineligible for benefits where "he has failed, without good cause . . . to accept available suitable work when offered him by the employment office of the employer."

Did Miss Sherbert have "good cause"?

In order for the South Carolina decision to be valid, it was necessary to find no infringement on free exercise of religion. If infringement was found, some evidence of "compelling state interest" must justify it. According to William Brennan, the South Carolina holding failed on both counts. First of all, he found that the state had imposed a burden on Miss Sherbert's religion by exerting pressure upon her to forgo a religious practice. He insisted: "The ruling forces her to choose between following the precepts of her religion and forfeiting benefits, on the one hand, and abandoning one of the precepts of her religion in order to accept work, on the other hand." As a practical matter, this type of burden was equal to "a fine imposed against appellant for her Saturday worship." And here is where the court found the crux of the infringement, for "to condition the availability of benefits upon this appellant's willingness to violate a cardinal principle of her religious faith effectively penalizes the free exercise of her constitutional liberties."

Justice William J. Brennan, a Roman Catholic, strongly defended religious liberty in the 1963 Sherbert v. Verner decision.

Yes, said the majority, the denial of unemployment compensation to Miss Sherbert was an infringement on her right to free exercise of religion. And the statutory protection given to those conscientiously opposed to Sunday work meant that "the unconstitutionality of the disqualification of the Sabbatarian is thus compounded by the religious discrimination which South Carolina's general statutory scheme necessarily effects."

Was there a compelling state interest which could justify this infringement? No, said the seven justices.

When the opposition brought out that the possibility of spurious claims for unemployment insurance might be argued as "compelling state interest," Justice Brennan cast the argument aside, since a state should first show that alternative means of regulation were not available to avoid the infringement. The alleged valid secular interest that the majority had clung to in the Braunfeld decision did not cast enough of a shadow in *Sherbert* v. *Verner* even to make a good argument. Said the justice: "No such justifications underlie the determination of the state court that the appellant's religion makes her ineligible to receive benefits."

Brennan carefully pointed out that the majority holding would not be construed as "fostering the 'establishment' of the Seventh-day Adventist religion." Instead it reflected simply the governmental obligation of neutrality in the face of religious differences. Nor was it "a case in which an employee's religious convictions serve to make him a nonproductive member of society," since the court had noted that of all the Seventh-day Adventists in the Spartanburg area, only Miss Sherbert and one other had been unable to find work and still keep the seventh day holy.

"This holding but reaffirms a principle that we announced a decade and a half ago, namely that no State may 'exclude individual Catholics, Lutherans, Mohammedans, Baptists, Jews, Methodists, Non-believers, Presbyterians, or the members of any other faith, *because of their faith, or lack of it,* from receiving the benefits of public welfare legislation.' *Everson* v. *Board of Education,* 330 U.S. 1, 16."

Both Justices Douglas and Stewart who, with Brennan, had gone on record two years before as believing that Sunday laws violated the "free exercise clause," wrote concurring opinions in the Sherbert case.

Douglas cited a variety of minority religious beliefs and customs and noted: "Some have thought that a majority of a community can, through state action, compel a minority to observe their particular religious scruples so long as the majority's rule can be said to perform some valid secular function." Justice Douglas made it plain that this was the reasoning in the series of 1961 Sunday-law decisions and "a ruling from which I then dissented . . . and still dissent."

The Sunday-law ruling "travels part of the distance that South Carolina asks us to go now. She asks us to hold that when it comes to a day of rest a Sabbatarian must conform with the scruples of the majority in order to obtain unemployment benefits."

Justice Douglas compared the state's interference in matters of religious conviction to similar conditions in Soviet Russia, "where a churchgoer is given a second-class citizenship, resulting in harm though perhaps not in measurable damages." He brushed aside the suggestion that a payment of financial benefits to Miss Sherbert might indirectly benefit her church. Such payment would be of no more benefit to a church than would the salary of any employed individual. In reality, Justice Douglas saw the issue as not "what the individual can demand of government" but rather "what government may not do to an individual in violation of his religious scruples."

Justice Stewart concurred with the majority finding that Miss Sherbert's free exercise of religion had been infringed. He said:

"I am convinced that no liberty is more essential to the continued vitality of the free society which our Constitution guarantees than is the religious liberty protected by the Free Exercise Clause explicit in the First Amendment and imbedded in the Fourteenth. And I regret that on occasion, and specifically in *Braunfeld* v. *Brown, supra,* the Court has shown what has seemed to me a distressing insensitivity to the appropriate demands of this constitutional guarantee.

More than mere passive protection, "the guarantee of religious liberty embodied in the Free Exercise Clause affirmatively requires government to create an atmosphere of hospitality and accommodation to individual belief or disbelief." The Constitution demands the positive government protection of religious freedom for small minority and large majority alike.

Under this view of "free exercise," Stewart had no difficulty in reaching a decision favorable for Miss Sherbert. But previous rulings by the majority that government-written prayers and sponsorship of Bible reading in public schools constituted establishments of religion, now impaled the majority on the horns of a dilemma. What Stewart deemed an insensitive and positively wooden approach to the "establishment clause" which "forbids the 'financial support of government' to be 'placed behind a particular religious belief' " now became an obstacle for a consistent finding which could approve compensation for Miss Sherbert.

The heart of the dilemma, as viewed by Stewart, was this: How could South Carolina pay public money to Miss Sherbert to protect her free exercise of religion without running at cross purposes to the court's mechanistic concept of the "establishment clause" which Stewart labeled as "historically unsound and constitutionally wrong"?

For so long as the resounding but fallacious fundamentalist rhetoric of some of our Establishment Clause opinions remains on our books, to be disregarded at will as in the present case, or to be undiscriminatingly invoked as in the

Schempp case, . . . so long will the possibility of consistent and perceptive decision in this most difficult and delicate area of constitutional law be impeded and impaired. And so long, I fear, will the guarantee of true religious freedom in our pluralistic society be uncertain and insecure.

In conclusion, Stewart leveled a blast at the Braunfeld decision, making it plain that a finding of infringement in *Sherbert* v. *Verner* should more than ever justify a finding of infringement in Braunfeld, for the sake of consistency.

The impact upon the individual's religious freedom in the Sherbert case was considerably less burdensome since there were no criminal sanctions involved and a maximum of twenty-two weeks of compensation was at stake. However, Justice Stewart found it difficult to believe there was any less of a burden upon religious practice in Braunfeld than in Sherbert. In fact, to find free exercise infringement in Sherbert, the associate justice was convinced that "the Court must explicitly reject the reasoning of *Braunfeld* v. *Brown*. I think the *Braunfeld* case was wrongly decided and should be overruled, and accordingly I concur in the result reached by the Court in the case before us."

As a practical matter, a finding of free exercise infringement in the Sherbert case was monumental, but it could not match the sensational overtones that would have reverberated had a similar finding by the majority come from the Braunfeld decision in 1961. Sherbert involved the power of a state to deny a citizen social welfare benefits created by a state. The blue law issue involved a religious tradition interwoven in social fabric, with criminal sanctions. To find curtailment of Sunday activity an infringement of Braunfeld's right to practice his religion, would likely have broken the back of Sunday laws in the United States.

Justices Brennan, Stewart, and Douglas had consistently found infringement of free exercise in both the Braunfeld and Sherbert cases. Justice Harlan had consistently seen no infringement in either case.

Justice Goldberg, who saw infringement, and Justice White, who took the Harlan view of no infringement, had not been members of the court at the time of the Braunfeld case.

Only Chief Justice Warren, Associate Justice Black, and Associate Justice Clark had seen infringement in Sherbert even though having gone on record as finding a public interest which outweighed any infringement of the free exercise of religion in Braunfeld. Had any two of these three members of the court seen violation of free exercise in Braunfeld, Sunday laws would have been dead, for all practical purposes, by the time of the Sherbert decision.

As it was, Miss Sherbert and her fellow church members were grateful for court recognition of a constitutional right to observe their chosen day of rest.

REFERENCES

1. Varner J. Johns, "A Sad State of Affairs," *Liberty,* Vol. 60 (1965), No. 1, pp. 27, 28.
2. *Religious News Service,* December 18, 1962.
3. *South Carolina Code,* Section 64-4. Quoted in *Sherbert* v. *Verner,* 374 U.S. 398 (1963).
4. *Sherbert* v. *Verner, Op. cit.*
5. *Ibid.*

Space-age science and invention raise new questions about time, the fourth dimension. Some propose a new World Calendar.

17. THE FOURTH DIMENSION

The most obvious and easily recognized time definition is "day." One complete rotation of the planet earth on its axis, although varying in length from sundown to sunrise, is one day.

So far, so good!

The orbit of the earth around the sun opens the door to a definition of another time period. Varying angles of the earth's surface to the sun produce temperature and climate reactions, and seasons are the result. The cycle of seasons is another logical category of time—the year.

As the moon circles the earth, the sun's light strikes the moon from different angles (as seen from the earth), which produces a changing sequence of shapes ranging from the slim crescent to the full round man's "face" chiseled in "green cheese." This continuing cycle suggests a means of measuring a time component intermediate between a day and a year—the month.

Creating an accurate chronology of history is confounded in mathematical attempts to blend these three categories of time measure which are tied to motions of orbiting masses. A year requires just under 365¼ days. Moon orbits around the earth are fewer than thirteen but more than twelve full revolutions per year.

The day, the month, and the year were comprehensible independent of each other. But how to devise a calendar integrating all three in a convenient package, when one year equals 365-plus days, or 12-plus months? The problem defies exact solution.

All three methods of measuring time shared one common denominator: They were tied to motion in space. The day was measured by the rotation of the earth; the month by the orbit of the moon; and the year by the orbit of the earth around the sun. However, the week was unrelated to space motion except by its accumulation of days. Napoleon thought the week should be ten days long. Russia tried a five-day week in 1927 and junked it for a six-day week in 1931, which was likewise abandoned shortly. Human experience for centuries seems to have demonstrated that the ideal weekly cycle is seven days, a maximum of six days for ordinary occupations relieved by a seventh day to serve as a change of pace. Physical health, psychological refreshment, mental relaxation, social expression, and spiritual dividends are derived from one day's rest in each consecutive seven-day period. And unlike the longer measures of time, the seven-day week was recorded in the Genesis story as part of the creation of God. It was not tied to a space movement per se as in the case of the day, month, and year.

Thus, the seven-day weekly cycle carries spiritual overtones and connotations beyond simple scientific measurements of space orbit. Any attempt to chronicle time outside the scope of this natural-law cycle outlines a blueprint for failure. The seven-day week is the core of chronological reckoning.

Julius Caesar came up with a calendar plan in the first century before Christ. He measured years in 365 days, with the excess time accumulated making a 366-day year every fourth year. Full-moon months were not the dominant consideration, and the year was limited to a twelve-month period, with no precise tie to lunar orbit. Julius gave his own name to the month of July and shortened February to twenty-nine days so his month could have a "lucky" uneven number of thirty-one days. Augustus Caesar followed suit, taking another day from February to give thirty-one days to his namesake, August. The leftover leap-year day was then added to February every fourth year.

The Julian calendar preserved the seven-day Genesis week. The only trouble with this calendar was that the full day added every fourth year made each year overflow its precisely allotted dimensions of 365 days, 5 hours, and 49 minutes. By the sixteenth century the Julian calendar was ten days off the normal season sequence, and Pope Gregory XIII determined to correct the widening gap.

In 1582 an Italian astronomer devised a formula which designated a leap year when the number of the year can be divided by four—except in cases where it can also be divided by a hundred. In that case, it is never a leap year unless the year's number can also be divided by 400.[1] This formula works to keep the seasons in pace with the years.

To put the year back on schedule, the Julian calendar October 5 was simply renumbered October 15. Although the old October 5 now had a different numerical designation, it remained the identical day of the week. The historic weekly cycle was not upset in the slightest by Pope Gregory.

The Gregorian calendar was still in vogue when the Supreme Court ruled on blue laws in 1961. Thus, the weekly cycle which exists today coincides exactly with the seven-day week of Julius Caesar. Resurrection Sunday is still the first day of the week, just as it was at the time the resurrection occurred. Similarly, the seventh-day memorial of creation on the twentieth-century calendar matches the seventh day on which Christ entered the synagogue to worship "as His custom was."[2]

Recent attempts have been made to revise the Gregorian calendar. Several of these attempts threaten to upset the seven-day cycle. One idea would cut the year to 364 days, making up thirteen months of 28 days each. Another would also adopt a

207

15—D.S.

364-day year, making use of four equal quarters composed of three months containing 31, 30, and 30 days respectively.

Both these plans would destroy the weekly cycle by inserting an extra day each year and two extra days on leap years. These "blank days" would be sandwiched into a "no-man's-land," independent of any calendar-designated week or month. Thus, when the blank day hits following a normal weekly cycle, it would not be the first day of the week but would dangle clumsily in space, with uncertain identity. What would have been the second day of the interrupted weekly cycle would now become the first day of the out-of-kilter calendar week. What would have been the first day would fall into a "blank day" pigeonhole. Specifically, if what should have been the first day, or Sunday, is given blank-day status, the former second day, Monday, would then be labeled Sunday and so forth, until the next blank day appeared, when the weekly cycle would be thrown even farther out of kilter.

This would continue at least once a year, and twice every fourth year, until finally there would be so many blank days around that only the most astute chronologist could calculate which day is really Sunday, the true first day of the week.

Some calendar revisionists suggest a formula which would doubly compound the confusion. "Why not," they ask, "rename Sunday the seventh day of the week and rename Monday the first day of the week?"

Those Christians who insist on honoring the resurrection on the first day of the week would be confronted with a serious dilemma. Should they go to church on the original "first day," now called the seventh, or should they worship on the so-called "first day," now Monday? Or maybe they should join those who observe the memorial of creation on the original seventh day, now called the sixth. Whatever their choice, before long the old "blank day" nemesis would appear, necessitating yet another adjustment. A world already split by language and ideological barriers can do without the added confusion stemming from a distortion of time.

Christians concerned with the precise day of Christ's resurrection look to the first day of the week—the Sunday of the Gregorian calendar. If Christ's resurrection is to be memorialized by weekly observance on the identical first day, the cycle of the week which now brings that day on Sunday should not be upset. The same thing applies to Christian observers of the seventh day as a memorial of creation. The Gregorian calendar preserves a weekly cycle which allows worship on the same seventh day which Christ observed. A blank-day calendar would distort that sequence so the actual seventh day would fall on Friday one year, Thursday the next, and so on.

The Vatican Council went on record as being open to calendar revision subject to one basic contingency: "The Church has no objection only in the case of those systems which retain and safeguard the seven-day week, so that the succession of weeks may be left intact, unless there is question of the most serious reasons."[3]

Efforts to streamline the calendar and at the same time effectively meet the interests of religious groups are displayed in the "World Week Calendar." Under this plan the year would be reduced to 364 days, divided into twelve months. Quarters would carry ninety-one days each. The first month of the quarter would always have thirty-one days and the last two months of each quarter would always have thirty days each. Birthdays, holidays, and other special events would fall on the same day of the week every year.

The resulting bonus time of one day, five hours, and forty-nine minutes each year would be accumulated until there was enough time for a full seven-day sequence—a "World Week." "World Week" could be incorporated between December 31 and January 1. Unlike the blank day, it would not upset the weekly cycle. Neither would it play havoc with calendar computations. From a business standpoint, it would fit in well with the New Year's holiday and year-end bonuses. And "World Week" would come only once every five or six years.

After a "World Week" the following Sunday would still be the first day of Biblical days, and the following Saturday would still be the seventh day.

Is the observance of a certain day of the week obsolete in the space age? Not at all, provided an individual's choice of a day of rest is a spiritual rather than a legal concept. For example, Christian observers of the seventh-day Sabbath as a memorial of creation believe it is meaningless apart from spiritual values. It was made for man, and was to be a "delight."[4] Secular benefits are incidental.

Spiritual relationships concern the individual and his God. In this sphere government is an unnecessary, interfering intermediary. Religion's acceptance of government coercion to achieve spiritual goals is an admission of spiritual weakness. An elevated spiritual purpose can be degraded by mechanical administration of the state, and the looked-for incidental secular benefits resulting from primarily spiritual observances can be obscured.

Sabbath observance is a personal symbol of loyalty and allegiance to the Creator of the universe. Once a week, the conduct of the Sabbath-keeping Christian tells the world, "We didn't just evolve by chance; we are here through divine power." To him, to accept another day for the observance as a mere matter of custom and tradition is to subvert divine authority to a level of personal convenience.

This is why the Christian uses the calendar to follow the weekly cycle in an effort to reflect the custom, example, and command of the One whose teachings he accepts. The Christian Sabbath keeper is conscience-bound to observe the seventh day of creation as Christ observed it, within the dimensions of personal environment and capability. This is why there is a spiritual

210

significance in putting a label on time and answering the question, "When is the seventh day?"

And this is why the seventh-day-keeping Christian objects to Sunday laws on two counts: First, he believes they symbolize a union of church and state incompatible with the religious freedom essential to a free society and the free moral exercise of the individual. Second, apart from the distasteful connotations of state action, laws commanding observance of Sunday honor a doctrine tied to a questionable tradition. Belief in God as the Creator can most effectively be expressed by a commitment to the fourth commandment. The Sabbath is permeated with spiritual symbolism which cannot be shrugged off in an age when the very existence of God is being attacked by philosophies of atheism.

A weekly Sabbath memorializing the creative power of God is a bulwark against atheism. It is a roadblock to the pseudoscientific hypothesis of an accidental evolution. And its elimination by theological theoreticians from the ten rules for better living sets the pace for a nonchalant social response to the remaining commandments. This in turn can contribute to a vague respect or disrespect for civil law.

Some nineteenth-century American jurists would have been jolted to discover that the Sunday laws they backed for purely religious rationale did not in fact honor the Sabbath day observed by Christ. Obsolete traditions relegating seventh-day-Sabbath observance to sectarian Judaistic ritual, while concurrently exalting first-day religious exercises as a Christian substitute for this worship concept, ignore reality.

Christ worshiped on the seventh-day Sabbath "as His custom was."[5] The disciples of Christ worshiped on the seventh-day Sabbath while Christ was in the tomb. And Christ's counsel to postresurrection Christians facing a prophesied siege in Jerusalem was to pray that their flight be not "on the Sabbath day."[6]

Romans led by Gessius Florus penetrated to the north wall of the Jerusalem temple in A.D. 66 and then mysteriously withdrew. Christians, heeding the warning of Christ given more than thirty years before, fled to refuge in Pella and Perea and escaped the massive destruction by Titus that leveled the city in A.D. 70.

The Sabbath day of Christians living after the resurrection was the identical seventh-day Sabbath that had been observed by Christ and His disciples. It is a vain quest to look to the practice or teaching of Christ for authority to substitute Sunday for seventh-day-Sabbath observance.

Dr. Ernest R. Palen, pastor of New York's Middle Collegiate Church for more than thirty years, created a stir by proposing in a sermon delivered March 13, 1966, that Protestants and Roman Catholics join in a return to observing the seventh day instead of Sunday as the Sabbath. A Reformed Church in America theologian, Dr. Palen startled listeners by quoting from Exodus 20:8 and suggesting "It should not be too great a break for us . . . to observe the same Sabbath day that Jesus Himself observed."

In the view of Dr. Palen, "If the Jews and Christians would join forces and have a common day to keep holy, we shall have taken the longest stride toward religious unity that our civilization has yet known." Observance of the seventh day as the Sabbath by Jews and Christians alike, Dr. Palen declared, would "place a stamp of greater sincerity on our pleas for ecumenicity."

He added, "one day of the week really kept holy by Catholics, Protestants, and Jews would give an uplift to the moral tone of our day that nothing else could do."

Dr. Palen proposed that Pope Paul VI take the initiative. He predicted that if the pontiff designated "the seventh day—the historical and Biblical Sabbath—as a day to keep holy," most of the major Protestant bodies would "go along."[7]

Today's realities demand a reexamination of the practicality of blue laws, as well as reexamination of the religious traditions which produced the blue-law concept.

THE FOURTH DIMENSION

REFERENCES

1. See Bertha Morris Parker, "Calendar," The *Golden Book Encyclopedia,* Vol. III (Golden Press: New York, 1960), pp. 237-239.
2. Luke 4:16.
3. See Dr. Sidney B. Hoenig, "The Days That Never Were—But Will Be," *Pageant,* December, 1964.
4. See Mark 2:27, 28; Isaiah 58:13, 14.
5. Luke 4:16.
6. Matthew 24:20.
7. George Dugan, "Christians Urged to Join Jews in Observing Saturday Sabbath," New York *Times,* March 14, 1966.

Those who crowd the freeways on Sunday, whether to attend church, sight-see, or watch a game, express individual option.

18·

FREEDOM
TAKES
A HOLIDAY

October 3, 1965, was a typical Sunday in Southern California.

The San Bernardino freeway bulged with the vehicles, of last-minute visitors to the Pomona Fair. The Dodgers played the last baseball game of the regular season, relishing a newly won National League pennant victory. The Los Angeles Rams and their football cousins, the Minnesota Vikings, trampled each other into the Coliseum turf. Disneyland, Knott's Berry Farm, Marineland, and Sea World beckoned to year-round adventurers. Sailboats caught the breezes at Balboa Bay and Lake Arrowhead. The "lively ones" rode the surf at San Clemente while stay-at-homes puttered in yards to please green-thumbed spouses. Early in the day, many Californians attended a church of their choice. Others had flown to New York to greet the precedent-shattering visit of Pope Paul VI.

Each of the reactions was an expression of individual option. There was no threat of fine or arrest for violating a blue-law code. Californians enjoyed an "atmosphere of recreation," do-it-yourself style, in contrast to the rigid blue-law language approved by the United States Supreme Court in 1961.

Amazingly, the California public seemed to relish a weekend with the family, blissfully unaware that this atmosphere of hap-

215

piness and free expression belonged to them without the aid of a police official grasping their collars and warning "have fun, make for rest, relaxation, repose, and recreation as you are ordered, or face fine and arrest!"

No one had to use a stopwatch to make sure the ball game started at a "noncriminal" hour. And fortunately no one had to argue with the supermarket cashier that a balloon could be classed as a "novelty" and sold legitimately, rather than as a "toy," which might make its Sunday sale nonessential and "criminal."

Californians had done without a general Sunday-closing law since 1883 and they had done very well, thank you. The state enjoyed a golden age of prosperity and growth, and the lack of blue-law "protection" did not stem the tide of immigrants who swept over the high Sierras, bringing newcomers to California at a rate confounding census takers.

The only thing to spoil California's "atmosphere of recreation" was an occasional invasion of smog. But freedom takes a holiday when the blue hue of coerced Sunday observance spatters the scene with arbitrary blots. It would take a lot of fast talking to convince the open-space-minded Westerner that enforced Sunday observance could offer him anything except a pain in the neck and the pocketbook. What, then, is the secret that makes the possibility of being "criminal-for-a-day" so tremendously attractive to some modern Americans?

The traditional blue-law attack has been aimed at three "evils" which supposedly inhibit the proper observance of Sunday: worldly amusements, Sunday labor, and Sunday commerce. Originally these "evils" were assaulted in order to foster religious practice and perpetuate a theological tradition. Now that the religious orientation of the blue law can be spurned, *a la* public welfare, what is the legitimate secular purpose that nourishes its future?

A very nebulous one, carefully camouflaged by prolific verbiage! Far from contributing to a carefree "atmosphere of recreation," Sunday laws actually curtail amusements and legitimate recreation, exposing the seeker of first-day pleasure to criminal sanctions. Free Americans can do without this form of paternalistic nonsense. Usually if given the opportunity to choose their own Sunday observance, they would say, "Please, I'd rather do it myself."

As to the labor issue, Sunday-observance laws offer no protection to an employee working in a Sunday "essential" activity. Under the typical scheme, the citizen is free to work Monday through Saturday in a "nonessential" job. Then he can punch a Sunday time clock within the "essential" labor category. Where is the protection for labor or the individual? It has to come from the legitimate health and welfare measures which provide minimum wages, maximum hours, and the "one-day-in-seven" statute, guaranteeing at least one full day's rest in each consecutive seven-day period. Also, labor organizations negotiate agreements designed to provide labor with a fair share of the nation's wealth and leisure. A blue law is a week-kneed substitute for genuine labor-oriented legislation.

Finally, the arbitrary restraint on commerce and competition demanded by Sunday-observance laws mocks free enterprise. In a totalitarian state the arbitrary selection of acceptable versus criminal classes of commerce one day each week might be compatible with philosophies which uphold confiscation of property. But in a free competitive system? Is there any reasonable justification for a system which proposes to approve the sale of film but ban the sale of a camera on Sunday?

The recently revitalized secular-purpose arguments of Stephen Johnson Field can hardly stand on their own two, or three, feet. And with these three undergirding secular-purpose objectives of blue laws tattered and torn, what argument is left to urge coerced Sunday observance in the space age?

Nothing except simple, old-time religious interest! It existed both before and after 1961. Without the sustaining support

217

of religious pressures, the entire blue-law scheme enmeshed in state lawbooks would collapse overnight. It would take some monumental haystack searching to find even one needle of secular concern that could make the public want the continued "benefits" of a "criminal-for-a-day" environment.

On the other hand, the blue-law scheme is so problem-plagued today that "what's wrong" can be told in twenty-five reasons or less without resorting to ivory-tower hypotheses.

Public opinion is a good place to start.

Who wants blue laws anyway? Certainly not religious minorities who worship on the seventh or some other day. It is highly unlikely that the non-Christian relishes the prospect of a fine for enjoying worldly pleasure on Sunday. Even a large number of Christians who attend church on Sunday have attacked blue laws with surprising vigor.

Said a Lord's Day Alliance speaker from Boston: "Legislation is not the answer, and we have found that out many times here in this land of ours. You simply cannot legislate morals, you cannot legislate good behavior, you cannot legislate the observance of the Lord's Day."[1]

The *Baptist New Mexican* questioned the fairness of requiring seventh-day observers to close businesses on Sunday and deplored "the fact that Houston ministerial groups asked for boycotts against businesses which remain open on Sunday."[2]

Two Lutheran clergymen from Milwaukee took issue with other area ministers seeking to force Sunday store closing. They appealed for a program which would allow employees to worship on Sunday if they desired and "asked churchmen who desire to legislate the Sabbath principles of rest and worship to consider [that] . . . the Christian church must not lean upon laws imposed upon those outside the church to secure Sabbath observance among her own people."[3]

Gilbert S. Fell, minister of Central Methodist Church in Atlantic City, noted shortly before the landmark 1961 Supreme

Court opinions that "whatever the cause—perhaps the so-called religious revival of the 1950's—there is increasing agitation for more stringent Sabbath observance laws." While affirming his personal belief in the great religious value of a weekly holy day, he went on record as vigorously opposing "the recent attempts to reimpose Sabbath laws." He cited several reasons for his opinion:

> First, these laws run counter to the First Amendment. . . . Since I would not wish to be made to observe Saturday as the Sabbath, I do not see how I can enforce other groups to observe my wish. . . .
>
> Second, to call such laws "health measures" . . . is a sham and a fiction. Perhaps at their inception these laws were to some degree intended as health measures—although this interpretation is questionable—but surely in these days we have ample leisure time, so much so that the sociologists see its amplitude as a problem.
>
> Third, these laws violate the Protestant affirmation of personal free choice. Let those who wish the Sabbath observe the Sabbath.
>
> Fourth, the Sunday laws tend to be discriminatory. In New Jersey it seems likely that a law will pass permitting a man to go out and drink himself under the table on Sunday but preventing him from purchasing a bathing cap or a toothpick on that day.[4]

Shortly after the 1961 Supreme Court decisions, the 174th General Assembly of the United Presbyterian Church in the United States heard a report from its Special Committee on Church and State. The report recommended that "this General Assembly affirms its conviction that the church itself bears sole and vital responsibility for securing from its members a voluntary observance of the Lord's Day. The church should not seek, or even appear to seek, the coercive power of the state in order to facilitate Christians' observance of the Lord's Day."[5] Though not demanding repeal, the recommendation urged Presbyterians not to support new Sunday laws, and to seek exemptions for seventh-day keepers under existing laws. The essence of this document was adopted by the General Assembly of the church meeting in Des Moines, Iowa, in the summer of 1963.

Allan C. Parker, Jr., pastor of the South Park Presbyterian church, Seattle, Washington, made a strong appeal: "I do not believe that because I have set aside Sunday as a holy day I have the right to force all men to set aside the day also. Why should my faith be favored by the state over any other man's faith?"[6]

Princeton Theological Seminary President James McCord, a leader in the ecumenical movement within Episcopal, Methodist, Presbyterian, and United Church of Christ congregations, sees blue laws as a part of the Puritan tradition handicap burdening the church today. "The church is still chock full of symbols about wildwood and Puritan America. It is amazing to me that New England has imposed itself on all America. It has become the stereotype for a religion with all the juice squeezed out of it." He decried the "blue laws and blue noses"[7] that had emerged.

Roman Catholic voices have also been heard. "Father Robert F. Dinan of Brighton, Massachusetts, dean of the Boston College School of Law, said 'the religious freedom of non-Sunday observers had been and is clearly infringed upon by the law's establishment of Sunday as the universal day of rest.'" A Georgetown University law professor, Dr. Chester J. Antieau, "said Sunday closing laws 'unquestionably do grave economic injury' to some religious minorities. He also challenged the validity of the argument that Sunday laws 'keep our families together.' He added that 'greater ease of police enforcement is hardly a justification' for Sunday laws. 'There is not one whit of evidence that it is impossible or even difficult to enforce the rest laws in any of the twenty-one states that exempt some minorities from Sunday controls.'" And "Father Charles E. Curram, of Rochester, New York, professor of moral theology at St. Bernard's Seminary, doubted that solutions lay in the enactment of more precise laws. He described as 'a fallacy' the general impression that law and legislation 'make Christianity.' "[8]

The public at large has registered some forceful reaction to Sunday laws at the polls. In a formal election the citizens of Toronto, Canada, made their thinking clear. On December 5, 1960, they found an occasion to be heard.

> Sunday movies and sports received strong support at the polls in the Ontario municipal elections despite the pleadings of Protestant and Roman Catholic church leaders. Here in Toronto, the Sunday movie vote ended in a lopsided score—81,821 for and 45,399 against. Meanwhile, the Toronto suburbs of North York and Scarborough voted two to one in favor of Sunday sports. In nearly all other areas where the two issues were on the ballot the voters approved.[9]

When Michigan tried a Sunday-closing law with a Saturday-closing option after the Supreme Court had spoken in 1961, only three of the eighty-three counties in the state implemented its provisions.

The people of a free country also vote with their feet. If they don't wish to go somewhere or do something, they won't be forced. If Americans didn't want to shop, stores couldn't afford to remain open on Sunday. Why not let citizens decide for themselves? If the majority of the people are against it, Sunday commerce will simply fade away. If the people want to shop on Sunday, why curtail free expression? A man shouldn't be forced to work on Sunday if he chooses to worship on that day. But why tell him how to spend his leisure?

With little evidence of popular public support, Sunday-law backers in the space age look to commercial interests for underwriting and religious interests for leadership. But Mr. Average Citizen stays rather consistently off the blue-law bandwagon.

When Maine Governor John H. Reed OK'd a 1965 bill allowing Sunday sales of liquor in his state, he explained "It is the will of a majority of the people of this state for this act to become law." Despite the protests of a Christian Civic League, which vowed to force a statewide referendum on the issue, the governor explained a reversal of his previous "matter of concience" opposition as due to the fact that citizens have had "ample opportunity to make their views known to their elected representatives."[10]

Arbitrary classifications. In 1956, then Governor Adlai L. Stevenson of Illinois vetoed a bill that would have sent a citizen to jail for ninety days for selling an auto on Sunday. Asked the governor, "If such a restriction on Sunday trade is sound for automobiles, why should it not be extended to newspapers, groceries, ice-cream cones, and other harmless commercial transactions? Carried to its logical extreme, any business group with sufficient influence in the legislature can dictate the hours of business of its competitors. And if hours, why not prices?"[11]

Once committed to the Sunday-closing principle, reason takes a back seat to pressures and special interests. Where can a legislature safely draw the line on Sunday conduct without facing the twin charges of "arbitrary" and "unreasonable"?

Here's an example: Under some blue laws it's a crime to sell a shirt. It follows that it should then be unlawful to clean or launder a shirt on Sunday—at least for pay. Then, how about coin-operated laundromats? The Canadian Supreme Court answered this in 1961 by saying that an automatic coin laundry infringed the "Lord's Day Act" despite the fact no one was actually employed on the premises.[12]

Once you forbid coin laundromats, to be consistent you must extend the ban to coin-operated candy and soft-drink machines, and from there to coin-operated telephones. After banning a coin telephone, the telephone lines should be shut off to private phones as well, because this use involves only a different method of payment.

Where can the legislature draw a consistent line?

When a crackdown was attempted on blue-law violators in Cincinnati, Judge Clarence Denning refused to call it a crime to wash a car when service stations could legally wash a windshield. Asked the judge, "How far does the person using a sponge to clean an auto have to propel said sponge before it can be said he is in violation of the law? And conversely, where shall he stop in the cleaning of an auto to be within the purview of the law?"[13]

The perplexing problem of arbitrary, irrational, and vague classifications reached hilarious heights in Michigan shortly after the Supreme Court spoke in 1961. Attempting to build on the shaky "secular" premise, the Michigan legislature devised a two-headed beast which forbade certain conduct on Sunday—or Saturday, depending on the day of rest selected. The bill tickled the funnybone of Michigan newspapers like the Jackson *Citizen Patriot*:

> Let's assume that the Saturday or Sunday store-closing bill becomes law and the state hires 23,789 special policemen to enforce it and arrest all violators. Among the typical lawbreakers could be a solid citizen who bought a hammer on Sunday for "emergency provision" but was caught using it to make a birdhouse. There will also be the felon who purchased a lawn chair "for exclusive outdoor use" and was nabbed red-handed with it in his living room, being used as an extra chair for a poker party. And consider the sad case of the housewife who bought a pillow, claiming it was for "outdoor camping use," but was apprehended by a special policeman while testing it indoors.
>
> And the court dockets will be jammed with such cases as the fellow who bought a hat to go with his legally-purchased raincoat, the defendant who added a camera to his film and flash-bulb purchase, and the accused who bought a radio tube and stuck it in a hi-fi amplifier.
>
> Legal questions will probably be raised, too, on such vague terms in the new law as "perishable fruits and vegetables," "power-operated grooming supplies," and "large

223

and small appliances." For instance, consider the plight of
the distraught judge who will have to rule on a plea of
"unperishable fruits" or of the defendant who claims the
appliance he bought on Sunday was neither large nor small
—but medium. Where will it all end?[14]

State Senator Carlton Morris of Kalamazoo challenged anyone to try to "figure out this hodgepodge." Said the senator,
"I hope you're happy with this bill when we get through it. I
gather, under it, you can buy a hot dog but not a bun. It's even
laughable to try to explain it."[15]

The Saline *Reporter* placed a call for King Solomon in an
impassioned, tongue-in-cheek plea:

> The dazzling inconsistency of Michigan's blue laws
> never fails to confound us. For years, we have had trouble
> explaining to out-of-state guests that they could drop the
> whole family budget at the race track if they chose but if
> they wanted to play euchre for ten cents a hand, we'd have
> to pull down the shades first. Now, if the proposed "Sun-
> day closing" legislation passes and isn't vetoed by the gov-
> ernor, we're going to have to tell them they can't buy a
> screwdriver on Sunday in any store with more than 4,000
> square feet of floor space . . . unless they want to drive
> down to Clinton County for it. It will be legal to buy
> aspirin on Sunday but purchase of toothpaste may turn
> out to be illegal and immoral. Question: Is tooth paste a
> drug?
> You'll be able to buy outdoor furniture, but sale of
> indoor furniture would be forbidden. Apparently reverence
> comes easier outdoors. Bread, but not coffee. Butter, but
> not jam. Perishables are exempted. No kidding, all these
> fine distinctions have passed the House of Rep. by a whop-
> ping vote of 86 to 12. The "Sunday closing" law pro-
> moted by some retail and church groups, has been bitterly
> fought by most of the supermarkets . . . and by the tour-
> ist and sportsmen's groups, who won their point: It will still
> be legal to sell ammunition on Sunday.
> The law, as written, will allow Saturday closing as an

alternate, for those who regularly observe the Sabbath on Saturday. Merchants may take their choice. The bill would apply only to the big-population counties, of 130,000 persons or more. So when we explain to visitors that they can buy camping equipment anywhere on Sunday, but it would be breaking the Sabbath to buy toys (in Washtenaw county, but not in Lenawee county) unless the store has less than 4,000 sq. ft. . . . may they be forgiven for thinking they're dealing with the White King?[16]

The Coldwater *Daily Reporter* couldn't resist some gentle needling of its own:

> We see where the Michigan House of Rep. passed a Sunday-closing bill this week. It's all right to sell food to eat on the premises, but you can't take it home with you. If you want bedding such as blankets or pillows, you can't buy it unless it's for outdoor camping. Footwear and headwear are out except for rainwear and overshoes. So if you see a bareheaded man camping out in his overshoes next summer, better stop and feed him.[17]

The Battle Creek *Enquirer and News* struck a more sober note by introducing the word "insanity" to explain the development of a "Frankensteinian monster":

> We'll ruefully have to admit we gave the majority of Michigan's state representatives more credit for sound judgment than they deserved. In the house last Tuesday more than 80 of its 110 members again voted for that fantastic, utterly ridiculous creation known as a Sabbath-closing law. After undergoing the state senate's scrutiny, during which the bill was amended to the point of inanity—or maybe we should mention (pardon, please) the word, insanity—there seemed to be some hope that the House would then recognize the Frankensteinian monster it had put together. Most political observers confidently predicted demise of the bill, but they were so wrong. They—and that includes this corner—completely underestimated the temper of the legislators. The house majority simply wanted a Sabbath-closing

225

law, and they were going to have one, no matter what! And now that they've got it, what are they going to do with it, assuming that Gov. Swainson signs the measure? Even if the governor vetoes it, the legislature probably will override him (here we go—predicting again) because the house surely wants the law. It's going to be fun watching the enforcement of this legislative creature. It's going to be quite entertaining to observe the way businesses will figure out tricks to outwit the law and its enforcers. And, we just can't wait for the first court case to learn how a judge is going to interpret some of the law's provisions. Best of all, we're going to enjoy the predicament of the ones who cooked up this mess of political pottage. They have succumbed to expediency without thought of the consequences. They can well be haunted by these words from Michigan's late Senator Arthur H. Vandenberg, "Expediency and justice frequently are not even on speaking terms."[18]

The governor did sign the bill, with some misgivings. But eighty of the eighty-three counties in the state took advantage of the local-option privilege and refused to implement its provisions. In 1964, all eight justices in Michigan's high tribunal lent a hand to give the modernized blue law the gate. One of three separate concurring opinions succinctly pinpointed the Achilles heel of the "secular" blue law: "When a law makes violation criminally punishable, it must be definite and certain enough so that violation thereof becomes ascertainable in some manner other than by extrasensory perception, moon gazing, or resort to a crystal ball."[19]

The arbitrary hodgepodge of post-1961 "secular" Sunday-closing laws raised the void-for-vagueness issue in a dramatic way and overlapped the potent enforcement problem.

Take a good look at the *enforcement* problem!

Police officers are overworked and underpaid. Epidemics of theft and criminal violence clog police blotters. Court calendars lag behind burgeoning civil and criminal case loads. Fires of civil disobedience and chaos bordering on anarchy char the landscape

226

and eat away established legal framework. The national crime rate skyrockets. Now dump the blue laws into the laps of the police and say, "Here's a 'criminal-for-a-day' list! Enforce it!"

Of course there will be the occasional prosecution and conviction. But realistic, uniform enforcement—impossible! And without consistent enforcement, another breeding ground for contempt of law is set in motion.

Imagine you have been charged with policing the average blue law. Then you can imagine what the police are up against.

Sunday "crimes" are by their nature limited to a twenty-four-hour period. In some cases arbitrary time slots within that period, such as after 2 p.m. and before 6 p.m., compound the confusion. The harassed enforcer had better be armed with a stopwatch. Next he has to check the geographic boundary. Is this a county which exercised its local option to operate outside some portion of the Sunday-law scheme? Or is this a city with a population level exempted by the legislature from the operation of the law? The police official had better have his map, his compass, and a recent census report.

But before he makes an arrest, he also should check through the forbidden list and cull out the "essential" from the "nonessential." Selling a car might be forbidden, but selling an auto accessory could be all right. A pair of tennis shoes would be a valid purchase as "sporting equipment" but might be banned if classed as "wearing apparel." The officers should have an up-to-date list in his pocket direct from the state legislature and be prepared to perform the functions of judge and jury to determine if a "crime" has actually been committed justifying an arrest.

No wonder the Cincinnati police took a good look at the enforcement mess late in 1964, and quit trying. No more whip cracking "against Sunday business operations unless the public itself files the complaints."[20] City Solicitor William McCain declared that the city lacked the police manpower for adequate

227

enforcement. It was a travesty to arrest only a few when summonses could not, as a practical matter, be issued to all businessmen breaking the blue law. It is also ridiculous to encourage a Gestapo-style police state where neighbor becomes an informer against his "one-day-criminal" neighbor. Americans like to think that such a system went out of style with the disappearance of the little man with the big mustache. Neighbor versus neighbor court cases are not compatible with the "rest and relaxation" goals of Sunday proposals.

Some dilemma! Push for full enforcement and everyone becomes suspect. Ignore the law and help yourself to a breeding ground for contempt of law and law-enforcement officials.

When a leading Maryland auto dealer promised not to sell any more cars on Sunday, the pending prosecution of a prior violation was pigeonholed. State Attorney Arthur A. Marshall, Jr., observed that blue laws "have been more of a detriment to the county than an aid," but since they were the law, there was no choice but "to enforce the laws whether I agree with them or not."[21]

Olmstead County District Judge Arnold Hatfield outlawed the Sunday-closing ordinance of Rochester, Minnesota, because it singled out business enterprises employing six or more persons.[22] A Fort Wayne, Indiana, superior court judge took issue with a colleague's ruling in the Gary City court and ruled the Indiana blue law unconstitutional because it was not explicit enough and was discriminatory.[23]

In 1962 the North Carolina Supreme Court junked the oldtime blue law, and the legislature responded with a new and modern version in 1963. This also got the judicial ax in 1965 because it exempted forty-eight of the 100 counties in the state and legislated against the state constitution, prohibiting trade regulation by local or special legislative act.[24]

An 1855 Kansas blue law was declared "so general, vague, and indefinite" that the state supreme court discarded it in

1962.[25] Five days after the state legislature came back with another one in 1963, a district court judge enjoined its enforcement against supermarkets which would be closed on Sunday by legislation that allowed the small neighborhood grocer to stay open.[26]

Although the 1855 Kansas blue law had been copied from the venerable 1821 Missouri model, the Missouri high tribunal resisted an attack on the Missouri Sunday law in a December, 1961, decision. But fifteen months later all seven justices of the Missouri high court joined in reversing the 1961 decision and threw out the old law because it was "so vague and indefinite" that it was "incapable of rational enforcement."[27]

This prompted a day of jubilee. A collective sigh of relief could be heard along the banks of Old Man River. A newspaper account described the scene in Kansas City.

> Drugstore clerk Billie Canon sold a pink-and-yellow Easter bunny Sunday and she wasn't arrested. In the same store, a year ago, another clerk sold a similar bunny. She was arrested for breaking a 137-year-old law that said only items of necessity could be sold on Sunday. . . .
>
> "People are coming in to shop and they don't have to ask, is it OK to get this," said Pete Reimer, basement manager at a store of the large Katz drug chain.
>
> Under the blue law, you could buy French perfume at one counter, but not soap at another; no light bulbs, but charcoal briquets. Paper napkins and facial tissues were considered necessary, but paper towels were not.
>
> On April 23 last year a desperate citizen paid for detergent and bleach at a Kansas City grocery store and made a clean getaway by pulling a pistol on two clerks. He phoned later to apologize: "I needed the soap to wash the baby's clothes."[28]

Although religious groups and other Sunday-law proponents still clamored for a new blue law, the "void-for-vagueness" point had been made. Although there were other post-1961 decisions which sustained blue laws, the enforcement and arbitrary classification basis for rejection had received more than incidental recognition in state supreme courts.

Free enterprise also runs at cross purposes to blue laws. To use Sunday-observance laws as tools to regulate or curtail competition is to give the voice of free enterprise a hollow ring. Adlai Stevenson vetoed the 1956 Sunday-closing proposal for Illinois auto sales while he issued a clearcut pronouncement for free enterprise:

> Under our free enterprise system, government should not interfere by regulatory or prohibitory laws in the business field except (1) where the activity in question is directly related to the public health, safety, morals, or welfare, or (2) to *enforce* competition. Traffic in automobiles does not qualify under the one, and, so far as the latter is concerned, its only purpose and effect are to *restrain* competition.[29]

Mayor James Baker of Pomona, California, used the same argument and put his political future on the line in the summer of 1961 when he opposed a Sunday-closing ordinance applicable to barbers. Despite the support given the measure by the city council, and in the face of pressures from local barbers, the Y.M.C.A., St. Joseph's Catholic Church, the First Baptist Church, and St. Paul's Episcopal Church, the indomitable mayor voted against the measure because he considered it an infringement of free enterprise. This, he said, would set a precedent in the city that could extend to other businesses. Although he lost the battle, the mayor made his point and quipped, "I've probably just made so many enemies among the barbers, I will have to go to Los Angeles for a haircut."[30]

The time-is-property concept of James Madison is compatible with the free enterprise system. Blue laws are inconsistent with the system and diametrically oppose the philosophy behind it. Businessmen have as logical a basis to contest the arbitrary confiscation of their time as any other portion of their property.

Colonial blue laws flourished in a predominantly rural society with isolated communities and limited communications. Individual ownership of business and needs unique to small geographic areas dominated business practice. Sunday-observance laws fit this framework in an effort to regulate the mores of a community, and, depending upon its heritage, each localized religious establishment had its own moral flavor. Since then there have been a nineteenth-century industrial revolution and a twentieth-century technological evolution. The pastoral scene of provincial colonial society is no more. Families live in an urban sprawl which spawns cities that overlap into megalopolises. Communications have telescoped time. Corporate interaction has partially replaced individual proprietorship. Labor organizations with bargaining power have dominated creative workmanship. Call it the space age, the atomic age, or the computer age—times have changed!

The dynamics of contemporary commerce transcend traditional boundaries of time, geography, language, and custom. The antiquated blue law is ill at ease in the modern environment. There is no horse and buggy to transport its tradition nor whipping post to support its enforcement. The law was implemented in a social-political context which no longer exists. And, unlike timeless principles of freedom, the blue law remnant was painful in the old days and is impractical in the new.

A weekly day of rest for the individual is needed today more than ever. But rather than futile efforts to force round pegs into square holes, the day and manner of rest should be guaranteed to individual choice, for individual need is the core of public health and welfare concern.

It is opportune to face the future with the emphasis on freedom. A future which can achieve the valid secular objectives supposedly achieved by Sunday laws can find alternative procedures compatible with freedom.

A true holiday, like the Fourth of July, has no criminal penalties. By contrast, blue laws make the workingman a criminal and a victim of the very law supposed to protect him! Unlike true health and welfare measures which protect the individual from being forced to live under improper working conditions, Sunday laws expose the individual to penal sanctions. Sunday laws protect and honor the observance of a day. They do not protect the individual.

Sunday laws have consistently failed to shake their religious overtones. Their essentially sectarian and oppressive nature will not disappear with some kind of blue magic. Colonial Sunday-observance laws represented religious establishment and impaired the free exercise of religion. In the 1960's blue laws still rely on religious interests for support and survival.

The existence of a church in a free society, along with most of its traditions, inevitably produces beneficial secular by-products. But to claim that indirect secular purpose flowing from a religious observance justifies government establishment of an observance is to leave the door wide open to infringement and usurpation.

A tax-supported church and a "Sabbath" enforced by penal sanction were earmarks of colonial church-state union. Coerced Sunday observance, symbol of that union, violates the spirit of the First Amendment. Government funds appropriated to religiously sponsored and operated "secular" programs of health and education is the logical next step backward. Seizing the primacy of secular-purpose excuse, proponents of almost any religious program can argue vehemently for some form of government cooperation, approval, or financial sponsorship.

Unless the blot of blue-law establishment is erased from state statute books, the camel's nose of something less than absolute religious freedom will remain in democracy's tent. Blue laws have pierced the wall of separation, and the slightest touch can widen the breach.

FREEDOM TAKES A HOLIDAY

REFERENCES

1. C. Gordon Brownsville (Senior Minister of the famous Fremont Temple Baptist Church, Boston, Massachusetts), in *Lord's Day Leader,* First Quarter, 1964.
2. *Religious News Service,* January 17, 1961.
3. *Ibid.,* November 16, 1960.
4. Gilbert S. Fell, "Blue Laws—A Minority Opinion," *The Christian Century,* Vol. 76 (Nov. 25, 1959), pp. 1373-1375.
5. *Presbyterian Life,* September 1, 1962, pages 30, 31.
6. Allan C. Parker, Jr., "I Don't Like Blue Laws."
7. James McCord as quoted by Ron Timrite, "Puritan Handicap," San Francisco *Chronicle,* October 30, 1962.
8. *Religious News Service,* April 26, 1963.
9. *Ibid.,* December 7, 1960.
10. *Ibid.,* May 24, 1965.
11. "Adlai Stevenson Speaks on Sunday Laws," *Liberty News.*
12. "Coin Laundries Held Illegal on Sunday," Long Beach, California, *Press-Telegram,* June 28, 1961.
13. "Cincinnati Court Favors Sunday Car Washers," *Gasoline Retailer,* February 6, 1963.
14. "Hardly Ever on Sunday," Jackson *Citizen Patriot,* April 24, 1962.
15. "Sunday Sales Ban Still Getting Laughs," Dowagiac *Daily News,* April 12, 1962.
16. "Calling King Solomon! We Need You!" Saline *Reporter,* March 30, 1962.
17. "A Few Rambling Ravings," Coldwater *Daily Reporter,* March 24, 1962.
18. "More Credit Than They Deserved," Battle Creek *Enquirer and News,* April 19, 1962.
19. *Religious News Service,* November 5, 1964.
20. *Ibid.,* December 30, 1964.
21. "Sunday Sales Charge Set Aside," Washington, D.C., *Evening Star,* June 9, 1965.
22. *Religious News Service,* June 3, 1965.
23. *Ibid.,* October 3, 1961.
24. *Ibid.,* June 29, 1965.
25. *Ibid.,* March 5, 1962.
26. *Ibid.,* July 9, 1963.
27. *Ibid.,* March 13, 1963.
28. "All Missouri Sunday Sales Finally Legal," Los Angeles *Times,* March 20, 1963.
29. Adlai Stevenson, as quoted in *Liberty News.*
30. "City Bans Sunday Hair Cutting," Pomona *Progress-Bulletin,* August 1, 1961.

APPENDIX

SUNDAY LAWS IN THE
EARLY CENTURIES

APPENDIX

SUNDAY LAWS IN THE EARLY CENTURIES

Although Sunday laws blossomed into their intolerant maturity during American colonial times, they date from a much earlier period. Over sixteen centuries ago, in A.D. 321, a political opportunist named Constantine proclaimed certain constraints on Sunday activity.

Traditions about Constantine are abundant. Eusebius, bishop of Caesarea and a contemporary of Constantine, wrote in glowing terms of the spiritual factors motivating the life of this Roman emperor. Subsequent observers have bestowed upon him the title, "The First Christian Emperor."

Modern church historians are not so generous. Schaff charges that Constantine "did not formally renounce heathenism, and did not receive baptism until, in 337, he was laid upon the bed of death." In support of the argument that Constantine's "progress in the knowledge of Christianity was not a progress in the practice of its virtues," Schaff cites Constantine's order to execute "his conquered rival and brother-in-law, Licinius, in breach of solemn promise of mercy (324). . . . He caused soon afterward, from political suspicion, the death of the young Licinius, his nephew, a boy of hardly eleven years. But the worst of all is the murder of his eldest son, Crispus, in 326, who had incurred suspicion of political conspiracy."[1]

236

Milman describes Constantine as "outwardly, and even zealously pagan" up to 313 and subsequent to 326 as one whose mind "appears to have relapsed in some degree to its imperfectly unpaganized Christianity. His conduct became ambiguous as before, floating between a decided bias in favour of Christianity, and an apparent design to harmonise with it some of the less offensive parts of Heathenism."[2]

Even "his coins bore on the one side the letters of the name of Christ; on the other the figures of the Sun-god, and the inscription, 'Sol Invictus,' as if he could not bear to relinquish the patronage of the bright luminary which represented to him, as to Augustus and to Julian, his own guardian deity."[3]

The Background

To resolve the riddle of this man one must view him against the backdrop of prevailing political and religious conditions.

Political turbulence and unrest greeted Constantine when he ascended the throne. The throne itself was shaky enough, and barbarian hordes threatened invasion. The iron monarchy slowly rusted, though until his death in A.D. 337 the emperor attempted in every way possible to restore stability and strength.

Paganism predominated. Not more that "a twentieth part of the subjects of the empire had enlisted themselves under the banner of the Cross before the important conversion of Constantine."[4] Nonetheless, Christians were a vocal and influential minority which held a certain appeal for Constantine. A union of church and state existed, in which religion played a subordinate, departmental role. Constantine directly concerned himself with religious affairs only as a lesser segment of his political sphere. However, he was "the first representative of the imposing idea of a Christian theocracy, or of that system of policy which assumes all subjects to be Christians, connects civil and religious rights, and regards church and state as the two arms of one and the same divine government on earth. . . . Christianity appeared to him, as it proved in fact, the only efficient power for the political reformation of the empire, from which the ancient spirit of Rome was fast departing."[5]

Constantine's political motives were showing when he strove "not so much for the cause of God, as for the gratification of his own ambition and love of power."[6]

For three centuries Christianity had flourished in a hostile environment, though persecution and suppression had been punctuated by moments of comparative tolerance. The brutal persecutions of the Emperor Diocletian had marked the opening of the fourth century of the Christian church.

Constantine's concern for Christianity was reflected in an Edict of Toleration, A.D. 313, which granted "to Christians, and to all, the free choice to follow that mode of worship which they may wish."[7] A new day had dawned for a dedicated religious minority.

The "Venerable Day of the Sun"

In a quest for additional devices of unity, Constantine noted the significance attached to the first day of the week by Christian and pagan alike. Many Christians had for a long time attached the "Lord's Day" label to the first day of the week and marked it for a weekly festival in celebration of Christ's resurrection. The Mithraists worshiped the sun as a deity, so the day of the sun was sacred to them also. Constantine found it politically expedient, therefore, to please these two diverse segments of his realm by honoring the "venerable day of the sun" through governmental edict in which "he expresses himself, perhaps with reference at once to the sun-god, Apollo, and of Christ, the true Sun of righteousness; to his pagan and his Christian subjects."[8]

The retention of the old pagan name of *"Dies Solis,"* or "Sunday," for the weekly Christian festival, is, in a great measure, owing to the union of Pagan and Christian sentiment with which the first day of the week was recommended

238

by Constantine to his subjects, Pagan and Christian alike, as the "venerable day of the Sun." His celebrated decree has been justly called "a new era in the history of the Lord's Day." It was his mode of harmonising the Christian and Pagan elements of the Empire under one common institution.[9]

At a time when forces were already at work which would tear the empire into shreds, the first Sunday law did provide a common denominator of unity. The law, promulgated on March 7, A.D. 321, ordered:

> Let all judges and all city people and all tradesmen rest on the venerable day of the sun; but let those dwelling in the country freely and with full liberty attend to the culture of their fields, since it frequently happens that no other day is so fit for the sowing of grain or the planting of vines; hence, the favorable time should not be allowed to pass, lest provisions of heaven be lost.[10]

Although the law carried religious overtones, it could hardly be called "Christian." The edict did not invoke the "Lord's Day." The day after the Sunday proclamation, Constantine revealed his pagan inclinations in a decree calling for consultation with "soothsayers" when "the palace or other public works shall be struck by lightning."[11]

The Sunday law exempted the rural Roman. It carried no criminal penalties on its face. But, mild as it seemed, it set a precedent for a succession of political and theological conflicts which were to mark sixteen subsequent centuries. Constantine himself found five more occasions, ranging from a law concerning the emancipation of slaves on Sunday to provision for the celebration of Easter, to enhance the legal status of the day.

The Council of Nicaea

Christian church leaders assembled for the Council of Nicaea in A.D. 325 at the call of Constantine. The "venerable day

239

Before the Battle of Milvian Bridge, Constantine gave ensigns with

symbolizing the Christian spirit in which the battle should be won.

of the sun" edict issued four years previously had not solved the doctrinal battle between churches of the East and the West with regard to Sunday and Easter observance.

The assembled delegates were survivors of a ten-year physical battle waged against the church by Emperor Diocletian, commencing about A.D. 303. The atrocities of Diocletian's rule marked and maimed the bodies of many churchmen in attendance at the council. Some had suffered physical loss of an eye or an ear. All had felt the sting of a government intent upon persecuting a religious philosophy out of existence. No wonder the delegates welcomed the official favor offered by Constantine.

The attention of the church now focused on a battle from within—the necessity for interpretation and formulation of church dogma. Of concern to all was the establishment of a proper memorial to mark the crucifixion and resurrection of Christ. Churches of the West favored the observance of Sunday as the day of resurrection. Churches of the East emphasized the significance of the crucifixion on the fourteenth day of the Jewish month Nisan, irrespective of the day of the week. For his part, Constantine was intent on pursuing his policy of national unity and harmonizing the disputing factions.

What were the backgrounds for the disputations at Nicaea?

Some church historians claim that early in the second century Sixtus, bishop of Rome, had called for observance of the resurrection on Sunday. Another tradition claims that while Pius I was bishop of Rome, his brother Hermes went so far as to claim that an angel had instructed the church to commemorate yearly the resurrection on the first day.

East Versus West

Christians in the East and in the West differed on the matter. When Anicetus was bishop, Polycarp, bishop of Smyrna, paid him a visit in Rome. This encounter, described by Irenaeus, Bishop of Lyons, took place in an atmosphere of calm and respect:

When the blessed Polycarp went to Rome, in the time of Anicetus, and they had a little difference among themselves likewise respecting other matters, they immediately were reconciled, not disputing much with one another on this head. For neither could Anicetus persuade Polycarp not to observe it, because he had always observed it with John the disciple of our Lord, and the rest of the apostles, with whom he associated; and neither did Polycarp persuade Anicetus to observe, who said that he was bound to maintain the practice of the presbyters before him.[12]

In a letter to the emperor, written about A.D. 155, Justin Martyr supported the views of Anicetus. What had started as merely an annual observance and continued as such until the time of Sixtus, had eventually become a weekly "assemblage" for the reading of "the memoirs of the apostles, or the writings of the prophets." Then a leader gave admonition and "exhorts to the imitation of these good things." Justin referred to prayers offered and voluntary offerings collected for orphans and widows. He continued:

Sunday is the day on which we all hold our common assembly, because it is the first day in which God, having wrought a change in the darkness and matter, made the world; and Jesus Christ our Saviour on the same day rose from the dead. For He was crucified on the day before that of Saturn (Saturday); and on the day after that of Saturn, which is the day of the Sun, having appeared to His apostles and disciples, He taught them these things, which we have submitted to you for your consideration.[13]

But the amiable spirit that pervaded the meeting of Anicetus and Polycarp faded. Late in the second century, Victor, bishop of the church in Rome, sought to cut off from the common unity the parishes of all Asia for their failure to agree on observing the resurrection on Sunday.[14]

Polycrates, bishop of Ephesus and a chief object of Victor's pronouncement, defended his position by citing the example of

Philip and John (two of the twelve apostles), Polycarp, "who was a bishop and martyr," Traseas (also a "bishop and a martyr") from Eumenia, Sagaris of Laodicea, Papirius, and Melito—all of whom "observed the fourteenth day of the passover according to the gospel, deviating in no respect, but following the rule of faith. Moreover, I, Polycrates, who am the least of you all, [do] according to the tradition of my relatives, some of whom I have closely followed. For there were seven, my relatives bishops, and I am the eighth; and my relatives always observed the day when the people [the Jews] threw away the leaven."[15]

Irenaeus, bishop of Lyons, embraced the theology of the West and maintained that the "mystery of the resurrection of our Lord" should be observed "only on the day of the Lord." But, "in the name of those brethren in Gaul over whom he presided," he admonished Victor "not to cut off whole churches of God, who observed the tradition of an ancient custom."[16]

Church Foundations Shaken

Despite these efforts at conciliation, the Easter controversy shook the foundations of the early Christian church. And just as certainly, the position of the Quartodecimans in the East (who celebrated Easter on the fourteenth day of the month Nisan) began to lose ground. The ultimate triumph of the Sunday resurrection observance advocated by the West hinged in part on the aggressive efforts of Christian church leaders in the city of Rome.

In primitive Christianity there had been no strong central church power structure. Local leaders assumed all administrative responsibilities. Members of the clergy who served several congregations in metropolitan areas were designated "bishops." Later, although bishops from diversified geographic centers were theoretically equal in rank, the bishop of Rome gradually acquired greater prestige and authority than the rest.

There were tangible reasons for his influential role which gave the victory in the Easter controversy to the churches of the

West. Rome was the communications center. A succession of able men had led the church in the empire's capital. The apostolic succession theory, coupled with the fact that Paul and probably Peter had been in Rome, was not without effect. Repeated interference with other bishops, such as the action of Victor; the right of hearing ecclesiastical appeals; and continuing orthodoxy—these forces and events united to lend strength and prestige to the supremacy of the Roman bishop.

While the Easter observance controversy was at its height, the church organization structure was embryonic at best. There was not as yet a firmly codified New Testament Scripture to use as a test for doctrine. Thus the church was susceptible to the dynamic influence of the Roman church leadership.

Where Sixtus, Anicetus, Pius, and Victor had favored the Sunday resurrection festival during the second century, Sylvester, who had the ear of Constantine, helped bring victory to the Western theologians. Sylvester urged the changing of the calendar names for the days of the week, so that the seventh day be called "Sabbath," and the first day, the "Lord's Day." As early as the third century the church had referred to Sunday as the "Lord's Day," to be observed concurrently with the Sabbath, since "we have said that the Sabbath is on account of the creation, and the Lord's day of the resurrection."[17]

Victory for the West

The subsequent involvement of Constantine opened the door to final victory for the Western point of view. In 314 the Council of Arles ruled that all Christians must keep the same day for Easter. Eleven years later the Council of Nicaea fixed Sunday as that day. Thus Sunday resurrection observance came into its own as an integral component of Christian church doctrine, while the celebration of the crucifixion on the fourteenth day of Nisan went into eclipse. This left the church with two significant weekly worship events: the "Sabbath" memorial of

245

creation, on the seventh day; and the "Lord's Day" resurrection observance on the first day.

However, already certain aspects of traditional Sabbath observance were under attack. The focus of theological conflict now shifted to the elevation of one observance and the concurrent decline of the other. Just as the arm of the state had reached into the Easter controversy, government continued to strengthen the dominant position of Sunday observance long after Constantine's historic proclamation of A.D. 321.

Actually, Constantine relaxed some aspects of his law in July of that same year, 321:

> As it seemed unworthy of the day of the sun, honored for its own sacredness, to be used in litigations and baneful disputes of parties, so it is grateful and pleasant on that day for sacred vows to be fulfilled. And, therefore let all have the liberty on the festive day of emancipating and manumitting slaves, and besides these things let not public acts be forbidden.[18]

Sunday Observance Strengthened

But in the century that followed, a succession of decrees was issued which commanded soldiers to worship on Sunday; freed Christians from tax collection on Sunday; forbade circus spectacles, horse races, and theatrical shows; and prohibited Sunday lawsuits.

Although some Christians had called Sunday the "Lord's Day" possibly as early as the second century, the terminology did not appear in Roman law until late in the fourth century, when it was connected to Sunday observance in a decree of the three co-emperors Gratianus, Valentinianus, and Theodosius:

> On the day of the sun, properly called the Lord's day by our ancestors, let there be a cessation of lawsuits, business, and indictments; let no one exact a debt due either the state or an individual; let there be no cognizance of disputes, not even by arbitrators, whether appointed by the courts or vol-

untarily chosen. And let him not only be adjudged notorious, but also impious who shall turn aside from an institute and rite of holy religion.[19]

Earlier, in 380, Theodosius had established Christianity as the official religion of the empire; now the union of church and state was absolute. Emperors were free to punish religious heretics, for under a monolithic church-state power, theological dissent could also be interpreted as a criminal act against the state.

In A.D. 538 the Third Council of Orleans forbade rural work such as "plowing, cultivating vines, reaping, mowing, threshing, clearing away thorns, or hedging," and promised punishment to violators "as the ecclesiastical powers may determine."[20] The Second Council of Macon in A.D. 585 threatened advocates with the loss of their "privilege of pleading the cause" if done on the "Lord's Day," and the countryman was to be "soundly beaten with whips" if he placed a "yoke on the neck of his cattle" on the Lord's Day.[21] The A.D. 813 Council of Mayence under Charlemagne decreed that "Lord's Days shall be observed with all due veneration, and that all servile work shall be abstained from, and that buying and selling may be less likely to happen."[22]

State-sponsored Religion Precedes Decline

Increased public clamor for a state-sponsored religion accompanies a decline in social morality. The anemic spiritual condition of a nation's religious experience is tacitly admitted where the church looks to government to codify religious practice.

The decline and fall of the Roman Empire and the subsequent headlong plunge of civilized social order into an age of stagnation is mute testimony that a monolithic church-state government failed to save either the purity of the church or the political power of the state.

In succeeding centuries the pattern continued. Whenever the Christian church united with the secular government, Sunday laws blossomed as the tangible symbol of this alliance. The dissenter felt the sting of intolerance as new penalties were added. There was no alternative to "ultimate truth." "Error" had to be eliminated, by persecution if necessary. The independent church functioning freely within the independent state did not exist.

Constantinople Versus Rome

The road from Rome to Constantinople seemed long and treacherous to Cardinal Humbert, bishop of Candida Silva. It was A.D. 1054. Threatening clouds of doctrinal dissension hung low over the cardinal and his two companions, Frederick, deacon at Rome, and Peter, bishop of Amalfi, as they began their journey. These churchmen carried with them a stern directive from Leo IX, bishop of Rome, to Michael Cerularius, patriarch of Constantinople. Leo demanded that the Greek Church give immediate recognition and obedience to the authoritative declarations of the pope.

A letter from Michael Cerularius, written to Leo the previous year, had inspired this firm action. Cerularius had challenged doctrinal interpretations fostered by Roman church leaders.[23] Specifically, he argued with the Roman custom of fasting on the seventh-day Sabbath. This was more than a simple disagreement in interpretation of disputed doctrine. Traditional strongholds of church authority were suffering a frontal attack, and no one realized the gravity of the battle better than Pope Leo.

Cerularius and his Eastern followers argued thus: Since the councils of the church had attacked the custom of fasting on the Sabbath, and since there was no mandate for the custom either from apostolic practice or from the Bible, the whim of a Roman bishop was insufficient justification for such a radical departure from established belief.[24] He later declared, "We are commanded also to honor the Sabbath equally with the Lord's [Day], and keep and not to work on it."[25]

The Western Church rejected both the challenge to its leadership and the doctrinal thesis upon which it was based. Humbert's Roman advocate accused the Greeks of following the example of the Hebrews:

> [They keep] holiday on the Sabbath by neither plowing nor reaping, and by reason of custom do not work, but they hold a festivity and a dinner and their menservants, maidservants, cattle, and beasts of burden rest. . . . They certainly observe the Sabbath, and you observe; they dine, and always break the fast, on the Sabbath. . . . They have a twofold reason for observing the Sabbath, obviously (1) by reason of the precept of Moses, and (2) because the disciples were saddened and heavy on this day on account of the death of the Lord, whom they did not believe to be about to be resurrected. Wherefore, because you observe the Sabbath with the Jews and with us the Lord's day, you appear by such observance to imitate the sect of the Nazarenes, who in this manner accept Christianity that they might not give up Judaism."[26]

Humbert Defends Sunday Observance

Humbert strongly denounced the Eastern attitude, and as positively justified Western practice. He cited the "compassionate regard for the Lord in suffering and death" by the Latin Church's rejoicing in the "resurrection on the Lord's Day, when concern much troubled the Jews as they were seeking to corrupt the guards of the sepulcher by means of money. Wherefore we, holding unto the present time the apostolic tradition concerning the Sabbath, and desiring to hold unto the end, are careful to subscribe to that which our ancient and venerable fathers declared and confirmed."[27]

At this juncture in the treatise, Humbert pointed to the leadership of Sylvester, bishop of Rome and contemporary of Constantine. He cited Sylvester as having declared:

> In every Lord's Day on account of the resurrection is to be kept in the joy of Christians, then every Sabbath day of

the burial is to be estimated in execration of the Jews. For all the disciples of the Lord had a lamentation on the Sabbath, bewailing the buried Lord, and gladness for the exulting Jews. But for the fasting apostles sadness reigned. Let us, therefore, be sad with the saddened on account of the burial of the Lord, if we would rejoice with them on account of the resurrection of the Lord. For it is not proper that we should observe an account of Jewish custom, the subversions of the foods and ceremonies of the Jews.[28]

Authority the Principal Issue

The issue between East and West was not primarily theological. Rather, it had become a conflict over the authority exercised by the bishop of Rome. It was here that the churches of the East refused to yield.

Cerularius resented the pope's demands that his decrees be recognized as *the* authority of the church. A public debate on June 24, 1054, between Humbert and Nicetas only widened the breach. Finally, on the morning of July 16, the papal legates in Constantinople publicly attacked the position of Cerularius at the church of St. Sophia and presented to the church the pope's written excommunication of the churches of the East. Local church leaders retaliated by publicly destroying the papal pronouncement.

Before Humbert completed his return journey to Rome, he received a communiqué from the emperor urging him to make one more attempt at church unity. But the damage had been done. Subsequent attempts at reconciliation failed, and more than nine centuries of separation between Christians of East and West followed. Seventh-day Sabbath observance in Western Christian worship went into virtual eclipse, as the majority of Christians believed Sunday had been sanctioned as the essential day for Christian worship. Ultimately Christian thought went the full circle and attached the "Sabbath" title to Sunday, the first day of the week.

REFERENCES

1. Philip Schaff, *History of the Christian Church,* Fifth Edition Revised (Grand Rapids, Michigan: Wm. B. Eerdman's Publishing Company, 1950), Vol. 3, pp. 15, 16.
2. Henry Hart Milman, *History of Christianity* (London: John Murray, 1867), Vol. 2, pp. 284, 328.
3. A. P. Stanley, *Lectures on the History of the Eastern Church* (London: John Murray, 1861), page 227.
4. Edward Gibbon, *The History of the Decline and Fall of the Roman Empire* (Philadelphia: John D. Morris & Company, c. 1900), Vol. 2, p. 152.
5. Schaff, *Op. cit.,* pp. 12, 14.
6. Augustus Neander, *General History of the Christian Religion and Church,* Torrey's translation (London: Henry G. Bohn, 1853), Vol. 3, p. 31.
7. Eusebius, *Ecclesiastical History,* Book 10, Chap. 5, Boyle's translation (Philadelphia: J. B. Lippincott & Co., 1879), p. 426.
8. Schaff, *Op. cit.,* p. 105.
9. Stanley, *Op. cit.*
10. *Code of Justinian,* Book 3, Title 12, Law 3. In *Corpus Juris Civilis,* Vol. 2, p. 108.
11. *Code of Theodosius,* Book 16, Title 10, Law 1. In *Codex Theodosianus,* col. 1611.
12. Eusebius, *Op. cit.,* Book 5, Chap. 24, p. 210.
13. "The First Apology of Justin," Chapter 67. In *Ante-Nicene Fathers,* American Edition (New York: Charles Scribner's Sons, 1899), Vol. 1, pp. 185, 186.
14. Eusebius, *Op. cit.,* p. 209.
15. *Ibid.*
16. *Ibid.,* pp. 209, 210.
17. *Constitutions of the Holy Apostles,* Book 8, Sec. 4, Chap. 33. In *Ante-Nicene Fathers,* Vol. 7, p. 495.
18. *Code of Theodosius,* Book 2, Title 8, Law 1.
19. *Ibid.,* Book 8, Title 8, Law 3.
20. Third Council of Orleans, Canon 28. Binius, Tome 11, p. 496.
21. Second Council of Macon, Canon 2. Binius, Tome 8, pp. 75, 76.
22. Council of Mayence, Canon 37. Binius, Tome 20, p. 357.
23. Michael Cerularius and Leo of Achrida, *Epistle to John of Trani.* In Migne, *Patrologiae Graeca,* Vol. 120, cols 835-845.
24. Nicetas Stethatos, *Libellus Contra Latinos Editus.* In Migne, *Patrologiae Graeca,* Vol. 120, cols. 1011-1022; *Patrologiae Latina,* Vol. 143, cols. 973-984.
25. Cerularius, *Letter I,* to the Patriarch of Antioch. In Migne, *Patrologiae Graeca,* Vol. 120, cols. 777-778.
26. Humbert, *Adversus Graecorum Calumnias.* In Migne, *Patrologiae Latina,* Vol. 143, cols. 936-937.
27. *Ibid.*
28. *Ibid.*

ACKNOWLEDGMENTS

The late Frank H. Yost, tireless fighter for individual freedom, scholar, and my greatest teacher, patiently directed the gaze of a would-be scholar to the history of church and state. R. R. Bietz, church administrator and crusader for religious freedom, provided the encouragement to study law. Though he may be unaware of his influence, Lewis Rodriguez, a physician and an exemplary Christian, provided the spiritual incentive to attempt this writing project.

The writing skills of editorial assistant Paula Becker refined the original rough draft of this document. Roland Hegstad, Editor of *Liberty: A Magazine of Religious Freedom,* added his unique flourish to the chapters dealing with the 1961 Supreme Court decisions relative to Sunday legislation. Richard H. Utt, Book Editor of the Pacific Press, directed the revisions, patiently united the pieces, and placed the finishing touches with professional precision.

I am especially indebted to the authors and publishers for permission to quote from the following works:

Frank H. Yost and Alvin Johnson, *Separation of Church and State,* University of Minnesota Press.

William Addison Blakely, compiler of first edition of *American State Papers,* Review and Herald Publishing Association.

Irving Stone, *Men to Match My Mountains,* Doubleday and Company, Inc. (1956).

E. M. Halliday, "Nature's God and the Founding Fathers," *American Heritage,* American Heritage Publishing Company, Inc. (1963).

Frank H. Yost, *The Doctrine of the Sabbath and the Sunday,* unpublished manuscript mimeographed under the auspices of the Seventh-day Adventist Theological Seminary (1951).

Dan A. Ochs, *A Study of Religious Legislation in California,* unpublished thesis submitted to College of the Pacific (1934).

My thanks to a patient and helpful family, who weathered more than three years of off-again, on-again efforts to make a typewriter talk. I also feel grateful to a nation with a people so great and a form of government so free, that whoever wishes to be heard, may speak.

No man is an island. An author real or imagined builds on the work of others. He owes a debt to many more than he can acknowledge. For any good that may find its way into these pages, I say a genuine "thank you" to those who made this manuscript possible.

THE AUTHOR.